The Miracle is Real

TANNIS NEBOZENKO-HAARSMA

WESTBOW
PRESS®
A DIVISION OF THOMAS NELSON
& ZONDERVAN

WestBow Press books may be ordered through booksellers or by contacting:

WestBow Press
A Division of Thomas Nelson & Zondervan
1663 Liberty Drive
Bloomington, IN 47403
www.westbowpress.com
844-714-3454

ISBN: 978-1-6642-8280-3 (sc)
ISBN: 978-1-6642-8279-7 (hc)
ISBN: 978-1-6642-8278-0 (e)

Library of Congress Control Number: 2022920464

Print information available on the last page.

WestBow Press rev. date: 01/12/2023

Go home to your own people and tell them how much the
Lord has done for you, and how He has had mercy on you.
—Mark 5:19 NIV

O Give thanks to the Lord. Call upon His Name.
Make known His good deeds among the people.
—Psalm 105:1 NKJV

He comforts us in all our troubles so that we can
comfort others. When they are troubled, we will be able
to give them the same comfort God has given us.
—2 Corinthians 1:5 NLT

I will exalt You, O Lord.

I am writing this book to give Glory to the Risen King, to give hope to the hopeless, to bring light into the dark, and to provide courage to anyone who needs it.

This book is dedicated to Jesus Christ,
my Rock and firm foundation.

CONTENTS

ACKNOWLEDGMENTS

This book is for all the people who were a part of our family's victory and who stood beside us as health professionals. Some of you became like friends, some like family, some like coaches, and some, I testify, were heaven-sent angels. We know that without you alongside us through this journey, I would not be writing this book. That's because there would be nothing victorious to share; the outcome would have been one of loss and pain.

The purpose of this book is to validate three things. Firstly, its purpose is to raise God higher and make Him even more worthy of all praise and glory. Secondly, it is to give hope to others when their situations seem hopeless. And lastly, it is to let everyone know that the impossible is possible with God. I urge you to allow these truths to sink into the depth of your soul and saturate into your bones. The reason for this is because everyone, at some point in his or her life, will be, or is presently, in need of a miracle.

INTRODUCTION

Well, here it is now February 7, 2018, and I now have time to share our story, it's a true story. At times when you read it you will think it really can't be true. I promise you 100 percent of the events in this book are true; none of them have been fabricated or exaggerated. So many people asked whether we were going to write a book. At the time while going through our storm, I had said no. I guess that was my answer because we wanted this season to be over and we wanted to forget about it. But when you go through something traumatic like this, you'll never forget it, especially when there is some kind of aftermath or ongoing effects. As time has marched on and our lives have taken on a new normal, our feelings have changed. Why wouldn't we share the miraculous? We know miracles are real. Miracles are available not only to our family or the deserving; miracles are available to everyone.

Something I also want to share with you that encouraged me to write this book is that when I was sitting beside Chuck's bedside, praying with him, one of Chuck's nurses in Ottawa said, "You should write a book, but really, no one would believe it. But if you do, I'll be the first to buy a copy, signed by you."

So let me begin now. The miracle is real.

CHAPTER 1

The Start of a New Year

Christmas 2015 was so wonderful. Anyone who knows me knows that Christmas is my favorite time of year. This obsession has been passed on to my daughter, Carly. Christmas was a bit different that year, as it was the first year that Carly did not come home to spend Christmas Day with us. So Christmas morning was just the three of us: my son, Matthew; my husband, Chuck; and me, Tannis. Later on, my aunt and cousin came over to join us for the Christmas Day feast.

On December 27, Chuck and I flew out to Calgary, Alberta, to visit Carly and her husband, Chris, and of course their little white bulldog, Winston. We spent New Year's Eve in Banff with them and had a marvelous week. "My sister Barb and her husband, Derek," also live in Calgary, so we had spent quite a bit of time with them. We visited with my nephews, their wives, and all their beautiful little children.

On January 3, it was time to come home. I had noticed over our weeklong stay in Alberta that Chuck had been experiencing headaches almost every day with some aches and pains. Also, he was feeling more tired than usual. I thought he was just fighting a flu. On January 4, we had both returned to work, and later on in the week, we had an appointment to meet at the bank and speak with our financial advisor, as we were planning to retire.

As a side note, I retired on January 31, 2018, with Chuck. The mere fact that I am able to say "retired with Chuck" assures me that the miracle is real. With the greatness of God, I am able to say that we made it into a healthy retirement. It is because of the Lord's mighty, supernatural power along with His healing, protection, and guidance that we are here together in this stage of our lives.

Back to the story. Chuck and I met at the bank. It was a rather nice day for early January in Winnipeg, which is also known as Winterpeg because winters can be so cold here. Not too long ago, Winnipeg was on the front page of the local newspaper for being colder than Mars. Anyway, we met at the bank, and when I walked in, my eyes immediately zoomed in on Chuck. He was sitting in the bank reception area with two jackets on—his regular winter parka and his big, heavy-duty work safety jacket—his head turtled into them. I sat down beside him and asked him what was going on and why he had two jackets on. He told me that he was freezing and he didn't know what was going on; all he knew was that he felt terrible. We spoke further and decided that we would still go ahead with the appointment but would make it short as possible.

The meeting was like any other financial meeting. We exchanged niceties and went on with business. During the meeting, Chuck kept mentioning that he did not feel well and that he really needed to finish up and go home. Patricia, the financial advisor, and I joked a bit, telling Chuck to toughen up. I could see that Chuck looked flushed, his eyes bloodshot and heavy, and he was shivering because he was so cold. Patricia dealt with our affairs and had Chuck sign the documents needed. I told Chuck to go home while I finished up at the appointment. All Chuck wanted was to go home and crawl under the covers. He left the bank, and that's exactly what he did.

I finished up with Patricia and went directly home. I was hoping to find Chuck feeling better, but deep inside my soul, I knew that wasn't going to be the case. I walked into the house. It was quiet and dark. I quietly went upstairs to find Chuck buried in the covers with two sweaters on and still feeling very cold. I thought, *I'll make supper, and Chuck will eat and feel better.* That's what I really wanted to happen, so I went downstairs and started preparing dinner. I always think food is good medicine for our bodies and souls, and isn't it? Supper was soon ready, and Chuck actually came down on his own, which I interpreted as a sign that he was feeling better. As I served dinner, Chuck sat on the couch, and I called him to come to the table. We sat down, said our evening grace, and prayed for Chuck to fight off this illness that seemed to be overcoming him. Chuck didn't have much of an appetite. He ate what he could and pretty much went straight back to bed. I cleaned up after dinner, did some household tasks, prepared my lunch, and got my clothes ready for work the next day. I called it a night and went to bed.

CHAPTER 2

Something's Not Quite Right

The alarm rang at 5:15 a.m. I was tired, as Chuck had been up several times during the night. When he woke up, he was extremely thirsty because of having a high fever during the night. I brought him a ginger ale and some Tylenol. Chuck obviously would not be going to work. He'd be staying in bed, hoping that this flu would break and he would soon start feeling himself again. I did a half-hearted workout, showered, and finished getting ready for work. I came to give Chuck a kiss goodbye and told him I would be calling our family physician for an appointment. Chuck resisted the idea, as he was feeling way too sick to get up and go. He said he wouldn't be able to muster up enough energy to get up, get dressed, and drive to the doctor's office. I assured him I would make the appointment in the late afternoon so that he could stay in bed and sleep most of the day. I also reminded Chuck that because of his prosthetic heart valve, he could not fool around with his health and well-being. I reminded him it was already Thursday and told him he really should see the doctor before the weekend. Chuck reluctantly agreed and went right back to sleep, and I went off to work.

As I drove to work thinking about Chuck's illness, I started worrying. The reason for my worry was that fourteen years before, in 2004, after a dental procedure, Chuck had developed endocarditis.

Endocarditis is an infection of the inner lining of the heart. If left untreated, it destroys the heart valve and can lead to life-threatening complications. The year 2004 was a nightmare I would never want Chuck to relive or our family to go through again.

This seems like the right time to give a brief history of Chuck's lifelong heart-health issues. Chuck was born on May 11, 1957, in the rural municipality of East St Paul, which is approximately five kilometers north of the city of Winnipeg. He was the only boy born into a family of seven children; he was the fifth child. When Chuck was born, the happy news spread that his mother, Gloria, and father, Buck (Albert James), finally had a baby boy. Just being a boy made Chuck pretty special—and, I will say, a bit spoiled, too. Chuck was immensely loved by his parents and six sisters. To this day, all his sisters refer to him as their "favorite brother."

Back in the day (this would have been around the early 1960s), doctors making house calls was more common than it is today. Because Gloria had seven children and lived outside the city, Gloria's chosen pediatrician would come out to the house from time to time.

Dr. Snyder had come to the house to see one of Chuck's sisters, and while he was there, he said, "Let's have a look at this little guy." Dr. Snyder examined Chuck and had a listen to his little heart. After listening with his stethoscope, he felt he heard a heart murmur, and he told Gloria he thought it would be a good idea for her to bring Chuck into the office to have an X-ray. Gloria took Chuck in for the tests Dr. Snyder had ordered. It was at that time that Chuck was diagnosed as having been born with a bicuspid valve instead of the normal tricuspid valve. This meant that Chuck's aortic heart valve had only two flaps instead of three. The amazing thing is that Chuck's aorta, the main artery in the human body coming off the left ventricle of the heart, had a kink or a bend in it. This actually worked in Chuck's favor. Because his aortic valve had only two flaps, the kink or bend in Chuck's aorta worked and moved his blood down into his abdomen exactly as a normal tricuspid aortic valve would have. As Gloria said, that perfect kink or bend was the beginning of the miracle. During Chuck's early childhood, he had regular visits to the doctor's office to check on his condition and growth. As a child, Chuck was quite small and had a difficult time keeping any weight on.

One day when Chuck was in grade three, he came home from school and told his mom that he was quite dizzy and not feeling well. After more clinical appointments with cardiologists, it was decided that Chuck would require his first open-heart surgery at nine years of age. The surgery was scheduled for November. Chuck remained in the hospital over Christmas and stayed for approximately three months. Dr. Mymin was hopeful that they would be able to clean his artery and Chuck would never require any more open-heart surgeries in his lifetime. Regretfully, that was not the case.

Chuck recovered at home for a while and returned to school in the spring. Like any other young boy, Chuck was active and curious. During a post-op follow-up appointment, Chuck asked his doctor whether it would be okay for him to start riding his bike. The doctor's answer to the question was yes. Chuck could ride his bike for the rest of his life, but he would always need to remember to save enough energy to ride his bike back home. As a child and a teenager, Chuck's life was normal; he went to school, played hockey, hunted, obtained his driver's license, graduated high school, went to college, fell in love, and married me in 1983.

In 1981 Chuck went for his yearly stress test and angiogram. At this time, they found decreased blood flow and therefore Chuck's heart was not functioning properly. Chuck had lost weight and was always quite pale looking. Chuck also had noticed a change in his stamina and endurance when doing any physical activity. Dr Mymin who was still Chuck's cardiologist advised Chuck that now would be the time for Chuck to have open heart surgery to replace his aortic valve with a prosthetic aortic valve. That 2nd open heart surgery took place that fall. Chuck's stay in the hospital was only 10 days and the surgery was a complete success with no complications.

As I sit here and write this story, I bow my head and thank God for the oh, so many miracles along this path. Just this very moment, as I remembered this segment of our life journey concerning Chuck's heart and life, I am so grateful that God was with us and continues to be with us. His mighty supernatural power has saved Chuck's life countless times. I so much understand and relate to the lyrics of the song "So Will I," written by Hillsong, especially these lines:

> That if the oceans roar His greatness and every painted sky is a canvas of His Grace.
>
> If creation sings of His greatness and reveals His nature, so will I.
>
> If everything exists to lift Him high, so will I.
>
> He is a God of promise; no word is spoken in vain.

Back to Chuck's heart history. In 1990, we heard that the Björk-Shiley convexo-concave valve, which was the one that Chuck had implanted in him, were found to be defective. The problem was with the design. The valve had a tendency to develop fractures in the outflow strut, which could result in catastrophic valve failure and possibly sudden cardiac death. Later analysis revealed that the strut was fracturing at the place where it was welded onto the metal valve ring. One end of the strut would fracture first, followed by the second strut some months later. Eventually 619 of the 80,000 convexo-concave valves implanted fractured in this way, with the patient dying in two-thirds of those cases.

We made an appointment with Chuck's cardiologist to discuss Chuck's valve. At the time, this was Dr. Hughes at the St. Boniface Clinic. Dr. Hughes laid out for us the pros and cons of the valve. We, along with Dr. Hughes, decided that the risk of fracture was less likely than the risk of surgery to replace the valve. In Chuck's case it was noted in his medical file that there was a vast amount of scar tissue and that his veins were on the small scale, which had made his 1981 open-heart surgery very difficult.

Fast-forward to the fall of 2003. This time of life was very busy. Our children, Carly and Matthew, were seventeen and fourteen years old. Carly was in her senior year of high school, and Matthew was in his first year. I was happy and felt comfort that they were in the same school. I'm sure I can speak for most moms in saying that there is comfort in knowing that your kids are in the same school. I will describe it as "the sibling connection." In this case, if something goes wrong, such as a forgotten lunch, they can help each other. They were very involved in pretty much everything: school, dance, sports, swimming, and the list goes on. And of course they had friends. It was a real benefit, too, that Carly had her driver's license and had access to a Dodge Neon.

So fall was here, school was in full motion, and Chuck was going to a safety conference in Quebec. Chuck worked at the Department of National Defence in Winnipeg as the wing general safety officer and headed up the safety program at the base. Chuck was feeling as though he might be developing a cold or something he just wasn't feeling quite right.

While Chuck was in Quebec, he fell very ill. He would call and share that he had a fever, sweats, chills, body aches, and headaches. At one point, Chuck even left one of his sessions because he felt so ill.

Chuck returned home looking very pale and sick. He had appointments with our family physician, who felt that Chuck was fighting flu. So the doctor prescribed him three rounds of antibiotics. I think it was on round three of the prescribed antibiotics that I took matters into my own hands and made the call to the doctor's office. I was very upset. I repeated all Chuck's symptoms and mentioned that Chuck was losing weight. I believe he had already lost seventeen pounds. And every day, he looked clammy. Chuck was finally referred to a see a cardiologist that requisitioned Chuck an echocardiogram.

Well, the results of that test were not good news. It was found that vegetation had grown on Chuck's prosthetic heart valve. Chuck was diagnosed with developing endocarditis for the first time. It was determined that this happened because of dental work Chuck had done in late September. The only solution for this was another open-heart surgery. It was a huge blow to us. As I mentioned previously, the risk of surgery was greater than the risk of fracture of Chuck's defective heart valve because of his small veins and the large amount of scar tissue.

As I said before, this was an extremely busy time of our lives, and even though we knew that ahead of Chuck lay a complicated surgery, the busyness of life continued. The cardiologist that discovered the vegetation instructed Chuck to go directly to St Boniface Hospital if he got any sicker.

It was Good Friday, April 9, 2004, and we were at a Good Friday morning church service at St. Michael's Ukrainian Catholic Church. Chuck was standing beside me, and I noticed he was wobbling. Besides being worried and frightened, I looked at his face and knew that this would be the day we would have to take Chuck to the hospital.

The service ended, and we immediately left. I dropped off the kids at home, knowing that this was going to be an all-day event. I'm sure we all can agree and confirm that hospitals are breeding and testing grounds for patience, so I took Chuck to St. Boniface Hospital on my own. To make a long story short, Chuck was admitted to the hospital, not to my surprise, where he waited for his surgery date, which was finally decided to be on Monday, May 3, 2004.

Of course, I wanted to see Chuck before his surgery, so that morning I was up early, getting ready to go. The phone rang, and it was Chuck asking me when I'd be on my way, because there were starting to prep him. I told him I would be there in about a half hour. I wasn't a minute too soon, because when I arrived Chuck was already on the stretcher, half wheeled out of his room. We were both glad to see each other. The hospital allowed me to stay with Chuck in the waiting bay outside the operating room (OR).

There are times in your life when you just wish the ones that you love wouldn't have to go through with some of the obstacles that lie ahead of them. This was one of those times. There wasn't much spoken; actually, we spent our time just holding hands and praying for the protection of the Lord over Chuck's body and the Lord's guidance over the surgeon's hands. I'll never forget what Chuck said to me while they placed the green hospital cap on his head to cover his hair. He looked at me and said I should have said yes to the valium.

The OR attendants came to take Chuck into the OR. They said they were ready and waiting for him. We kissed several times, and Chuck said, "See you in a bit." I assured Chuck I'd be waiting for him in the family room and would see him when his surgery was over. Little did I know this entire ordeal being over was forty days away.

CHAPTER 3

The Unexpected

It was just after 8:00 a.m. when I was told that Chuck's surgery would be over around 4:00 p.m. Some of the doctors would come to the family room and give an update to waiting family members as the surgery was going on. I was told from the very beginning that Chuck's surgeon did not give in-person updates. But I could call in on the phone located in the family room to the Surgical Desk, and I would be connected directly to a nurse that would update me on the status of the surgery.

At around 10:00 a.m., three of Chuck's sisters and his mom, Gloria, came up to the family room, which was on the second floor, just outside the OR wing. I welcomed their company and appreciated all the food and snacks they brought with them for the day. There were at least eight other heart surgeries going on, with families waiting in the family room. There was a large TV screen with each patient's name and the number of the OR room he or she was in. I spotted the name C. Haarsma on the screen and could feel a twinge in my belly. As the morning went on and noon was creeping in, I was very aware of the other surgeons coming in and updating the other anxious families. The very lucky ones were told their loved ones' surgeries were successful and complete.

Well, I did and didn't want to make my first call. I was hoping to hear that everything was going well, but truthfully, I also feared the opposite. I nervously picked up the phone and dialed in to the surgical desk. The nurse picked up the phone, and I asked how Chuck Haarsma's surgery was going. The voice at the other end of the phone asked, "Who?" Again I said Chuck's name. She put me on hold and came back only to say it was still going on and would be going on for quite some time longer. I thanked her and hung up the phone. I updated my sisters-in-law and mom-in-law; they looked the way I felt inside when I repeated what she had told me.

The afternoon passed, and the clock on the wall read 4:30 p.m. I noticed there was only a man and his son left waiting in the family room, other than I and my mom-in-law. Chuck's sisters had gone home because of other commitments and obligations. In the family room, there was a smaller room with a door for confidentiality and privacy during surgeon updates. I remember very vividly this distraught, somber surgeon coming into the family room, touching a man on the shoulder, and gesturing for him and his teenage son to go into the small room. I thought to myself that it didn't look positive. They were in the small room for probably ten minutes. When the door opened, only the surgeon came out, taking off his surgical cap with his head down, letting out a big sigh. After he was gone, I walked past to see in the little room. It was empty—no man, no son. It was then that I noticed the several boxes of Kleenex in the room and another door that led into main hallway, which was open. I'm sure that other door is there so that when you are told and hear the words, "Sorry, I'm so very sorry," you can exit without having to go back into a room full of people. I think that door is the door to the beginning of a new life for anyone who passes through it—a life that is shattered and continues on without a precious, sweet loved one. My heart sunk and ached for the man and his son. My mind wandered on as to what was going on with Chuck, as his name was the only name left on the OR screen. Every other surgery had been over for hours. About an hour and a half later, at twilight, Chuck's surgeon came into the family room. I froze, and my heart started to pound when he asked us to step into the small room, as we were the only people left in the waiting room.

I'm sure you can imagine what I was feeling. My body instantly stiffened; I could feel my heart in my chest, and my throat tightened up. I feared we'd been leaving out the back door into the hallway. We went into the small room, and the surgeon closed the door behind us. Chuck's mom and I sat down, and the surgeon remained standing. He began to explain that most of the surgery had gone well. They had managed to get through the scar tissue. It was difficult, but they had been successful in doing so. He continued, saying that he had cut away Chuck's infected heart valve, and that, too, had gone well. At that point, he started to draw a picture on the whiteboard that was hanging on the wall of the small room. He drew a picture of the new valve he had placed in Chuck's heart. He said, "It was a perfect fit, *but* ..." When I heard the word "but," I froze. To tell you the truth, though, I had been waiting for it. The entire time, I was thinking to myself we had been brought into the small room for some reason and most likely it was not good news. I noticed my mom-in-law shift her body and wait for his next words. His words came out, and he shared that where he had sewed the valve into Chuck's heart, Chuck's blood was coming out from the small needle holes around the valve where he had sewn it in. He said they had given Chuck several types of drugs to try to coagulate his blood to stop the bleeding. So far nothing was working. He said they had one more drug they could try, called factor VII. They were waiting for the drug to be delivered. Factor VII had to be ordered from the outside, since it was not stocked in the hospital. The reason for this was that it was used very rarely and was extremely expensive. I think the cost back then was $7,000. The doctor said he hoped that it would arrive soon, since time was critical. That was it; he was finished. He said he must get back into the OR. He opened the door and quickly left.

Well, to say the least, my mom-in-law and I were stunned. I guess you could say we were somewhat relieved that our time in the little room didn't lead us into the hallway of a shattered life. I would describe this time of our life as Chuck lying on a tightwire, teetering from side to side, with one side being life, the other side death. Can you envision the safety net under a tightwire in case an acrobat stumbles and falls? Well, Chuck had a safety net all around him—above, beneath, left, and right. That was the presence of God in the entire situation.

My mom-in-law, with her great strength, gathered her composure and said, "We need to start praying. We need to start praying and get others to pray that Chuck stop bleeding around his heart valve." Gloria called her friends from her Bible study that she was attending at that time. Our family was attending two different churches, and I think that was a real benefit to Chuck. I called both prayer contacts, one from St. Michael's Parish and the other from Springs Church. We were surrounded by and knew many people who believed in the miraculous healing power of Jesus Christ. This was lifesaving for Chuck. Thank you to every one of you who may be reading this book, for your prayers for Chuck and our family. Whether you were from a church or Bible study, or whether you were a standalone prayer warrior, we know your prayers came back full of power and life. There is tremendous miraculous power in prayer. Prayer is the most powerful tool I know of.

As I sit here and continue writing, I'm well aware that I added this part of the book to give only a brief summary of Chuck's medical history. But I can't overlook, deny, ignore, or forget any part of the miraculous healing and protection of God in our lives. It was there and covered us back then, and it continues to do so at present and will do the same in our future. I know this is true not only for our family now but also for the generations ahead, as it is one of God's promises. His promises are true, his promises are "yes" and "amen," the latter of which means "so be it." "[Praise to the God of All Comfort] Praise be to the God and Father of our Lord Jesus Christ, the Father of compassion and the God of all comfort, who comforts us in all our troubles, so that we can comfort those in any trouble with the comfort we ourselves receive from God" (2 Corinthians 1:3–4 NIV).

Back to Chuck's medical history. Chuck's mom and I called everyone we knew that would pray. I know that the people we contacted called others to pray, so there was a vast amount of people praying. That gave us some comfort not only because it was the only thing we could do, but also because it was the best thing we could do.

I had been in contact with my kids and mom through out the day. My mom was staying at our house to be with Carly and Matthew after school and in the evening. Carly and Matthew had been up to the hospital after school in hopes of seeing their dad. They were really disappointed to find out they couldn't visit him, but I think they found comfort in seeing their grandma and me. Plus, they had the comfort of just being in the same place where their dad was.

It was getting late, so my kids went home. We hugged, kissed, and hugged again. I told them not to worry, as everything would be okay. I think they believed me. Chuck's mom was by herself, and she still had to drive home to East St. Paul. I assured her I'd be okay and told her how much I appreciated her and thanked her for spending the entire day with me. We hugged, kissed, and hugged again. I now was all alone. No one was there but me. No one's name was on the surgery screen but Chuck's. Everything was quiet. The hospital was quiet. The family room was quiet. The cleaner had already cleaned the room, so I wasn't expecting to see anyone other than the surgeon, who I hoped would be bringing good news.

The surgeon came back out to the family room around 11:30 p.m., and when I saw him, I didn't know what to expect. I noticed he had papers in his hand. He explained that he had done all he could with Chuck to this point. He went on to say that they had given Chuck the factor VII (the coagulant.). It would take some time within a twenty-four- to forty-eight-hour window to see whether the factor VII would work. He mentioned that Chuck was still losing blood from the needle holes around the valve. Then he said he didn't know which way this situation would go and that there was a 50 percent possibility that Chuck may have to go back into the OR. He then unrolled the papers in his hand and requested that I sign the consent form for him to be able to do that. He said he hoped that factor VII would begin to work and another surgery for Chuck would not be necessary. If there was going to be an additional surgery, he could only give Chuck a 30 percent chance of survival. Because there was a chance that Chuck may be going back into the OR, the surgeon had decided to keep Chuck's chest open so that he would not have to cut and crack Chuck's chest for a second time. Chuck would be packed with sterile dressing and wrapped tightly with a sterile plastic wrap. He said they were just finishing up with Chuck and I should be able to see him in about two hours or so. He said Chuck would be unconscious, as they would leave him in an induced coma. He told me where to relocate myself into the Intensive Care Unit (ICU) family room and sit and wait for a call, at which point I could come in to see Chuck. That was it; he left to return to the OR. I moved myself and waited for the call.

I really can't remember whether I called into the ICU or they called me. It really doesn't matter. What matters is that I was finally able to go see Chuck. I remember walking down the hall to the ICU and seeing doors that had written on them in big, bold letters, "ABSOLUTELY NO ADMITTANCE / AUTHORZED PERSONNEL ONLY," framed in high-visibility tape. I pressed the button to open the double doors. I walked into the room and will never forget what I saw. There were patients lying in beds motionless, lifeless and still. The nurse at the desk knew who I was; she knew that Chuck belonged to me and I belonged to Chuck. She told me that Chuck was in bed seven, right across from the nurse's station. I walked up to Chuck's bed, absolutely shocked and taken back, even though I had seen him after his surgery in 1981. My high school sweetheart, my husband, my love was in a critical state, lying there with his chest wide open. I could see the soaked dressings that he was packed with. I was scared that his heart was going fall right out from his chest. All I could hear was the beeping of machines and the noise of Chuck's respirator breathing for him. Also, I could hear something trickling like a fountain beside my feet. I looked down beneath the bed. I can only describe what I saw as a machine that looked like a radiator. It was white with four eighteen-inch cylinders bearing milliliter markings, and in them was Chuck's blood. All I could see was wires and tubes going and coming into and out of Chuck's body. There were bags of blood and bags of antibiotics and bags of saline and bags of whatever else on every pole surrounding Chuck's bed. There were two nurses looking after Chuck. One of the nurses was rushing around Chuck without stopping, and the other was charting all of the different medical monitors. The nurse rushing around was changing bags, hooking up more IVs and checking monitors. It seemed to me that she was practically running. I asked her two questions. Firstly, I asked what the purpose of the radiator-looking thing under Chuck's bed was. She said that was Chuck's blood and that they had to monitor how much he was losing. My heart sunk. Secondly, I asked her whether there was anything I could do. She answered, "Yes. You can pray for a miracle." I did exactly that. I prayed for a miracle. I stood by Chuck's bed thinking that this was not the way things were supposed to go.

When I was back in the family room, a vision came to my mind. It was of the three of us—Carly, Matthew, and me—walking behind Chuck's casket at his funeral. I quickly removed that thought from my mind. I knew that wasn't right thinking according to God's Word.

As I mentioned previously, we were attending two churches at that time. The new church we had started going to was an interfaith Bible-based church, the other a Ukrainian Catholic church. Both churches were Christ centered, acknowledging Jesus Christ as humankind's Saviour and the Son of God. The difference was that the Bible-based church was more hands-on and taught that as we learn about the Bible and we put into practice what we learn, we become operators of it. It also taught about the importance of having a relationship with Jesus. According to that church's teachings, if you accepted Him as the Son of God and your Saviour, you would begin to see changes in your life, and you could conquer anything with His wisdom, leadership, and help. We were learning that the Bible was a remarkable book. By "remarkable" I mean miraculous. I was realizing just how ignorant we were of the Bible. The Bible is amazingly resilient. It has survived its critics, and it seems as though its most outspoken opponents come and go but the book continues to lives on.

I know it isn't in vogue or very sophisticated to talk about biblical facts today. Nevertheless, by experience I can tell you that Biblical facts really come in handy when the bottom drops out from under one's life. When your life or the life of your loved one is hanging on by a thread and your future seems uncertain, you really don't want to hear about a book on philosophy. You want to know what God says about your future or whether you even have one. You want to know what it says about your life, your grief, and fear. The best thing you can do is get a Bible in your possession and read it. Do you know that in countries where the Bible is banned, it goes underground and the church flourishes? The Bible is a resilient book that survives all attempts to destroy it. Thousands of years after it was written, God's Word still changes lives and the outcomes of life-threating situations today. His Word has the power to perform the miraculous if you know it, see it, have it written on your heart, and speak it. His Word is our ever-present help, speaking truth when we cannot find it. You must do as Hebrews 11:1 in the NIRV instructs us to do: "Faith is being sure of what we hope for and certain of what we do not see." You have to envision in your mind the miraculous. What I'm telling you is truth, and this truth works. I feel that if you're taking time to read this story, our story, it's my responsibility to share the faith that got us through the toughest times of our lives. I hope not to come off preachy or have you think I'm tying to convert you, because I'm not. It is genuinely a gift to know that there is a God that cares for you and your loved ones and that He can do the impossible. Also, the gift of family and friends—and their love, support, and care—is precious, but they can't do what only God can do. Only your faith in God to choose wisdom regarding which path to take in critical situations can bring about the supernatural and the unexplainable. He can see what we cannot; He can do what we cannot. His will brings life into dead situations. All we have to do is acknowledge Him as the One who can and ask Him to do so in prayer.

Back to the story. I stood there and prayed, and I prayed some more. The prayers were nothing fancy or elegant. I just asked for God to help and keep Chuck alive and to stop Chuck's bleeding. It was probably 3:30 a.m. when I decided I was staying at the hospital. I wanted to be there. If I went home, I'd just want to come back. Even though there was nothing I could do physically for Chuck, I could do heavenly things, such as praying and thinking and speaking life in and over him. I kept going into the ICU, probably every hour on the hour. Nothing changed, but daylight did come.

On Tuesday morning, I called home. The phone was picked up on the first ring. I can't remember who answered, but Carly and Matthew did not go to school that day. Transcona Collegiate was tremendous in supporting Carly, Matthew, and me during the entire forty days Chuck was in the hospital. We as a family had great relationships with the teachers.

Carly and Matthew arrived at the hospital around 9:00 a.m. I explained to them what had happened late in the night and in the wee early morning hours with their dad. I told them as best I could what to expect when they saw Chuck in the ICU. We went in. Of course, they were anxious and, I think, a bit scared to see their dad. We walked up to his bed, and I stood very close to them as they looked at Chuck. Both of them had tears in their eyes. I could see them looking at all the machines, their dad's open chest, the multiple bags of IV antibiotics, and bags of blood. It was terribly upsetting for them to see their dad in such a critical state. To Carly, Chuck was her real-life superhero; in fact, he still is to this day. To Matthew, Chuck was his best friend, his sporting event partner, his fishing partner, and, most definitely, his wrestling opponent—so much so that in one of their after-supper evening wrestling matches, they accidently tore down the blinds at our family summer cottage. They asked me whether there was anything they could do—exactly the question I had asked the nurse when I first saw Chuck. I answered exactly as she did. I put my arms around them and said, "Yes, we have to pray for a miracle." We prayed over Chuck with the laying on of hands, our hands touching Chuck's body. We prayed and asked for total healing and, specifically, for Chuck's blood to stop leaking and start clotting. I could hear the sniffling of tears as I myself wiped my cheeks. We did believe our prayers were heard, and I can tell you that they were. Yes, indeed they were. We blew kisses toward Chuck, as it was impossible to get near him; there were too many wires, machines, and tubes to get near to his cheeks. We left the ICU and went back into the family room. We sat for quite some time, saying nothing.

Carly and Matthew brought comfort to me just being by my side. I had to talk positively about the situation to them, because this was their dad, who meant everything to them. Life without him would be undoable for all of us. In speaking life into the situation and repeatedly saying Chuck was going to be made healed and whole through the power of Jesus Christ, I was putting my faith into action. The power of this promise is written in His Word. By declaring it out loud, not only was I hearing myself say it, but it was coming out from my lips, going in through my ears, and sinking in and on my heart and being embedded into my bones. Not even knowing it, I really began to think we were going to beat this situation. Actually, when I look back, I think people thought we were naive or ignorant of the fact of how sick Chuck really was. But we weren't. We put all our trust and hope in God Almighty, and He saw us through. We put into practice what we had been taught from both our churches. I had the pastor, Pastor Ernest from Springs Church, come pray and lay hands on Chuck, as His Word instructs. Also I had the priest Father Michael come from St Michaels Parish come and anoint Chuck's body as His Word instructs. His Word is truth, and it never comes back null or void. No word from His Word is spoken in vain.

The kids and I went in and out throughout the day to see Chuck, but there was no change. Evening rolled around, and it was time for Carly and Matthew to go home. I had decided to stay at the hospital day and night. My mom had sent an overnight bag with the kids, so I had the few things I needed to do so.

Chuck's surgeon spoke with me a few times throughout the next few days. He came into the ICU regularly to see whether there was any progress in Chuck's condition. In fact, the surgeon stayed overnight on the first night just in case on a moment's notice he would have to take Chuck back into the OR. His plan if Chuck's blood did not begin to clot was to take Chuck back into the OR on Friday morning and do another valve replacement. As much as he didn't want to do that because it was such a great risk to Chuck, the alternative was Chuck bleeding to death. I heard what he was saying, but I didn't want either of those outcomes for Chuck. So, I stood firm in my belief and just didn't waver in what we were believing and praying for. Tuesday night passed. Wednesday morning passed. Wednesday night passed. Then Thursday morning rolled around; it was the break of a new day. It was before 6:00 a.m. early Thursday morning when I woke up from sleeping on the cold plastic couch in the ICU family room. The hospital had provided me a pillow and a blanket, which I appreciated.

There's a sidenote I'd like to share. One night, two Hutterite women also stayed overnight at the hospital as their husband and father had cardiac surgery. They, too, slept on the cold plastic couches. I spent a lot of time with them over the next few days. They were very nice and very concerned and worried for Chuck and me. They sewed me a beautiful notion bag to keep my personal items and toiletries in, which I still have. They also invited my kids to visit their colony one day, which never happened. The night they stayed over in the room with me, we all prayed before we lay down. You know those little black kerchiefs (niqabs) they wear on their heads? Well, when they pray, they take them off and put them over their faces. I never did ask them why. Even the women who leave the colonies put the niqabs back on when they pray. In doing a quick Google search, I found that that custom goes back to the veiled woman that prayed to God in Biblical times.

As I was saying, Thursday morning had dawned. I washed my face, fixed my hair, put some makeup on, and brushed my teeth. Okay, I was ready to go see Chuck. I called in to the ICU, and they said I could come in. When I walked in, I noticed that the two nurses looking after Chuck looked calmer and almost seemed to be half-smiling. As I came to Chuck's bed, the nurse looked at me and said the words we had been believing and praying for and longing to hear. I can see her clear eyes, her sandy brown hair, and her angelic mouth saying, "Chuck's blood is starting to coagulate, and this is a good sign." I'm sure you can imagine my relief and the joy I felt when I heard what she had said. The first thing I did was thank God for what He was doing. I left the ICU and went back into the family room. I couldn't wait to tell the Hutterite women! Then I called home with this astonishing news. I'm sure you can imagine the joy, relief, and thankfulness at the other end of the phone. This good news quickly spread to all the people who had been praying and standing with us for Chuck to begin healing. Our daughter Carly told one of our family friends, "Keep praying, because it's working." And yes, we all kept praying with our eyes were fixed on the Divine Physician, the Healer, Christ Jesus. I can assure you that He is alive and capable of cleaning and getting us through our messes, no matter what they may be. He truly loves and cares for us and can be and is our true help in times of trouble. Our responsibility is to seek and ask in prayer, and believe in His mighty power. I can promise you this: He is faithful and can do the impossible—and not only once, but over and over again.

Carly and Matthew came to the hospital and spent the day with me. All the people that I had come to know in the hospital that week were so happy for us and somewhat surprised to hear that Chuck was beginning to heal. I guess that was because Chuck's situation was critical and looked so bleak. Chuck's surgeon had come to see me to say that if Chuck kept moving the in the right direction, Chuck would be going into the OR on Friday morning for the surgeon to close up his chest.

Even though Chuck was in an induced coma, he began to wake up and move. I think this was because his body was beginning to feel life again. They couldn't have Chuck wake up, because his chest was open and he was still on the respirator, which meant it would be shocking and stressful on him. But it was good for me and the kids to see him stir. It was a sign there was life in him. Chuck kept progressing throughout the day. His blood was coagulating, his blood pressure was stabilizing, and everything was looking promising.

Friday morning rolled around; it was a beautiful, bright sunny day. The day had come; Chuck was going into the OR to be closed up. The plan was that as soon as they finished up with Chuck, they would wake him up and slowly let his recovery and rehabilitation begin.

You can imagine the surprise it was to Chuck when I told him what day it was. When he first heard it was Friday, I'm sure he thought I was joking or kidding. He muttered something in French—a slang term. He ran his hands through his hair, trying to understand how it got to be Friday when he was well aware that he went into surgery on Monday. It took a while for everything to sink in. I slowly shared with him all the events that had taken place over the past week. Chuck was very weak—so weak that a plastic spoon was too heavy for him. His heart rate was extremely high; I remember that his heart was beating in the 180s per minute. The reason I can recall this so easily is because I thought to myself, *How long will his heart be able to keep this up without something going wrong?* Chuck's rehabilitation was a very slow and lengthy process, but he was making progress, and we were so grateful for this.

On day thirty after the surgery, Chuck called home to say

he was finally discharged. The kids and I were ecstatic. It was a Saturday, and Carly had a dance rehearsal downtown at Pantages Theatre. I told Chuck I would be there as soon as possible, but it wouldn't be as fast as he hoped for. Chuck understandably was very anxious to get out of the hospital and come home, He called several times, asking where I was and what was taking me so long. I assured him that I would be there right after I dropped Carly off. I didn't want Carly to have to worry about parking all day, so that's why I chose to drive her. Doing so meant it took me longer to get to the hospital to pick up Chuck, which ended up being a blessing in disguise. These little coincidences or circumstances that happen to us, I can assure you, don't occur by chance. I believe and promise you that all these little things are orchestrated by God for our protection. Sometimes we don't even know it until we take time to look back into our lives.

I finally arrived at the hospital, and I was so happy that Chuck was well enough to come home—so I thought. Chuck's room was at the very end of a long hall that was right next door to the chapel. I had spent a lot of time there, and when Chuck got progressively stronger, he joined me, praising and praying to God for what He was doing.

When I walked into Chuck's room, I was shocked I at what I saw. In my mind I thought I would see Chuck sitting in on the edge of the bed, dressed, with his bag ready to go. Instead, Chuck was in his jacket, buried under the covers. I was so taken aback; I was actually in disbelief. Chuck had gone downstairs to get himself a drink, and while doing that, he thought, he caught a chill. I told Chuck we had to call a nurse back in to assess him before I took him home. He looked pale, and he was shivering. The nurse came in and took his vitals, and sure enough, he had a fever. Instantly coming home was no longer the plan. Chuck landed back in a ward called Stepdown, which is the ward you go in after the ICU. It's lesser care than that of an ICU but more individualized care than a regular ward offers. There were only eight beds in the ward, and there were always two nurses charting and looking after the patients. Chuck was diagnosed with having a bacteria shower. A bacteria shower is a pocket of bacteria somewhere in a person's system that eventually bursts and goes through the entire body, making the person very sick. Chuck was back on a heavy regimen of IV antibiotics. He ended up staying in the hospital an extra ten days. The delay in picking Chuck up that day was, as I said before, a blessing in disguise. Had I picked him up earlier that morning, he would have again had to go through the whole process of going in through the emergency ward. I couldn't even begin to think what may have happened had I taken Chuck home. We might have waited, hoping it would pass, and waited too long. God's protection was over our lives back then, as it is now. God is for us, and He had proved Himself faithful again. The best thing I can hope for you is that you begin to trust God completely, should you not already.

In the next week leading up to ten days, Chuck got better slowly as the antibiotics fought the bacteria shower. Chuck came home on Wednesday, May 19; his stay in the hospital was a total of forty days. The IV antibiotic treatment continued at home for eight weeks, and Chuck kept getting stronger and heathier. Chuck returned to work in a year's time, and life returned to normal. Normal … how good normal is. I think we all take our normal for granted; at least I do, at times. Our everyday life is such a gift. Just to have the ability to get up in the morning and walk into the bathroom to use the toilet is a gift. There are so many people who can't even do that, never mind having all five senses—the abilities to see, to hear, to touch, to taste, and to smell—and the ability to walk and to talk. These are all gifts that many of us consider normal, but for many others it's not this way. The good stuff, the normal stuff in our lives, is all so very precious; we cannot take any of it for granted.

I realize that I have spent a lot of time going into Chuck's medical history, but even that journey testifies to the goodness of God. None of it was good luck, circumstance, coincidence, or karma. It was none of that. The outcome was a result of the miraculous—the supernatural power of Christ, activated by us putting our faith in Him. The time will come in all our lives when our hearts will beat their last beat and we will take our last breath. Until then, I can guarantee you this: every one of us will have to face challenges, trials, storms, troubles, obstacles, and unfavorable situations in our everyday lives, and we are going to have to fight to overcome them. The best way I know how to do this is by putting my faith in the One God and speaking about the problem as fixed, resolved, and done—not in our own strength, but in His. We must speak about it not as what we see, but rather as what we are hoping for. That is exactly what Hebrews 11:1 (NIV) says we have to do. I can tell you from experience that it works. But it comes from within you and what you believe and believe in.

I believe in the scriptures written in the Bible. The Old Testament prophesizes about what would happen and how Jesus would come into this world and how He would die. After His death, He told us He had to leave the earth to ascend into heaven to send down the Holy Spirit, who would become our helper and our comforter. Jesus said we would be able to do even more than He Himself did. But to do this, you have to know His Word, believe it, and follow His instruction. It's not about rules and regulations; It's about neither religion nor traditions. It's about believing in the Son of God, who was renamed the Son of Man, who came into this world not to condemn but to save humankind. To operate in the Holy Spirit's power, you need to read about Jesus's miracles while He was here for His short time on earth, as laid out in the New Testament. He gives us the keys to the kingdom, the miraculous, and tells us how to operate in them. He gives us the authority and the power to speak over situations. I choose to believe, and He did the impossible for our family. That's all I can tell you. The reason I'm writing this book is to give you hope in a hopeless situation and in your times of challenge, for you to conquer your giants. I want you to be able to fight the good fight of faith. He fights our battles, and no matter the outcome, He is God, and I believe that with Him we are victorious in our circumstances. I'm not telling you this hypothetically; I'm telling you this from experience. This is ultimate truth; Jesus is the ultimate truth. He does what He says He will do. To make these promises available to you and your loved ones, you need to read what they are, know them, and speak them over your life. Now, on with the story.

CHAPTER 4

This Can't Be

Now let's go back to where we left off before I went into Chuck's medical history. I'll just give a small recap of January 7, 2016. We had just come home from spending New Year's in Calgary, and Chuck had been feeling very ill and had a fever. It had been a very rough night for Chuck on January 6, so I had made a doctor's appointment for Chuck in the late afternoon. Chuck felt he couldn't muster enough energy to go; he was feeling that sick. With my persuasion, he agreed and went to the appointment Thursday afternoon. I tried calling him on his cell to see what the doctor had thought his sickness was. He didn't answer his cell. That was because when I arrived home, he was sound asleep, nestled under the covers.

I nudged him to wake him, as I was anxious to hear what the doctor had said. He slowly awoke and told me that the doctor was not sure what was going on but had given him a requisition to get some blood work done. Chuck seemed extremely groggy to me; he was definitely not himself. I asked Chuck whether Dr. C—— had prescribed him any antibiotics. When Chuck said no, I became instantly infuriated. I knew Chuck's prosthetic heart valve put him at risk and that Chuck was more vulnerable than the average person. I tried to make sense of it but couldn't reason why Dr. C—— wouldn't have prescribed him antibiotics to nip in the bud whatever this illness was. I was so upset that I called the doctor's office, praying that the doctor was still there. I dialed the number, the phone rang, and his receptionist answered the phone. I asked to speak to Dr. C——, and she put me on hold. To my relief, the doctor picked up the phone and asked how he could help me. I asked why he hadn't prescribed Chuck antibiotics, as he was well aware of Chuck's medical history. I asked him to please call the pharmacy and call in some medication so Chuck could get some kind of remedy and treatment going on. To my vast disappointment, he refused. This moment right here was a blessing in disguise, but I didn't realize it at the time. Right here, at this moment, we were under God's divine protection, and His way would prove better than mine. But as I said, I didn't know that at the time and sure wasn't feeling it. Dr. C—— told me he would get Chuck's blood test back probably midmorning and would call me as soon as he looked over the results. I couldn't argue about it anymore; he wasn't going to change his mind. I hung up the phone and hoped for the best.

I had made dinner. Chuck had eaten a small amount—not much, but it was better than nothing. I think food fuels our bodies. Exactly what we put into our bodies; we get out of our bodies. What we eat either promotes disease or fights disease. I was hoping the greens, the broccoli, and the salad would nourish and fuel Chuck's body with health. It was Thursday evening, and Chuck had made arrangements with his mom to take her to an appointment on Saturday morning. I thought that the best thing to do was for Chuck to let his mom know he was feeling very ill so that she could possibly get someone else to take her or reschedule the appointment.

My stomach is tightened as I capture this memory in my writing. I passed him the phone. He looked at it and paused. I said, "Chuck, call your mom."

Chuck had called his mom on a regular basis; Chuck knew his mom's number. He looked at the phone and said, "What's the number?"

I said the number, thinking to myself that everyone forgets a number now and then. Again, he looked at the phone and paused. I asked him what was wrong and why he wasn't dialing. So he began to dial, but the numbers he chose were not his mom's; in fact, he was just pressing numbers randomly. I asked him what he was doing. He put the phone down.

I said, "Chuck, you have to call your mom. Chuck, is everything okay?"

I knew it wasn't. I passed him the phone again, not because I couldn't or didn't want to dial for him, but because my senses immediately went into high alert. He tried again, and he couldn't do it. Of course, I didn't know what was going on, but I knew this was not normal and not good, and I could definitely tell this whole situation with Chuck was getting worse. So I dialed the number and passed the phone to Chuck. His niece Charlene answered the phone. Chuck's conversation with her was broken and didn't make any sense. He said bye and hung up. At this time, I led Chuck back to the couch, and he laid down. I called Chuck's mom again to give her the message that he would not be able to take her to her appointment on Saturday, but more importantly to talk about what just had happened.

Again I dialed the number, and our niece Charlene again answered the phone. I asked her how she was and so on. Then I asked her whether she had spoken to Chuck, and she said yes. I asked her whether what Chuck had said made any sense to her. She answered, "No, not really." I talked to Chuck's mom about Chuck not being able to take her on Saturday. Gloria completely understood and just said for Chuck to take it easy and look after himself and rest.

I remember getting off the phone and thinking I needed to do something. I actually was of clear mind, strong and certain of what my next steps should be. Trust me; this was not of my own strength, direction, or wisdom. My steps were set before me and ordered by the undeniable supernatural power of the Holy Spirit, and I listened to Him. Although I could feel this situation move down into my stomach, I remained calm. The Holy Spirit put me into motion.

This was to keep us safe and protected; no weapon formed against us could prosper, as the Bible tells us in Isaiah 54: 17. I truly believe this because it's true. As a Christ follower, this is a guarantee. But *you* must know it, believe, and speak it. He makes us brave as we lean in and trust in Him.

I remembered that I had taped into one of my cupboards a brochure of important phone numbers that we had received in the mail. I went and opened the cupboard, and there was the phone number to Health Links. I dialed he number and was put through to a nurse. I spoke with her, telling her about Chuck's history and what had been going on the last week or so. I told her about the incident that had just taken place on the phone with his niece. She asked for me to put Chuck on the phone.

I went to the couch, nudged Chuck, and told him Health Links was on the phone and a nurse wanted to speak to him. To be honest, Chuck was not very happy with me, most likely because I woke him up again, but he did speak to the nurse. She asked him a couple of questions, which I could not hear, but I could hear Chuck's answers, which gave me a good idea he most likely was not answering them correctly.

Chuck passed the phone back to me. Actually I think he just let it go and dropped it to the ground. I put the phone to my ear and remember the nurse asking where we lived and saying, "You must take him to the hospital now."

It was not really a surprise to me to hear the nurse say those words. Even though I wished this wasn't happening, it was, and the only way we were going to get out of this was by going through it. I started having flashbacks of 2004. I thought there was no way this could happen to Chuck and our family again.

It was about 9:45 p.m. when I told Chuck I was going upstairs to get dressed and that I was taking him to St. Boniface Hospital. Chuck grumbled a bit about it, but to my surprise he didn't resist the idea. I did explain to him that we needed to find out what was going on with him and that waiting for Dr. C—— to call the next morning was too long to wait. I got dressed and gathered Chuck's medication and glasses. Chuck already had his jacket on, and I could see that this was a huge effort for him because he was feeling so poorly. We got in my Jeep, and I drove to St. Boniface Hospital. I remember it was snowing.

Our ride to the hospital confirmed to me that the hospital was definitely the place we needed to go. Chuck and I didn't talk much, but when we did, I was well aware that Chuck was becoming more confused. When we arrived at the hospital, I parked at Emergency. I explained my situation to security, and they allowed me to leave my vehicle in the Emergency parking longer than the ten-minute maximum. To my relief, there were probably only five people in the waiting room. So we went to register Chuck as a patient. The nurse asked the regular questions: name, address, birth date, and why we were there. She took his temperature, which confirmed that Chuck still had a fever, which was no surprise to me; she also took his heart rate, which was normal. I explained the situation and made her aware of Chuck's prosthetic heart valve. I also mentioned that Chuck had had a dental appointment for a cleaning on December 8, which he had been premedicated for. All patients with prostheses require premedication prior to dental work to resist any bacteria that may enter the bloodstream from the mouth. As I mentioned the dental appointment to the nurse, to my surprise, Chuck spoke up, commenting that he'd also had another appointment with the dentist on December 17 that he had not been premedicated for. When he said that, I doubted what he was saying, firstly because I knew nothing of the appointment, which was unusual; secondly because Chuck and his dentist—who, by the way, is no longer our dentist—knew that Chuck required pre-medication; and thirdly because Chuck was experiencing confusion. So Chuck and I had a side conversation in front of the nurse debating the December 17 appointment. I could see we weren't going to come to an agreement on this, so I just stopped debating and went on with the process. The nurse had gathered all the information she required of us and told us to be seated and wait for Chuck's name to be called.

The waiting room was pretty quiet, other than a girl in front of us who was not well. She was there with her partner, who was very attentive to her as she kept moaning and throwing up in a pail. We moved our seats a few more rows behind them. I wanted to give her some space, and I also didn't want Chuck or myself to catch a flu bug if that was what she had.

Chuck and I talked quietly more about this "phantom" dentist appointment on December 17. As we did, a few things were running through my mind. *Could it be that he didn't tell me because he wasn't medicated and he knew very well that I would have cancelled that appointment until he was premedicated?* I determined I would confirm this appointment with the dentist's office. Being as it was Thursday night and his office was closed Fridays, I would have to wait until Monday to do so. I really couldn't help but wonder whether this appointment was just a figment of Chuck's imagination, because by this time he was very confused. He was so confused that when the nurse asked him what the date was, he answered with a date in the 1930s.

Our wait wasn't too long before they called Chuck's name. We went in through the big secure door. They gave Chuck a bed in the Emergency Ward. The area was small, but it had a privacy curtain all around, a tray table, and a chair, which I was thankful for. We got settled behind the curtain, they gave Chuck a gown to change into and a bag for his personal items, and they told us a doctor would be in shortly. So we sat and waited.

At this time, I decided to call Matthew and Carly. I couldn't reach Matthew, but Carly picked up right away. She was so shocked and distraught to hear what was going on with Chuck because we'd had such a great time the week before with her and her husband Chris in Calgary, ringing in the New Year. She instantly wanted to come to Winnipeg. I told her I would make travel arrangements for her to be here the next day, which I did.

At this time, Chuck wasn't doing too badly. The time was close to midnight, so we were both pretty tired. He was dozing off from time to time, and I was sitting and waiting in the chair for the doctor to come in. It wasn't long until I heard the shuffling of feet and saw a few pairs of shoes from under the curtain. Sure enough, it was our turn; the team of doctors came in to see Chuck. I remember seeing that the doctor was a petite woman when they pulled back the curtain. Actually, I would describe her more as a girl. She introduced herself and started asking Chuck and me some questions.

Chuck was able to answer most of the questions, but some of his answers were wrong and vague. So the very young petite doctor looked at me for some answers. I did my best to answer correctly. I made the point of repeating the fact of Chuck saying he'd had a second dentist appointment on December 17 that he claimed he had not been premedicated for. I had a very hard time believing this and convinced myself that Chuck was confused. It was so concerning to me and was bothering me, especially the fact that I wouldn't be able to confirm whether it was true until Monday. The doctor's bedside manner was very caring and thorough. Even though she looked around fifteen years of age, I felt very confident in her ability.

All that was in my mind was the second dentist appointment. I knew the consequence of infection after dental work concerning Chuck with his prosthetic heart valve. Back in 2004, only by God's grace did Chuck make it through. I can't even explain how I was hoping that this sickness was not the result of the dental appointment. I couldn't believe that Chuck would ever have dental work done without premedication, or that our dentist would perform work on Chuck without premedication. I was so well aware of the risk of endocarditis. Never did I want Chuck or our family to have to go through that nightmare again.

They decided to start Chuck on an IV to keep him hydrated and give him some Tylenol to help with his fever. They took some blood samples to run further tests to determine what was going on with Chuck. Chuck seemed somewhat settled—as settled as he possibly could be in an Emergency Ward. I remember looking at the clock and seeing it was sometime around 4:00 a.m. The doctor came in and said Chuck would not be going home and they would be keeping him and most likely taking him onto a ward. They suggested I go home and get some rest and come back later. I wasn't 100 percent comfortable with doing this, but I was extremely fatigued and wanted to offload Chuck's clothes, winter jacket, and boots, since there was no room to store them behind the curtains of the emergency bay we were in. I asked Chuck whether he was okay with me leaving and coming back later, and he agreed. Reluctantly I gathered Chuck's and my belongings and put on my jacket as I got ready to leave. I kept on asking Chuck whether he was certain it was okay for me to go home. He kept on saying yes, so I kissed Chuck goodbye and assured him I'd be back around 9:00 a.m. After a couple more kisses, I left.

I'll never forget the feeling I felt when I was walking back to my car that night. So many things were running through my head. I remember it was a clear night—actually it was the wee early morning hours, sometime just before 5:00 a.m. There was no one around, and there was no traffic—maybe the odd car. It was cold, but there was no wind and the moon was full. I felt very alone and distraught, wondering where all of this was going to take us. I was relieved to reach my car but sad that I was going home alone. I didn't have a good feeling. I knew the hospital was the best place for Chuck to be. I knew that something big was going on with him, but I didn't know just how big it was going to be.

CHAPTER 5

Please Don't Tell Me

When I arrived home, I was relieved to see Matthew's Jeep in the driveway. I walked in, took off my boots, and went up and gave him the snapshot of what was going on with Chuck. I told him to get a couple hours' more sleep and said we would go to the hospital at 8:00 a.m.

I washed my face, changed into my nightgown, and very tiredly crawled into our bed. Doing this brought back a lot of memories of 2004, when Chuck was in the hospital for forty days. I fell asleep immediately, but not into a deep sleep; I was in and out.

It didn't feel like I had slept much, but yet it felt as though I had left the hospital days prior. I called the Emergency Ward to see how things were going with Chuck. They put me on hold; a doctor came on at the other end. His report wasn't what I wanted to hear. Chuck's confusion had rapidly progressed since I had left. At this time, they had Constant Care (a health-care aide) assigned to him one on one, as Chuck was now deemed an at-risk patient. My heart sank; this was not what I had been hoping for. I thanked the doctor, told him I'd be there shortly, and hung up the phone. My mind was racing. I went into Matthew's room, shook him, and woke him up. I told him we needed to get to the hospital as soon as we could. Quickly we both got ready to go; the plan would work well, as he would have time to come and see Chuck, and then he could go get Carly at the airport as she was coming in at 11:30 a.m. Matthew called in to work and told them he would be out because of a family emergency.

In my heart, I knew this was bigger than just a few days in the hospital. I knew that we were going into deep waters, but I had no idea how deep those waters were going to be. Not only did I want Chuck to have the best care in the hospital, but I also knew we needed God in this. Just before we were leaving the house, I told Matthew that we needed to pray urgently. We joined hands and prayed that God would watch over Chuck and us, and that we would conquer this victoriously with His help. Although at the time I had no clue what was going on or where this was going to lead, I felt secure, and I honestly can say I wasn't fearful. I knew God was with me and was walking beside us every step of the way through all this.

I remembered that back in 2004, when Chuck was in a fragile state, the one and only thing that turned the situation around was prayer. I thought I needed to get as many people as possible praying immediately. I called our urgent prayer line from our church. I told them our circumstance, and they said they would get prayer going for Chuck and our family. I thanked them and hung up the phone. It was not too long before the phone rang. I picked up, and to my surprise—but also to my relief—on the other end was our dear friend Pastor Ernest from Springs Church. He asked me what was going on, and I told him as much as I knew, and he said he was going to go down to St Boniface Hospital to see Chuck. I said that I was going to the hospital shortly and I would see him there. I was so thankful he called and was grateful that he was going to the hospital.

When Matthew and I arrived the hospital, Matthew dropped me off at the door and went to park the car. I checked in at the patient desk, and they allowed me in to go see Chuck. I remember turning the corner and seeing Pastor Ernest already there, standing at the foot of Chuck's bed. When I reached Chuck's bed, I was taken aback and shocked to see Chuck's worsened condition. Chuck was standing up, jostling with his Constant Care aide. I was in disbelief and was shocked to see him in such a state. When I said, "Hi, Chuck," he looked right past me and uttered words that weren't English. They weren't words of any language; they were rumblings, mumblings. It was complete gibberish.

I walked right up close to Chuck and said, "Chuck, I'm here."

Again Chuck was talking a fabricated language; he was slipping in and out of normalcy. He was getting very loud and kept asking, "Where is my wife?"

I kept saying, I'm here, Chuck, right here." But he couldn't see me; it was as though I was a ghost.

Chuck kept on physically struggling with his Constant Care aide, whose name was Elmer. With all the turmoil going on, I finally greeted Pastor Ernest. I know Pastor Ernest was as shocked as I to see Chuck in this turbulent state. Pastor Ernest asked me how long this confusion had been going on. I explained that when I had left at 4:30 a.m., Chuck had been relaxed and understood why we had come to the hospital. In the short time I had been gone, Chuck's condition had spiraled downward and had deteriorated by 100 percent.

I could hear Matthew's footsteps coming down the hall. When Matthew came around the curtain and saw Chuck robustly jostling with Elmer, Matthew instantly became distraught as he witnessed Chuck's state of disorientation. Matthew tried everything to get Chuck's attention, including softly talking and directly looking into Chuck's unfocused eyes. Matthew joined in the struggle with Elmer in trying to keep Chuck at bay, calm and manageable, but the situation was escalating. To give you a clearer picture of what was taking place, I'll say it this way; Elmer was definitely earning his pay. Actually, he probably wasn't earning enough. Elmer clearly had a way with Chuck; he was able to calm and settle Chuck to sit down, but it didn't last long. Elmer would talk with Chuck, and for the most part Chuck would listen to Elmer and do what Elmer told him to do. Basically, the goal was just to get Chuck to stay on the bed or sit in one of the chairs.

Matthew, Pastor Ernest, and I did not know what to make of all this. We all knew one thing, though: that Chuck was rapidly going into a tailspin. All the doctors in Emergency were very good and extremely concerned, running all kinds of tests on Chuck. One of the sicknesses they were trying to test for and either confirm or rule out was meningitis. I kept on telling them about the second dental appointment Chuck said he'd had on December 17. As I stated previously, I would have to wait until Monday to confirm with the dentist's office whether he had his required antibiotic premedication or not. Monday seemed years away in this chaos.

Time flew by. It came time for Matthew to leave to pick up Carly from the airport, and Pastor Ernest had to leave to continue with his other obligations. Pastor Ernest said goodbye to Chuck and told me to keep in touch with him. Matthew spoke to Chuck, assuring him that he'd be back and that he was bringing Carly back with him. Although Chuck's mental condition was altered, I think Chuck understood—or maybe it was me, just hoping that he knew what Matthew had said to him.

Elmer handled Chuck extremely well. He was practicing every skill and attribute of patience, understanding, care, and concern to keep Chuck somewhat controlled. Elmer was exceptional at his job, and luckily Chuck liked him. I thanked God for Elmer, hoping that he would keep Chuck safe at least until Carly had a chance to see her dad.

It didn't seem too long before Matthew was back with Carly. It was so good to see her. Somehow, I felt more secure with my kids around me. Carly was so happy to finally see her dad. She was visibly shaken when she walked into the situation, which had escalated to a whole new level since Matthew had left and returned with her.

The jostling between Chuck and Elmer had now turned into all-out wrestling. Things were starting to get tossed and shoved around, such as the tray table, the chairs, the bed, and the IV pole. The situation and Chuck were getting very loud. doctors were coming in the surrounding curtain frequently, assessing the situation. By this time, Matthew had stepped in to help Elmer wrestle Chuck.

It was taking the two of them to keep Chuck in his bay. Carly was extremely upset; she was crying and doing everything she possibly could to try to settle Chuck into a calm state. Also, the other people in the Emergency Ward were getting very curious and were trying to see what was going on. A doctor told everyone to please stay in their own bed areas. I can best describe what was going on as a nightmare that I was hoping I would wake up from soon.

Elmer was beyond spent. A second Constant Care aide was called in to help manage Chuck, and his demeanor and approach were very different than Elmer's. It was quickly evident that Chuck didn't like his approach or him. Elmer was told to go for a break and also asked whether he wanted to stay overtime, to which, not surprisingly, he said no. Elmer grabbed his backpack and went off for a very deserved break.

The new Constant Care aide was trying to settle Chuck, but in reality, all he seemed to be achieving was making Chuck angry. Because of the fact that Chuck wouldn't listen to him, he himself was getting very frustrated at Chuck, which was elevating the chaos. He almost seemed to be borderline threatening Chuck, which was the wrong thing to do. Matthew's keen sense picked up on the conflict and stepped in, being the primary caregiver and wrestler.

Matthew's experience of wrestling with Chuck was a skill that was much needed right now. For years, since Matthew had grown big enough to jump on his dad, Matthew and Chuck had wrestled. I'm not sure who enjoyed it more, Matthew or Chuck. Actually, they both loved the matches. As the years went on, the matches became more challenging for both of them. I specifically remember one time at our cottage after dinner, which was the usual time the wrestling to took place. Once the matches began, it was often difficult to stop them, and this was one of those times. I was in there with my weapon, a wooden spoon, tapping each of them while shouting for them to stop. But neither of them was listening to me; really, they probably didn't even hear me. Before I knew it, someone's foot got caught in the blind cord, and crashing down came the blind.

Yeah, that stopped the match. Of course, Carly, Chuck, and Matt all looked at me. Back then I wasn't too impressed, but now we all laugh at it when we reminisce about it. Luckily the years of wrestling practice were now helpful and useful, because Matthew knew all of Chuck's moves. I say this seriously; wrestling truly was a valuable skill set in this chaotic situation.

As I said before, Chuck wasn't having any of this second Constant Care aide, and he was now getting aggressive with Matthew. Matthew wrestled Chuck onto the bed and pinned him. The Constant Care aide then called for help. Two security guards came in to help calm the situation, so they thought, but they weren't enough. The next thing I knew, over the intercom came the announcement "Code white in Emergency." The doctor pulled me aside in all the chaos and explained that Chuck was chewing through the drugs they were using in trying to settle him down. He further explained they had no other choice but to put Chuck into an induced coma, which meant he would be put on a respirator, intubated and unconscious. I couldn't really believe this was happening, but at this point there honestly was no other option.

Of course, this was devastating to me. Chuck on life support meant him being "out." The thought crossed my mind, and I questioned whether the doctors would be able to measure whether his condition was deteriorating or, as I hoped, improving. But really, the situation was very unruly and chaotic; something had to be done.

Security had to call for help; Chuck was that strong. It took at least ten people to get Chuck to lie down so the drugs that would knock him out could be administered. The doctor told us to step outside the curtain, as they were going to intubate Chuck. So, with tears in our eyes, Matthew gave Chuck a hug, and then Carly and I gave Chuck a hug and a kiss. I told Chuck we would see him in a short while, fully knowing I didn't know when that would be. Sadly, Chuck didn't know or understand what was going on. Regrettably, at this point Chuck honestly didn't even know where he was.

I took this time as an opportunity to call family. Some of my family—my sister and Chuck's family, his sisters—live in different provinces, so they asked me whether they should come to Winnipeg. I couldn't make that decision for any of them. I couldn't make that call and didn't want to, especially because I had no idea where this situation was going. I knew one thing though—maybe two. Firstly, Chuck wasn't going to be coming home anytime soon. Secondly, I needed God in this, because He would oversee what was going on and what was going to take place; only He could give Chuck the protection he needed from here on in. I truly believed this.

Both of Chuck's sisters flew into Winnipeg on Friday, January 8, 2016, Janice from Vancouver Island and Beth from Montreal. Also, "my sister Barbara and my brother-in-law Derek" came in from Calgary. Carly's husband, Chris, flew in early Saturday morning to see Chuck and be with all of us. To this day, I am so very grateful for everyone—Chris, Barb, Derek, Janice, and Beth—coming in from out of town and to all the family for their love, support, kindness, care, meals, help, and just simply being there in our darkest hours, which there were many of.

Carly, Matthew, and I were sitting at a desk in the hallway of Emergency. It became very quiet from Chuck's bay. It wasn't long after that the doctor told us that they had finished the intubation procedure on Chuck and we could now go see him. Even though we had seen Chuck on a respirator before, to me it was still shocking; it was never an easy thing to see. Chuck was now in a room off to the side behind glass doors. It looked like a smaller version of an operating room. The doctor opened the door to the cold and sterile room, and he left us there, alone with Chuck. There we saw Chuck lying completely still, covered with a white sheet hanging down, almost touching the floor. His handsome face now had two tubes coming from his mouth, and he seemed completely gone. To see him like this brought on a very lonely feeling for me. All I could hear was the sound of the respirator breathing for him. Carly and Matthew were also visibly shaken. The doctor came back into this room and told us that Chuck was now going to be moved to the second-floor

MICU (medical intensive care unit). There he would have his own nurse 24-7 to care for and look after him, as he was now deemed in critical condition. They told us to gather our belongings and go upstairs to the second floor. There we would stay in the MICU waiting room until someone would call and give us the okay to come see Chuck.

CHAPTER 6

What's Next

When we went up to the second floor, it was all too familiar. This was the ward in which my mom was admitted to the hospital back in 2012 with a blood infection. My mom was never released from the hospital; she passed away on August 19, 2012. To this day I wish that she would have beaten her illness, but that's not the way things worked out. I miss her every day.

Carly, Matthew, and I remained in the waiting room that was outside of the MICU. It was late afternoon, and we all were absent from our everyday lives, having been suddenly immersed into this family emergency. I guess this was one of those life changes that people describe as happening in "the blink of an eye" or "a moment's time." I think the biggest gift in my life is the gift of faith that God placed in me. This seed was watered by my mom, who took me to church from the day I was born. Over the years, I have nurtured and studied the Word of God. In doing so, it has seen me go through many obstacles and trials with victory. It has kept me protected, and my feet have never been snared in a trap of defeat, depression, anxiety, or fear. This is because I don't rely on myself or others to fix or save me. I put my trust in God and pray and talk to Him, and I pray for the wisdom of the Holy Spirit to guide and protect me. I live in that realm and try my best to remember His promises and live my life according to His written Word, and He keeps me under His wing every time.

Even though I would have wished this ordeal to simply go away, disappear, it wasn't going anywhere. I knew we would have to go through it. I remembered He makes a way when there is no way, and He has never failed me yet. So, as we were waiting, I had to call Pastor Ernest. He would help see us through all this, always reminding us of the miracles God did in biblical times, and how His promises still stand true for believers today.

I made the call to Pastor Ernest, explaining to him what had taken place since he had left the hospital in the morning. He said he'd drop by the hospital that evening.

The phone hanging on the wall of the waiting room finally rang. It was a nurse from within the MICU asking whether I was Chuck's wife, whom I replied yes to. She said we could come in. I remember the ward within the heavy steel doors and the "restricted personnel only" signs. It was large area with patients in their own rooms, still and lifeless. As I write this, I can still hear the beeping of life support machines. The nurse told me that Chuck was in Room 8. As we entered the ward, it seemed most of the staff knew who we were and directed us to bed 8, where Chuck lay. As soon as I saw Chuck, I was well aware that Chuck was in the same room as my dear mom was in back in 2012. Of course, it brought back sad memories of my mom that still linger in my mind and heart. But I couldn't dwell there, as in this moment there was too much going on with Chuck to think of the passing of my mom. Only with the help of the Holy Spirit was I able to operate, think, and decide what to do next when decisions were required of me.

It wasn't an easy thing to see Chuck lying there, still and lifeless like all the other patients around him. I remember his first nurse, Kim; she was very professional. She told us that Chuck was critical and still had no diagnosis. She reminded us that Chuck was a very sick man. I thought to myself, *What's next?* Never in a million years did I think that we would be going through another critical illness with Chuck. I thought 2004 had been enough and we would never experience sickness to that degree again. All I can say is, was I ever wrong. Carly, Matthew, and I sat quietly around Chuck, hoping that someone could tell us something, but that wasn't the case.

To my surprise and relief, Pastor Ernest lightly tapped on the large sliding glass door to Chuck's room. I motioned for him to come in. Pastor Ernest had been alongside us in 2004; he was just as perplexed or, better said, "caught off guard" by this as much as we were. I told Pastor Ernest as much as I knew. He listened, and I'm sure he was tuned into our uncertainty. He quoted scripture that told of Jesus's supernatural healing power. The scripture he quoted went through my ear gate, right down into my spirit, and was written on my heart. It didn't wake up Chuck; nor did it change the situation. But it did change me. It fed me, strengthened me, and gave us all hope. It confirmed in us that the impossible was possible, and we would choose not to believe what we saw in front of our eyes. Instead, we would choose to believe what the scripture said—that God was able to do the impossible.

It was getting late; Pastor Ernest was getting ready to leave and said he would be back in the morning. I realized that Chuck was in the safest place he could be. He was unconscious, and we were so tired and decided we would leave the hospital and go home and get some rest.

It's funny; as tired as I was, leaving the hospital didn't bring any sense of relief. Actually, I felt like turning around and staying, but I knew that tomorrow would be a big day regarding decisions concerning Chuck. We went straight home and straight to bed. Receiving no calls from the hospital made it a good night.

My sleep was short but good, and I felt rested when I woke. I wanted to make it back to the hospital for doctors' rounds, which usually started at 9:00 a.m. I quickly got ready and told Matthew and Carly to come up later in the morning, adding that if there was any urgent news, I'd be sure to reach them. I made it to the hospital on time and waited for the doctors to start their rounds. Chuck's nurse said that when I saw the doctors gather outside his room, I could come out and listen to what they had to say. They would have the latest updates and results on any tests or stats on Chuck's vitals, and possibly a plan for going forward.

I saw the doctors gather outside Chuck's room. This was all new to me, so I was a bit nervous to go out and join their group. Perhaps I was scared as to what they were going to say about Chuck, but I got up and went out anyway. As I joined the group, I got a few head nods and acknowledging glances. They started with Chuck's information—that he was a fifty-eight-year-old male brought in by his wife on Thursday evening, January 7, 2016, with a fever and confusion.

One of the doctors recounted the events up to this point, and then said, "Endocarditis for the second time has not been ruled out. We are waiting for the cultures to be reported from the lab, which should be here sometime later today. Mr. Haarsma's white count is extremely elevated, at eighteen point five. Mr. Haarsma at this time is being treated with a broad antibiotic until the diagnosis is determined." The doctor then looked at me and asked, "Any questions?"

I did have one: "What is a normal white count range?"

One of the doctors answered, "Between four point five to eleven."

Chuck's white blood cell count became something I inquired about every day. I knew that an elevated white count meant one's body was fighting an infection of some kind. They continued in saying they were waiting on lab results before any added treatment plan could be set in place. With that being said, the round was done. I thanked them, and they moved on to the next patient.

I went back to Chuck's bedside and looked at him breathing through the respirator. All there was to do was wait. Always waiting was the hard part. I guess that's because you're in the middle of a standstill and you can't do anything but wait. To move forward, you're waiting on something or someone, and you're no longer in control.

Being as it was Monday, January 11, 2016, there were two things I had to do. One was to call my work and tell them I would not be in. The second was to call the dentist's office and confirm the December 17 appointment without antibiotics, which was still baffling me.

I remember I went back to my Jeep to make the calls to both my work and the dentist's office. First I called my work, and my boss, along with my coworkers, was completely understanding and supportive through the entire situation.

Second, I called the dentist's office. I was so thankful that the receptionist I knew very well picked up the phone. I told her Chuck was in the hospital and his doctors needed to know about any dentist appointments and procedures Chuck had done recently and whether he was premedicated or not. She became very worried for Chuck and was very concerned. She put me on hold while she looked in his records. She came back on the line and confirmed that Chuck did have two appointments in December: one, on the eighth, which he was medicated for; and another, on the seventeenth, which he was not premedicated for. When I heard those words, my heart sunk. I knew right then and there, with 99 percent certainty, that Chuck was fighting endocarditis for the second time.

I immediately was extremely upset that the dentist did not premedicate Chuck. He knew about Chuck's prosthetic heart and the guidelines concerning it. I couldn't understand why he wouldn't take that precautionary measure! Because of it, Chuck was in a critical dark place. I asked the receptionist whether I could speak to the dentist to ask why he didn't medicate Chuck for the second appointment. She obliged and put me on a very long hold. In fact, I thought she had either forgotten about me or we had become disconnected. I continued to patiently wait. She finally picked up and said the reason he didn't premedicate Chuck was because there was no drilling required and no bleeding with the procedure. I didn't want to challenge his decision at this time. In case I needed to get more information from him, I did not want him to boycott my calls. I thanked her and said goodbye.

Hearing that confirmation of no premedication just as Chuck recalled from December 17 was a real letdown. My heart sunk. I remembered in 2004, after Chuck's sixteen-hour surgery, how the surgeon had said everything was so difficult because of vast amounts of scar tissue in Chuck's chest, just as the previous surgeon said in 1981. I now sadly and fearfully realized that the only cure, fix, remedy, and plan to go forward was another open-heart surgery for Chuck. My heart was in my throat, and I felt sick to my stomach. I felt overwhelmed and scared, but I knew there would be no other choice. The only way forward would be to go through another open-heart surgery again!

When there's not a lot of choices in your circumstances, you can't hover or burrow in the negative. It's of no benefit to either the situation or to you. To rely on yourself is a quick road to disaster. We are only human and cannot do anything past our own abilities of education, knowledge, and connection. A crystal ball, tea leaves, or tarot cards are not going to solve our problems either. Trust me; the only answer is faith, and your faith has to be put into something that is true and has been tested. You *cannot* believe what you see in front of you. We can all believe in things that are tangible, real, actual, and definite. Anyone can do that, but that's not faith.

Seeing miracles does not produce faith either; the process works the other way around. It's faith that produces miracles. Miracles are only signs of faith; they are actually the evidence of the faith you had before you received the miracle. "Faith shows the reality of what we hope for; the evidence of things we cannot see" (Hebrews 11:1 NLT).

I had a great deal of information rolling through my mind, such as the confirmation from the dentist, the voices of Chuck's previous surgeons saying he would not survive another surgery, the Canadian and American Dental Associations' and the Heart and Stroke Foundation's guidelines for medication requirements for prosthetic heart valves, and mortality rates on second-time endocarditis survivors (which I discovered on the Internet are quite high). I needed to discard all these things and all this information and remove it from my mind, so this is what I did.

In your mind, I want you to imagine a garage sale table with a whole bunch of stuff on it that someone no longer wants or needs. You walk up to the table and you take you both arms and aggressively take a sweep at everything on the table and clear it all off—everything. Everything is gone. Not one object is left. The table is wiped clean.

While I was still sitting in my Jeep, that's exactly what I decided to do. I cleared both my mind and, more importantly, my heart of all the junk. I wiped away all that stuff from within me and stood against what I'd heard and saw before me. I choose to believe what God said about going through trials and tribulations.

I turned my focus and put my faith in Jesus Christ and what the Bible says about the only man that could, and still can, raise people from the dead and heal all kinds of sickness and disease. Not only could Christ heal physical bodies, but He also drove demons out of people's minds, and He still does those things today. I had a choice to make, and I chose to believe in Him and His power. I'd like you to listen to a song by Jeremy Camp called "Same Power." That song, along with a couple others, saved Chuck from death and gave me the courage and strength to keep moving forward in the darkest of times. When Chuck was on the line between life and death, at his very lowest times, we—Chuck's sisters, my sister and brother-in-law, my son-in-law, and my kids—used to sit in the family room (which, by the way, became home for us) and sing along with Jeremy Camp's "Same Power." In Christian teaching, Jesus taught that you must speak words as if the outcome you desire is so. So I felt that we needed to sing about Chuck having that same power as Jesus, being raised from the dead, living in Chuck himself. So we substituted Chuck's name in the song where we could. One line in the song is "The same power that rose Jesus from the grave lives in us, lives in us." We would intentionally sing it as "The same power that rose Jesus from the grave lives in Chuck, lives in Chuck."

These words being sung by us as we gathered in the family room had tremendous strength and were so powerful that they kept Chuck alive, when truthfully in the natural realm Chuck should have not been able to survive all that he did. When I think back, I can hardly believe it myself. Many of you may be tempted to think we were just lucky. No, we weren't. Luck had nothing to do with it. It was the miraculous power of Jesus Christ to perform miracles. Jesus Christ is alive and available to all humankind to tap into.

These few scriptures scribed for us in God's Word (the Bible) proved true.

- "Jesus Christ is the same yesterday, today and forever" (Hebrews 13.8 GNT). This is talking about Jesus's power and ability to perform miracles, such as when He healed the blind, healed the crippled, and raised Lazarus and Jairus's daughter from the dead. He Himself did rise from the dead. So Jesus is alive today, and in His Word, He says to ask Him in His name for what you want. You can't ask for foolish things, but you can ask for anything in His name that aligns with His Word, and you shall receive it. We wanted total healing, protection, and restoration for Chuck. We prayed for complete healing for Chuck, even though in the natural realm nothing looked farther from the truth. We believed with unwavering prayer and faith that it was going to happen. What we saw before us was only for a moment; it was not to be in our future. God was and is and will be able to do exceedingly and abundantly more than we could ever ask, think, or dream of. That is who He is.
- "To Him who by means of His Power working in us, is able to do so much more than we could ever ask for, or even think of" (Ephesians 3:20 GNT). God did this time and time again, from beginning to end, in every situation we were in concerning Chuck and us.

- "Words kill or give life; they're either poison or fruit – you choose" (Proverbs 18:21 MSG). It's so crucial to speak miracles and life-giving words into your life. Words are containers of power. Words can either encourage or discourage, heal or wound, build or tear down; they can minister death or they can minister life. Your words steer the course of your life. Yours words can carry your faith to the kingdom of God and release angels to help you. Or your words can carry your fear to the kingdom of darkness and just release more trouble into your life. We need to choose our words carefully and be accountable for the words that come out of our mouths. Always try to find the treasure in your trial.

The words in the song "Move (Keep Walkin')" by TobyMac were such a blessing. They were like medicine to me as I was going through this journey. These words were immensely strength-building, comforting soul food for me. In fact, I find it miraculous that these two songs in particular—"Move (Keep Walkin')" by Toby Mac and "Same Power" by Jeremy Camp—were playing on the radio at the time of our crisis. I believe it was "God's" perfect timing when these life-building, strength-giving songs were released. The words from these songs resided in me; they were in my mind and, more importantly, deep down in my heart. When I thought that we were over a hurdle and then something else would go wrong, I could hear a line from Toby Mac's song "Move (Keep Walkin')": "Hold on, God's not finished yet." Those words gave me strength to make decisions and, at times, challenge some doctors. With confidence I could stand against and question some certain methods of care. With direct leading of the Holy Spirit, I was able to put forth ideas and suggestions on alternative ways of care. To my amazement, the doctors listened to me. Together as a team, Chuck's doctors, specialists, and nurses, with their skill, knowledge, experience, and never-ending utmost care, along with myself in knowing Chuck best, were able to come to a consensus on how to deliver Chuck the very best care possible.

There is no doubt in my mind that Jesus Christ oversaw everything and was there and never left the situation. I know this for certain. He kept me strong both at Chuck's side in the hospital and in my everyday life outside the hospital. Jesus Christ also spared Chuck from death several times over. He is the Alpha and Omega, from beginning to end. He is the author of our lives. "But the Lord is faithful, and He will strengthen you and protect you from the Evil One" (2 Thessalonians 3:3 NIV). Amen (so be it.)

CHAPTER 7

The Next Step

I was so disappointed regarding the confirmation from the dentist's office that Chuck had no pre-appointment antibiotic treatment before his December 17 appointment. I had a hard time believing it, never mind understanding it. I couldn't understand how, between both Chuck and his dentist, there was no prophylactic treatment before the dental work being performed. Actually, I was beyond disappointment; I was completely devastated and deflated. I parked my Jeep and went back up into the MICU. I passed on the information to the Chuck's nurse, who would scribe it in his chart and verbally communicate it to the doctors, as I would also.

I sat next to Chuck's bedside. I knew that we were in for a long haul and quite certain this meant that Chuck would be going for yet another open-heart surgery. Chuck was still intubated and in an induced coma, so I couldn't have a conversation with him, but I talked to him and prayed for him continually.

The morning passed, and Carly and Matthew came up to the hospital. Chuck's nurse Kim was an exceptional caring nurse. She reminded me again of how sick Chuck was. I know she did not do this to frighten me; I think it was to prepare me for the worst. I know she was just being transparent, honest, and open about Chuck's critical condition. She told us that a few doctors would come up later in the afternoon to discuss next steps with Chuck. So we waited beside Chuck.

I guess it was 4:30 p.m. when Kim came in and told me there was a doctor outside Chuck's room that would like to talk with us. So Carly, Matthew, and I went outside Chuck's room to hear what he had to say. This doctor reminded me of the type of doctor you might see in a soap opera, and we didn't like much of what he said or did. The doctor started by saying the lab results confirmed Chuck did indeed have endocarditis for the second time and that the bacteria were not only on his prosthetic valve but also had attacked the sternum. He said the surgery would be extremely difficult and he could give Chuck only a 15 percent survival chance and would not recommend surgery. He would perform the surgery if that's what we decided, but he was definitely not hopeful regarding the outcome. I heard what he said, but I didn't absorb it or believe what he said. I let it bounce off me as best I could. I think my disbelief in what he said was possible only because of what I did and do believe, which I will believe to my life's end. My belief system tells me that everything is possible with God. Even what is impossible in this world is not impossible for God.

Kim said there would be two other surgeons that would come in and talk to us. Again, we would sit and wait expectantly, hoping for a better report. Waiting became a game we would play a lot in this situation. Maybe it was a time-out provided by God so we could use that time to pray, to strengthen ourselves, and to set the miracle in motion. We did just that; we prayed. We waited a lot, and we prayed a lot.

I can't remember exactly when the next surgeon came to talk to us, but again we met him outside Chuck's room. The doctor introduced himself; I'll refer to him as Dr. S——. (At this time, I will note I decided not to write in full names of doctors and specialists because I did not want to pursue those permissions.)

I'll be honest; I was nervous as to what Dr. S—— was going to say. There's no doubt about it. But I was hopeful for a better report. Every scripture that I knew that had a promise of getting one through valleys and trials was pounding on my heart and in my mind.

Dr. S—— said exactly what the first doctor said—that Chuck had endocarditis and that the bacteria were attacking Chuck's prosthetic heart valve and his sternum. He continued by saying that there was no option other than surgery. He himself had already spoken to his colleague, Dr. P——, because of Chuck's fragile state, and he felt he needed to have further discussions with him. Dr. P—— was exceptional and dealt with the extreme difficult cases. Dr. S—— said that he would come back with Dr. P—— when he was out of surgery to discuss the plan further. He said they were going to slowly start lifting the sedation on Chuck to see whether the confusion and aggression had subsided. Dr. S—— said that because Chuck had been getting the heaviest IV antibiotics since Friday, he was hopeful Chuck would be in a better frame of mind. If that was the case, they would be able to take out the breathing tube, and Chuck would again be able to breathe on his own. I can't even explain how happy I was to have a little glimpse of hope and progress. I wanted to see Chuck again, off the sedatives, and to be able to hear his voice and talk with him. I wanted to have Chuck back in this life, awake, moving, breathing, blinking, thinking, and back to life. I wanted to see for myself what state he was in. I hoped and prayed for the best. I was happy to be able to know that maybe in a short while I would be able to kiss my husband and have him be responsive. I needed and wanted Chuck to stay in my life as well as Carly's, her husband's, and Matthew's. Dr. S—— gave Chuck's nurse the orders to start easing back on the sedation and said he'd come back later to see how things were going. I went back beside Chuck's bedside and whispered in his ear that he would be waking up soon and that I and the kids would be there. I started to give thanks and pray; it was the best thing.

CHAPTER 8

The Plan

It seemed almost immediately that they started reducing the sedation, and soon Chuck started stirring. Just to see his leg or hand move provided a sense of relief and gave us hope. What I mean by that is that Chuck had been out since early Friday afternoon and I really didn't know what had been going on under there. I was concerned mostly about Chuck's mind, because the infection had traveled into his bloodstream and into his brain fluid.

The process of waking up took a couple hours at the most. I've seen Chuck in this state a few times, and I think the best part of this, if there is one, is when he opens his eyes. The eyes, being the window of the soul, can tell the story of someone's inner spirit without words being spoken.

After the waiting and expecting, the time came, and Chuck's eyes opened. Our hearts were in our throats, and our eyes welled up. Chuck recalls this time as a blur. As he says, "You're coming out of an induced coma, but you're still on a basketful of drugs."

As Chuck wakened slowly, he looked around the room, and I know he was trying to figure out what had taken place over the last few days. The breathing tube was still in and very uncomfortable for him, as he squished up his face and moved his mouth around the tubes. His nurse came in frequently to check on Chuck and talk to him about how he was managing, and to ask him how everything was going. His nurse would be the one who would report back to the doctors, who would decide whether or not the breathing tubes would come out. The more Chuck came to, the more he realized where he was. Carly, Matthew, and I talked to Chuck to keep him calm and explain to him what was going on so he could try to understand his situation as best he could. Chuck was doing really well, and it seemed that he was no longer in a state of aggressive confusion, which was such a relief for all of us. Chuck told me at a later time that he was relived to be alive.

The nurse came in the room again with the information we'd had all been hoping and waiting for. It was time for the breathing tubes to come out. She spoke to Chuck directly while she touched his arm, and Chuck understood and nodded his head. We had so much hope that this was going to turn out well. We immediately thanked God for this, as we believe that it's His breath in our lungs. He is the One who gives us life, from beginning to end, and He is faithful to the end. Yes, that's right—until the end.

The doctor and a respiratory specialist who were going to remove Chuck's breathing tube had arrived outside Chuck's room. The nurse came in and told us we would have to leave the room for a short time, as they were going to perform the removal procedure. We left the room and shortly were allowed to go back in and see Chuck. Chuck was breathing on his own and immediately said hi as we entered the room. His voice was a little scratchy, but it was so great to hear him. His nurse was standing by his bedside; she had given him a cup of water to drink. I went up to Chuck and gave him a kiss, as did Carly, on his cheek; Matthew gave him a hug. Chuck was talking again. It was such a relief to have Chuck both conscious and coherent. In the upcoming days, there would be so much to decide and settle on. With faith we would do it. Chuck was now able to hear and discuss the way in which his future journey would unfold.

Chuck was in a much better state of mind. He was no longer combative, but he was very groggy, and his eyes showed how sick he was. He wasn't as healthy as I wished or in the condition I hoped for, but having him awake was better than him being unconsciousness.

I called the family to tell them the news that Chuck was conscious and able to talk. Like me, everyone was happy for this small step in the right direction. Chuck's best friend, Calvin, had come in from Kelowna, British Colombia, after a call from Chuck's mom letting him how ill Chuck had become. So later in the day, Chuck would see his sisters and Calvin. I told Chuck that his sisters from out of province, Janice and Beth, were in, as was Calvin. Chuck was taken aback on hearing this and asked why. The answer to his question was easy; it was because they loved him.

Chuck was so groggy and sick that he needed help with eating and drinking. The nurse came in to tell us that the two surgeons, Dr. P—— and Dr. S——, would be in shortly to talk with us. We waited. The time came, and both surgeons entered the room. They greeted Chuck with soft handshakes and said hello to Carly, Matthew, and me.

I don't know what I was expecting, but I was anxious to hear what they had to say. I was hoping they had a solution that did not involve another open-heart surgery, but deep down I knew those weren't the words we were about to hear.

Both doctors looked genuine, caring, respectful, understanding, and concerned. When they spoke, all of those qualities and characteristics were confirmed in their words. Dr. P—— took the lead and did most of the talking. He began by acknowledging to Chuck that Chuck had had quite an eventful weekend and was one tough guy. He explained the results of the tests and reconfirmed that Chuck had endocarditis and that the bacteria found in Chuck's bloodstream were *Staphylococcus aureus.* His latest blood tests and vitals showed that the antibiotics were helping in fighting the bacteria, and that was the reason why Chuck's fever was down, his mind was much clearer, and he was in a better state of mind with no confusion. Then came the words I didn't want to hear, though I knew that they were coming. Dr. P—— explained that a vegetation of bacteria had grown on the prosthetic heart valve and it looked like a tadpole. The IV antibiotics would never be able to dissolve the vegetation, and when Chuck's valve opened and closed, the vegetation flapped, and bits of the vegetation were breaking off from the movement of the valve and going into Chuck's bloodstream. There was no way to remedy Chuck's medical condition other than another open-heart surgery. In Chuck's case, time was of the essence. They were concerned that if the majority of the vegetation broke off and traveled into Chuck's bloodstream, the result would be fatal. Dr. P——, with the agreement of Dr. S——, said the surgery was required and no doubt was going to be very difficult, but really there was no other choice. When I asked about Chuck's chances of surviving the surgery, Dr. P—— and Dr. S—— gave him an 80 percent likelihood, but the surgery would be the easier part of this journey. The difficult part come be after the surgery, as Chuck's road to rehabilitation and healing would be a tough uphill climb. Dr. P—— was quite confident he would be able to successfully perform the surgery, but the success of the post surgery rehabilitation would depend on Chuck's entire being and his body's ability to heal. The surgery was going to be a tremendous stress on Chuck's body, and it was going to be a very steep uphill climb. It was Monday, January 11, 2016. Dr. P—— wanted to slate Chuck for surgery at 7:00 a.m. on Wednesday, January 13. He told us that the sooner it could be done, the better, because of the risk of the possible breaking off of the vegetation. Chuck's response to all of this was fearless and courageous. Chuck replied with a question, as always: "Where do I sign?" With Chuck's comment, Dr. P—— chuckled and said Chuck was a champ. He said he would come back later with the document for Chuck to sign and that he would get the surgery and prep process rolling. Both Dr. P—— and Dr. S—— gave Chuck gentle handshakes and left the room.

As strong as I am—and let me be clear that my strength comes from faith—all of this information was a heavy load on me. When Chuck said, "Where do I sign?" the next step for the surgery became a reality, and it was inevitable; there was no other choice. I have to say again, as I mentioned at the beginning of our story, never had I even pondered the smallest thought of Chuck going for yet another open-heart surgery. There was nothing I could do to change the situation. This was one of those times and places that I felt scared, that I felt the knot in my stomach, and that I wanted someone to wake me from this bad dream, but the only way out was to go through. We were going to have to go through; there were no other options on the table before us. I knew that we were never going to be able to do this on our own. Right then and there, I put my faith into action, even though my heart was in my throat. I grasped and clasped on to God and His Word. I grasped on to all of His promises—the ones that say He will get us through darkness and valleys, leading us through to the light and the mountaintops. I grasped on to those verses, as difficult as it was.

CHAPTER 9

The Day in Between

It was Monday, January 11, 2016, and Chuck's surgery was going to take place Wednesday, January 13. Tuesday, January 12, the day in between, would be precious. I realized that come Wednesday, Chuck would again be under and out, going through a very difficult surgery. I spent all my time at the hospital; there was no other place for me to be. Everything normal had stopped: work, daily routines, and daily life. I had decided to stay the next two nights in Chuck's room on a cot. I wanted to make most out of the time we had in front of us.

Chuck remained in the MICU with his own nurse. Chuck's sisters Janice and Beth, and his best buddy, Calvin, came up to visit with Chuck. All of us were feeling so many emotions. We were in regular contact with Pastor Ernest, who kept very close contact with us, and us with him. He, too, would be up to visit Chuck later that day. Chuck was just not himself; he was so sick. No matter what words I use to try to paint the picture of endocarditis and its symptoms on the body, I most likely will never be able to describe the degree of the illness. There was no doubt about it; my heart was heavy. This surgery was going to be massive.

All of us put on our brave faces and brave hearts. Chuck, being the one who was going to have to go through it all, was the most courageous and fearless. Never once did he ever feel sorry for himself; nor did he express his fears verbally, emotionally, or mentally.

Spiritually speaking, Chuck's spirit man was strong. When I asked Chuck how he remained so strong, he told me this: "When you're faced with a perilous journey, and when the circumstances are stacked against you and you don't have any other alternatives, you have to go through it." Chuck attributes his strength and his ability to go through adversity to his foundation in Jesus Christ. Chuck totally surrendered his circumstance to God. His thinking was that if he came out of this, then he would deal with his recovery. If he didn't make it through the surgery, then he was going to where and what he believes in, which is heaven, where he would meet Jesus Christ, his Lord and Saviour. There is comfort in believing in Christ, because His promise of believing in Him guarantees you heaven. Of course, Chuck wanted a successful surgery. As Chuck said, "It's sad to think you may leave behind your world as you know it, especially the possibility of leaving the people you love and no longer being with them. But, as a believer in Jesus Christ, the promise of heaven is comforting, knowing when our time comes to pass on, we are going to a better place with no more disease, pain, hurt, sorrow, or loss."

I think it's really important for me to mention at this time how important it is for you, yourself, to make a personal decision to make Jesus Christ your personal Saviour and to acknowledge the reason why He came here to earth. Christ came so we could enter heaven and save us from hell; it's that simple. I do feel responsible telling the people I have in my life and have relationships with, including the people I love, about why it's so important to make this decision. The people I meet and get to know, and the people I love, will all have lives after their current lives. Eternity is exactly that—forever, never ending. For me as a believer, not saying anything makes me irresponsible. As I've read and studied the Word, it has become very clear to me that I am to go out and share the good news and make believers or, even further, disciples of those I can. This is not done by force or coercion. It's done by you being open to receiving in your heart what I tell you. My words go through your ear gate and up into your mind, and the most critical and important part is that it goes from your mind down into your heart. If you are willing and open to allow this revelation to happen to you, you will never be the same. Whatever lies before you in this life you will be able to handle with grace and ease. The precious things in your life will become more significant, prominent, worthy, and valuable; I guess that's because you will become more genuinely aware of how valuable these treasured gifts are. You can begin to live with no fear, anxiety, dread, panic, worry, or fright. You will begin to live in trust, hope, faith, belief, protection, and care in the custody of a God whose promises are a positive yes and amen. He promises never to leave you, forsake you, or fail you. How can you not live with that, my friend? I am not telling you this out of what I think I know, or from a list of rules or regulations. I am telling you from experience and encounters with the miraculous.

On with the story. Monday night rolled around quite quickly. I guess it was around 9:00 p.m. It had been a very long day; everyone was tired, and Chuck was exhausted. Everyone said their goodbyes, and Chuck and I settled in for the night. I wanted to stay with Chuck, so I slept in his room on a reclining chair. Chuck was extremely fatigued, but he was also understandably anxious and uneasy. I myself was weary, and I needed some downtime just to close my eyes. I dimmed the lights, and Chuck and I held hands and prayed for protection, for strength, for courage, and for God's hand to be in and over everything. We kissed one another good night and tried to sleep as best we could.

I was out so much so that the nurses told me in the morning that Chuck had climbed from his bed over the railing and had knocked over his IV pole. Chuck had been up, with his nurse and a health aide trying to settle him back down. I myself hadn't even stirred or heard anything of what was going on. That is not me; I normally wake at the turn of a key. I was completely exhausted and spent. Being Tuesday, January 12, the day prior to the surgery, there would be a lot of prep going on with Chuck. I got up and got ready for the day. Carly had brought some of my notions in for me, as well as a change of clothes.

Today was a big day. Chuck's surgeons and doctors would be in to see Chuck, plus the anesthesiologist, the lab technicians, the PICC line team, and a whole sea of other medical people who were preparing for Chuck's surgery. Some of the events are a blur. It's not that I don't remember them, but I don't remember them in detail. But there are two events that I do recall.

The first was Chuck's signing authorization for his surgery. It was early afternoon, and Carly, Matthew, Janice, Beth, Calvin, and I were visiting with Chuck when Dr. P——, Dr. S——, and the anesthesiologist came in to see Chuck. One thing I should mention is that the anesthesiologist, Dr. M——, had come in late Monday afternoon, so this was the second time he would see Chuck. When we first met him, we noticed he had a unique surgical hat on, which we had commented about. When he met Chuck and us on Monday, there was an immediate connection, and we had a great conversation together. Dr. M—— told us that he had a seamstress make all the surgical caps he wore for him. He would shop for the fabric, and his choices of material had personal meanings to him. He had one with palm trees, another with skis, and one that was his favorite color; he used any pattern that captured his passions. I think he had a total of something like twenty-five caps. On Monday, Dr. M—— had asked Chuck about things he liked or had done during his life. Chuck told him about his days as a plumber. We thought Dr. M—— was just a nice, kind guy, which indeed he is. Dr. M—— is an extraordinary, brilliant, remarkable human being who has done much humanitarian work and medical work in third-world countries overseas, plus work here in Canada and the province. We could see through the words he spoke and his bedside manner that he cared about how Chuck was feeling as he faced this challenging surgery ahead of him. But Dr. M——'s eyes expressed his concern and care for us as he read our hearts, which were obviously showing through onto our faces. Dr. M—— finished his final medical assessment on Chuck, and then he pulled from his hard-covered medical clipboard a surgical cap. He handed it to Chuck, saying it was for Chuck to wear in the OR during his surgery. It was red, white, and black, and it bore a strong man's arm with several different kind of tools. Scribed on it was the slogan "Tools Rule." This is one of the moments in my life I will just never forget. Chuck appreciatively thanked Dr. M—— and, with help, put the cap on his head. Chuck, as sick as he was, looked so handsome, and of course he raised his arms and did his strongman pose, and he made us all laugh and cry. All of us, including Dr. M——, fought back tears in our eyes. Dr. M—— inquired of me whether I needed something to help relax me for Chuck's surgery day. I gratefully declined his offer. Along with the love of my family, what I needed was already with us, and that was God. God would get us through Chuck's surgery day. He would be our Strong Tower and Comforter tomorrow and for all the days ahead. He was, He is, and He will be, then, now, and forever and ever.

So next on the agenda for Chuck was the signing for his surgery. Dr. P——, being the primary surgeon for Chuck's surgery, was the one holding the documents for Chuck to sign. Dr. P—— explained again what the procedure was going to be. The thought at the start was that a tissue valve was going to be used to replace Chuck's infected heart valve. Dr. P——, with his caring and attentive bedside manner, spoke directly to Chuck and then passed the clipboard and pen to Chuck and showed him where to sign. Chuck, with his new surgical cap on, gripped the pen as best he could while Dr. P—— supported the clipboard. As I watched Chuck sign his surgery papers, it looked like the pen in his hand did nine consecutive loops with a sprawling tail and then a landed period. Think of this happening in slow motion, because that was exactly what it was like. I could feel, taste, sense, and hear the emotion in the room. I could hear that everyone was choked up by the sound of their sniffles. Dr. P—— touched Chuck on the shoulder and commented, telling him that was quite a signature and that should do it. Dr. P—— shook Chuck's hand and said he would see Chuck tomorrow morning in the OR. There was no denying that the atmosphere in Chuck's room was heavy. This was going to be Chuck's fourth open-heart surgery and third replacement valve surgery. We all remembered 2004 and the surgeon back then saying how difficult the surgery was because of Chuck's small veins and vast amounts of scar tissue.

At this time, I chose to take a time-out. There was a chapel at the end of another ward on the same floor as Chuck was on. I excused myself and went to spend some alone time in the peace under the wings of God.

This time I wouldn't spend a long time there, as Pastor Ernest was coming up to see Chuck and us. Calvin referred to Pastor Ernest as the "positive guy." There was a time when Chuck was hanging on only by a thread and the only thing that was holding him up was God's powerful hand; other than that, Chuck's life was on the line. In that dark time, Calvin said someone should call the "positive guy," as things always seemed to get better for Chuck and everyone when he was around. So I wanted to make sure I was there when Pastor Ernest arrived, but I also wanted to pray in solitude.

I want to take a minute to give a small description of this tiny chapel in St. Boniface Hospital. This chapel became my fortress and my hiding place. This little sanctuary was my resting place at times when I had to get away from it all, both back in 2004 and in 2016. St. Boniface Hospital is a Catholic hospital, so the chapel is like a small Catholic church. It has the pictures of the stations of the cross on the wall. For those of you who are not familiar with what those are, they are pictures of the significant events leading up to Jesus's crucifixion, and there are fourteen of them. But my absolute favorite feature is the huge cross of Jesus, front and center on the wall behind the altar. The cross is approximately sixteen feet high and eight feet wide. Jesus is not hanging on the cross. On this cross, He is dressed in fresh garments with His hands not nailed to the cross. Instead, His hands and His arms are outstretched as He is there, waiting and wanting you to come to Him, right into His arms. On this cross, He is not dead but fully alive. By His cross and on this cross, He is fully resurrected. I have stared at it, knelt in front of it, cried in front of it, felt confused in front of it, had my heart break in front of it, and felt anxious in front of it. His outstretched arms reminded me to come to Him, as if He were saying, "I am your everything." His desire is for every one of us to draw close to Him. Remember: He has the power to calm the wind and the waves.

As I prayed, I acknowledged that God had chosen Chuck to be my husband, and I his wife. I knew I needed to be strong. His Word says He will make me strong in my weakness; I knew I was going to have to stand on that promise. I asked God to protect Chuck and to be in the OR with Chuck to oversee the entire surgery. All my faith was in God alone, and I wanted Him to know that. As I prayed, I acknowledged that I truly believed He would be in the OR with Chuck. I believed that He would be the light in the dark and would make the crooked paths straight. I believed that He was going to go before us and that He already had handpicked Chuck's surgeons, Dr. P—— and Dr. S——, plus Chuck's anesthesiologist, Dr. M——. I believed He knew and already had chosen every person that was going to be in the OR with Chuck. I told Him I trusted Him, and I thanked Him for all He had done for us in the past, all that He was continuing to do, and all He would do for us in the future. I thanked Him for it all. I got up from my knees and made the sign of the cross.

The timing was perfect, Pastor Ernest pretty much arrived just as I got back from the chapel. All of us greeted him with a hug, and Pastor Ernest mainly focused in on Chuck. Janice had left to go pick up her daughter Kristen from work, and I can't remember whether Beth and Calvin were still there. Pastor Ernest is an energetic, happy, adventurous, intelligent, smart, witty guy with true and sound knowledge and belief in Jesus Christ.

This visit from Pastor Ernest is the second event that I vividly remember that took place that day in between Chuck becoming conscious again and the day of his surgery. When Pastor Ernest came to visit Chuck, he always had a Biblical story he shared that would give us hope. On this particular visit, he told the story of the eagle. It is from Isaiah 40:31: "But they who wait on the Lord, shall renew their strength. They shall mount up with wings like eagles. They shall run and not be weary, they shall walk and not be faint" (Isaiah 40:31 KJV). Further, he explained to us what the eagle represents throughout the Bible. Primarily the eagle is found in the Old Testament. The eagle, with its keen eyes, is a symbol of perspicacity, courage, strength, and immortality, and it is able to bear much weight. God refers to Himself as an eagle for several different reasons; one of these is His protective nature, as described in Psalm 91:1–4:

> Those who live in the shelter of the Most High
> will find rest in the shadow of the Almighty.
> This I declare about the Lord:
> He alone is my refuge, my place of safety;
> he is my God, and I trust him.
> For he will rescue you from every trap
> and protect you from deadly disease.
> He will cover you with his feathers. He will shelter
> you with his wings.
> His faithful promises are your armor and protection.
> (NLT)

Eagles represent sovereignty and supremacy. This is fitting, since God is the real ruler over kings and presidents; but also, when a storm hits, eagles can fly far above them, indicating that God is never affected by conditions, for He is also sovereign over nature. Pastor Ernest referred to many of the verses in the Bible that mention the eagle's strength and powerful characteristics. Every verse Pastor Ernest quoted gave us the hope that we would be able to rely on God's strength and power.

When Janice returned from picking up Kristen from work, she

came into the room excited, saying that we wouldn't believe what she had seen. As it was January, it was super cold out, and the outside world had become still and frozen. Janice proceeded to say that on her drive back she noticed something flying above and around the cross of the hospital. She was having a hard time making out what it was, but as she got closer, she realized it was three eagles!

We all were taken aback. Actually, we felt a tingling down our spines, as Pastor Ernest had just finished talking about the strength, courage, and symbolism of the eagle. You may think this is just a coincidence, but no, my friend, the timing of the eagles' presence was a sign and wonder. There is no doubt in my mind about this. As you continue on, you will read that there was another visit from an eagle—another sign and wonder.

"My sister Barbara and her husband, Derek," had arrived from Calgary in the late afternoon. It was great to see them and have the extra support from my sister and brother-in-law was extremely comforting. Chuck was appreciative and happy to see them before his surgery.

Around 6:00 p.m., Pastor Ernest had some alone time with Chuck. He then called us back into the room to pray, as the time for Chuck's surgery was drawing nearer. None of us were looking forward to Chuck's surgery day other than Chuck. When Chuck had signed his authorisation papers, he'd said, "Let's go and get her done."

I wished we could skip that day—the waiting, the anticipation, the anxiety—but that was impossible. I had to trust. I had to trust the doctors and all those who would be with Chuck. My saving pill was my trust in God. That's where I put all my cares, fears, and emotions. By allowing me to do that, He made me strong. I would be ready to handle what lay ahead for both Chuck and me.

CHAPTER 10

Surgery Day

The night before surgery was one of tossing and turning; not much sleep was had by anyone. Carly had offered to stay with Chuck so I could sleep at home and try to get some rest. I took her up on her offer. Carly was always a daddy's girl and to this day still is. Carly said that Chuck had told her not to worry, as he would make it through the surgery, and through the entire night Chuck had held on to the toe of her boot. Chuck wished for the night to pass so he could just get the surgery done. Chuck would have preferred it if they had come earlier for him. Not me; I was the polar opposite, completely in a different zone. I guess that was because I would have to wait all day long, wondering and worrying, knowing somewhat of what Chuck was going through. I'm not making light of any kind of surgery, but this was not a minor surgery; this was as enormous as a surgery can be. Just the entry into Chuck's body to get near Chuck's heart worried me, but again and again my saving grace was believing that God had this and He would be there.

The time came, and I saw outside Chuck's room that the medical team and stretcher had arrived for Chuck. All of them looked clean, crisp, bright, and ready to take Chuck into the OR. I spotted Dr. M——, the anesthesiologist, with one of his unique surgical caps on. Carly helped Chuck put his "Tools Rule" surgical cap on. This choked me up inside. The moment was here, and it was real. I will mention that all the nurses, especially the male nurses and other medical staff, were jealous of Chuck's cap. Everyone mentioned that never in all the years of working with Dr. M—— had they ever seen him give one of his caps away to a patient or any other colleague or staff member. The connection between Dr. M——, Chuck, and our family was unique and is one we'll never forget.

Chuck's days in the MICU were now coming to an end. I felt those days were precious, as they gave us the time to talk, laugh, joke, hug, and kiss each other. But those three days were also very hard because Chuck was so very ill in suffering the symptoms of the endocarditis. As I mentioned before, Chuck was going to be out for the next few days, so I thought. This made me feel as if I were going into another cold, frozen, still, lifeless winter season.

Chuck's room became abuzz. They started to transfer Chuck, moving all the IVs from the pole by his bed onto the stretcher IV pole. Next, they helped Chuck transfer onto the stretcher. I felt another hard gulp in my throat. Dr. M—— laid the steel surgery slate on top of Chuck's stomach. Chuck and all his stuff were arranged on the stretcher, and he was ready to go. Now came what I would describe as the grand finale; they opened the double glass doors of Chuck's room to be able to wheel Chuck out into hallway and then down to the OR.

I was trying to walk beside Chuck as best I could, but there were quite a few people around him. That was when Dr. M—— pulled me aside and pulled out a little brown envelope from inside his surgical coat. He said he'd brought me a little something to help calm my nerves and help me relax throughout the day. Dr. M—— has a heart of gold; he was truly concerned for me. I graciously declined, as I had another path out, which was my heavy reliance on God and prayer. I had the King of Kings and the Lord of Lords on my side. I was counting on Him to get me and the kids through. I don't know what I would have done if I hadn't had my faith in Him.

One of my favorite definitions of faith is as follows: "faith is going against all logic to think or act based on a belief."

We walked alongside Chuck as they wheeled him to the Surgical Ward. I have to say again how brave and courageous Chuck was. To this day, I ask him how he managed everything, and he gives all the credit to his faith in Jesus Christ. Additionally, Chuck is a determined, strong-willed, and patient man. Without Jesus Christ and without Chuck's characteristics, I would be writing a book of a different kind.

We had reached the big doors of the Surgical Ward, and Carly, Matthew, and I could go no further with Chuck. This was it; it was time for us to say goodbye to Chuck. This was a hard one. As much faith as we all had and have, there is always a little shadow of doubt, a what-if. So the medical team stopped in front of the doors and stepped back as Carly, Matthew, and I gave Chuck our final kisses and hugs. Now we stepped back, losing the fight of holding back our tears. Dr. M—— pressed the button on the wall to open the doors to the long hall of several operating rooms. We watched as Chuck went through the doors. We watched through the windows until he was out of sight. It left us with quite a lonely feeling, as there was absolutely no one in the hall. Carly, Matthew, and I gathered our emotions and made our way to back to Chuck's room in the MICU. We gathered the few things of Chuck's, along with our coats and jackets. Feeling somewhat overwhelmed, we decided we would go downstairs into the cafeteria for coffee. We did that, I remember, around 8:30 a.m. I saw both Dr. P—— and Dr. S—— get up from the table they were sitting at. I knew that it meant Chuck must be asleep and ready and waiting for them. It seemed as if it were in slow motion as I watched them walk through the hallway to the elevators. Again my heart was in my throat. Right then and there, I bowed my head and prayed.

We decided to go up into the second-floor family waiting room just outside the Surgical Ward, where Chuck was. There were a few comfortable chairs and a couple of TVs. It was the same room in which I had waited for Chuck back in 2004. The little room with the two doors and boxes of tissues was still exactly the same. I'll coin it as "the little room of life or death." The door to the family room meant life, and the door to the hall meant death.

The day was long, as I'm sure you can imagine. As the day progressed, the family gathered at the hospital to come be with us. They all brought bags with them that were filled with drinks, food, snacks, magazines, and other time fillers to help make the day pass as easily as possible. To have the family around us was very comforting and calming; it filled the spot and lessened the room for fear and anxiety to creep in.

Chuck's name was on the surgical TV screen in the family waiting room, displaying which OR he was in. I remember seeing his name, A. C. Haarsma, but I don't room remember the room number of the OR. As the day went on, other people's names were removed from the slate because their surgeries were done, but Chuck wasn't that lucky, and his name remained on the screen.

I appreciated everyone being there with Carly, Matthew, and me. I am so grateful for all of my family, but I did make my way, by myself, to the chapel a few times during the day. A person can pray anywhere—that I know—and I pray outside of churches often, but I needed to just sit and gaze at the cross with Jesus's open arms. Seeing his arms outstretched reminded me that we were protected. I think it was near 7:00 p.m. when a nurse came in to tell us that Chuck's surgery would be at least a few more hours. She continued to say that the surgery was taking longer because they had run into a few things that they weren't expecting. After hearing those words, we all felt the same—worried and quite anxious. Well, those three hours turned into after midnight. The feeling in the room was one of worry, and we were all wondering the same thing: was Chuck still hanging on?

It was around 1:30 a.m. when Dr. P—— and Dr. S—— walked through the doorway and into the family room. By the looks on their faces, I really didn't know what to expect. I remember that Dr. P—— sat down across from me, slightly to my left. And I think

Dr. S—— remained standing. Then Dr. P—— began to speak. He said that Chuck's surgery had been very difficult and they had run into many situations that they weren't expecting. He continued in saying that he did not use a flesh valve, because when they went into Chuck's chest, they unexpectedly had to graft Chuck's aorta because it was ready to burst. A new mechanical valve had to be attached to his new grafted aorta. He said that Chuck had bled a lot and they'd had to give him many bags of blood throughout the surgery. I started to get tense, as did everyone else. He said they finally got it all together, started to take Chuck off the bypass, and started his heart. It seemed everything was going well. Chuck's heart was beating for about half an hour, and then Chuck went into cardiac arrest.

My body went cold and started to tremble under my skin when I heard this. My family covered me with coats. Dr. P—— said they tried to start Chuck's heart again, but they were unsuccessful. I thought he was telling me Chuck had died. Then came the words that allowed a mustard-seed sized bit of hope to kindle. At this time, they had to put Chuck on ECMO, which is a heart and lung bypass. Right now there was nothing more they could do for Chuck. They needed to let Chuck be until they could figure out what they could do. He apologized that he didn't have better news. He told me that Chuck had been left open. Dr. S—— didn't say much other than that Chuck was in an extremely critical state and they hoped for the best throughout the night.

Dr. P—— asked whether we had any questions, and I don't think anyone did. Dr. P—— told us Chuck would be taken over to the Asper Building to Intensive Cardiac Care Sciences (ICCS). He told us that we could get there without having to go outside by following the signs reading "ICCU" in the tunnels below the hospital. He got up from his chair, touched my knee, and said, "We hope for the best," and both doctors left the room.

Everyone got up and started gathering all the stuff and their coats. I was still shaking, and someone asked whether I wanted to be taken over in a wheelchair. I declined, as I thought walking over would help me shake off my trembling.

Since it was close to 2:00 a.m., there was absolutely no one around. The walk through the tunnel was quite long and somber to me. I felt that Chuck was in the hospital somewhere, but I didn't know where or whether he was really here. What I mean is that his body was not functioning at all on its own. Chuck had experienced cardiac arrest on the OR table and was now on a heart and lung machine (ECMO machine). The scenario in that tunnel was surreal. To tell you the truth, I don't even know how I did walk to the Asper Building, as I was trembling so much. But I did, and doing so was the beginning of many things I would have to walk through without knowing the outcome but trusting that God would get us through every obstacle, twist, and turn.

We found our way to the Asper Building and located the family room. Little did I know it would become our room for the next four months. Dr. P—— had asked me to wait in the room and told me someone would call the phone hanging on the wall to say when I could come in and see Chuck. I don't know how long we waited or whether they called me or I called them, but the time came when I was able to go in. The guidelines were that only two people at a time were allowed in the room. I guess because Chuck's condition was so critically unstable, they allowed Carly, Matthew, and me to go in together the first time and going forward.

I didn't know what to expect, but we—Carly, Matthew, and I—all got up from our chairs and walked down the two halls to the ICCS unit. The two big steel doors were marked with reflective tape, and in huge black letters were words reading, "ABSOLUTELY NO ADMITTANCE / AUTHORIZED PERSONNEL ONLY." Also, there was another phone hanging on the wall right outside the doors with a red plaque beside it reading, "YOU MUST CALL IN BEFORE ENTERING ICCS unit."

We walked though the doors, and I remember the charge nurse and the ward clerk sitting behind the counter. The charge nurse looked very familiar, and then it came to me; she was the nurse who had looked after Chuck in the ICU back in 2004. There was a sign saying that we must wash our hands. The sink was in front of the ward clerk, who acknowledged us and said Gerri, the charge nurse, would take us to the room Chuck was in.

Gerri got up from behind the desk and walked us down the hall. As we walked through the doors of Chuck's rooms all I saw were machines everywhere; it looked nothing like any other surgery I had ever seen. There were at least twelve to sixteen IV monitors hanging on poles. There was a respirator with tubes that were taped to Chuck's mouth. Then there was the ECMO (extracorporeal membrane oxygenation) machine, a heart and lung bypass machine, which is very hard for me to describe. The ECMO was huge and was set back from Chuck's bed; it had so many tubes and lines running to and from it. ECMO is used when a patient has heart or lung damage or, as in Chuck's case, the entire cardiovascular system is in failure. ECMO works by removing blood from the person's body, oxygenating it, and removing carbon dioxide from it via an artificial lung before pumping the new blood back into the injured body. A bedside ECMO specialist would stay with Chuck 24-7 to monitor the system and take readings to ensure the system was operating properly.

It was all overwhelming and was definitely not what we had hoped for. We walked over to Chuck's bedside and looked at Chuck. I remember Carly and Matthew touching and rubbing Chuck's arm. Their eyes were filled with tears as they talked to him, in hopes that he was hearing them. As we found out later, Chuck did hear people talking at certain times even though he was on complete life support.

Chuck looked so lifeless and so very stressed. Actually, he looked dead to me. Chuck looked as if he had been through a war zone and back, which indeed was exactly what he had been through. On his pillow by his head lay his "Tools Rule" surgical cap that Dr. M——had given him to wear during surgery. When I saw the cap, I was shocked and taken aback, as it was wet and three quarters of it was soaked and stained. It made me physically weak. I can't remember who did so, but someone put it in a bag for me to take home.

I stared at Chuck. the whole situation was more grim, solemn, and critical than I could have ever imagined. I focused on the one thing we could be thankful for, though—that somehow Chuck was still considered medically alive. Chuck had a band around his head to monitor both his pulse and oxygen levels, as they could not get either reading from the finger clip. Along the band, Chuck had developed egg-sized bumps that were purple in color, which brightly contrasted against the rest of his face, which was a tawny yellow. Chuck's chest was also left open, just as it had been back in 2004. I couldn't think back, and I surely couldn't think ahead. We were stuck in the moment. From this moment on, we would be living in moments, hanging on by a frayed thread.

It was close to 2:30 a.m., and surprisingly, Pastor Ernest had arrived. I guess Carly had texted Pastor Ernest, as he had requested us to do, to let him know Chuck was out of surgery and had been transferred to the ICCS. We certainly did not expect him to come at this time, but he did. Gerri, the charge nurse, asked me whether it was okay for him to come in and see Chuck. I confirmed that Pastor Ernest was allowed in to see Chuck any time, day or night. He came into Chuck's room and quietly greeted Carly, Matthew, and me. He walked over to Chuck's bed and looked at Chuck and looked around the room. Pastor Ernest, too, was taken aback by everything: all the machines, tubes, lines, wires, poles, and monitors. Pastor Ernest's face was full of compassion, concern, and sincere care for Chuck and us. I remember that he put his hands on Chuck's arm and on the top of his head, careful not to tug on any lines or tubes. The laying on of hands is a significant practice of healing written about in the Bible.

Mark 16:18 says that believers would lay their hands on the sick and they would recover. There are at least twenty-four verses in the Bible that speaks of the laying on of hands. It is both a symbolic and formal method of invoking the power of the Holy Spirit during baptisms, dedications, confirmations, and healings. There is power in this ritual, but again it all comes back to the practitioner having to believe. As Pastor Ernest prayed, we stood and agreed with every word he spoke and believed it in our hearts. Every time Pastor Ernest prayed and laid his hands on Chuck, he would say, "The same spirit that rose Jesus from the dead, lives in you, Chuck." Also, we would lay our hands on Chuck with one hand on each other so we would all be united together. We agreed with the words Pastor Ernest prayed over Chuck mentally, emotionally, physically, and spiritually.

I didn't want to leave Chuck, but I was exhausted and knew there was nothing more I could physically do for him. When we were finished praying, I said good night to Chuck, telling him we would be back in the day, in hopes he could hear our words and feel our love. The nurse and the ECMO specialist nodded their heads as we all left Chuck's room.

We didn't say much on the walk back to the family room. Seeing Chuck in the state he was in was deflating and heartbreaking. The family was patiently waiting to hear an update on Chuck. Pastor Ernest stayed with us as we talked as a family. We all gathered in the large family room, and I sat in a chair that was in the front of the room and told them everything I knew about Chuck's condition. It was around 3:30 a.m. Chuck's mom was at home alone, and it was mentioned that maybe someone should go get her and bring her to the hospital. I thought that maybe instead of that, Chuck's sister Marilyn should go over and just be with her until daylight hours. I was so very grateful for all the love and support from the family all around me. The situation we were in was grave and dire; I couldn't imagine doing this alone, as some people have to.

Around 4:00 a.m., everyone was beyond tired and spent. As much as I wanted to stay, I knew I needed to go home, even if it was just to have a shower and put on a change of clothes. We all agreed we'd leave and be back in later in the morning. Even knowing there was nothing I could do for Chuck; I was so reluctant to leave. I wanted to be there if Chuck was going to pass away. Hesitantly, we gathered all our things and made our way down the halls to the elevator and then through the tunnels in the basement, back to the parking areas. It was a bit of a journey—one I didn't like at all. I didn't like the tunnels, and I never did get used to them. I was always relieved when I reached the last stretch of the tunnel. It was a wall painted with pictures of various areas of care administered by the Gray Nuns, who founded the beginnings of St. Boniface Hospital.

It was cold and still outside. Carly, Matthew, and I drove home together, and on the ride home all I hoped for was that I wouldn't receive a call from the hospital. Gerri, the charge nurse, had taken our contact information (Carly, Matthew's, and mine) in case they would need to get a hold of us. I didn't want to hear the phone ring in the middle of the night or early morning hours, because I knew it wouldn't be good news.

It seemed that I hadn't been home for a long time. Walking into the house knowing that Chuck wasn't there was shattering and left me definitely realizing our lives had changed. We were all ready to crash, to just lie down and lay all of this stuff down. Matthew still lived at home, and having Carly home and staying with me was comforting. We all went into our beds and rested as best we could. I prayed to God, praying that in the rest of the darkness things would be still and He would keep Chuck in His care tonight and always. I crawled under the covers and reached my hand over to Chuck's side, imagining that my arm was resting on him. I closed my eyes and caught some sleep.

Even though I was dog-tired, I woke up early, as I usually do. I was so grateful that we hadn't received a call from the hospital overnight. I got ready to go as quickly as possible and decided that we would take two vehicles to the hospital in case I would decide to stay later than Carly and Matthew. Carly and I would combine our efforts daily and started the routine of packing a midsize cooler with drinks, sandwiches, and snacks to have at the hospital because of the long hours and days we would spend there. I was ready and said goodbye to Matthew and Carly and made my way to the Asper Centre. The walk was quite long from the parking lot through the tunnels to the Asper Centre. I usually would drop off the cooler at the security guard desk in the Asper Centre, go park my Jeep and walk through the tunnel back to the Asper Centre, and then pick up the cooler and head up to the family room on the fifth floor. This was all very new to me. It felt cold and empty, but it did become home to us, as we spent so much time there.

Finally, I was there—the fifth floor at ICCS. I didn't see anyone other than the security guard, which made it feel even more barren than it already was. I put my stuff down, took off my coat, and walked up to the phone on the wall, scared as to what the voice at the other end might possibly tell me. I was trusting and putting my faith in the healing power of God, but I was still mighty scared. What I had seen the night before had been so unexpected, but with God's strength in my weakness I picked up the phone and called in. The voice at the other end knew who I was and put me on hold. I waited, of course wondering what the hold was for. She came back and said I could come in. You don't know what a relief it was to hear that I could come in and see Chuck. Instantly I thanked the Lord that Chuck was still alive. I had been down this path with Chuck a couple times before, and never was the post surgery experience of seeing Chuck for the first time ever like this.

I made my way down the two halls to the doors of "ABSOLUTELY NO ADMITTANCE / AUTHORIZED PERSONNEL ONLY" to the ICCS. I pressed the button on the wall to open the doors. When the doors opened, whether or not it was real, it felt as though all sets of eyes were on me. I said good morning to anyone who made eye contact with me. I washed and dried my hands in front of the ward clerk, took a breath, and made my way to Chuck's room, which was the last room down the right side of the hall. Chuck's nurse was in his room, attending to him, and so was the perfusionist that was monitoring the ECMO. I said hi to both, and then came the hard part of walking up to Chuck's bed. I don't know what I was expecting. I guess I was hoping for some kind of improvement. But when I saw Chuck, he didn't seem any better from his rest overnight. In fact, he looked more yellow, the purple bumps on his forehead looked bigger and darker, and it also looked as though he was sweating, but yet when I touched him, he felt cold and clammy. I looked around the room; it was all so very overwhelming. Chuck had actually been placed in a double room because he was hooked up to so many machines and monitors; all the equipment wouldn't be able to fit a normal-size room. Although I saw everything that was in front of me with my human eyes, I switched my focus to the possible miraculous healing, which was possible only through Jesus Christ. In doing that, I was able to stand beside Chuck longer than I would have been able to do on my own strength. It allowed me to speak and pray words of life over him.

The nurse brought me over a chair. I'm sure she could see my brokenness and uneasiness with the whole situation. I stayed near Chuck, praying, because that was all I could do. Praying was the best thing I could do, because it requested and allowed the supreme power of God to work beyond what medicine and surgeons and doctors could do. Don't get me wrong; I believe and know that 90 percent of the doctors, surgeons, specialists, nurses, and health-care aides were handpicked by God to care for Chuck. But they, too, could only do so much. They could only do what was possible in the natural realm, but God, and only God, could do the supernatural—the impossible. He was and He is the God who can move the mountains in our lives.

The morning passed, and Carly and Matthew arrived at the hospital before lunch. They called in from the family room, and the head nurse allowed them in. I was happy to see them, and I could tell by their faces and body language that, like me, they, too, were overwhelmed with everything. As they looked around the room, trying to absorb everything from the way Chuck looked to all the machines, tubes, wires, lines, and monitors in the room, their eyes filled with tears, which made me weep because I knew of their love for their dad. This was all so shocking and upsetting.

I think it was probably that day that Carly decided she would not be going back to Calgary. She decided she would take a leave from work and stay with us for the next while. I was so grateful to her for doing this for us. I needed her love and support here with me, at the hospital and at home. Matthew and I worked for the same company, Manitoba Hydro. I was definitely not going back to work during this emergency, but Matthew would have to return after being off for a little more than a week. Manitoba Hydro was very good to both of us. Even though Matthew couldn't be off, Manitoba Hydro was very generous and allowed Matthew time to attend any large decision-making meetings with Chuck's team, or any other situation of high importance or crisis.

We spent the entire day there, going into the room repeatedly just to see Chuck and pray for him. Pastor Ernest came to the hospital to see Chuck every day, sometimes two or three times a day, especially when Chuck was lying on death's doorstep and so unsteady. As I mentioned before, Pastor Ernest would often pray over Chuck and lay hands upon him. This was one of those days. Pastor Ernest kept us strong in reminding us of the promises in God's Word. Thankfully Pastor Ernest spent a great deal of time staying and talking to us, telling us stories from the Bible of miracles and of signs and wonders.

As the day went on, everyone gathered in the family room. Daily, there were usually eight to ten of us. This day there were a few more, as there was family in from out of town. We were sitting in the small room in the family room, when all of a sudden we heard Carly come bursting in, screaming and crying. She had just been on the phone with her husband, Chris. Everyone heard her boots as she entered the room, and she sounded frantic. We all got up to meet her and find out what was wrong and what was going on. My first thought was that Chuck had passed away, but no; it wasn't that; it was exactly the opposite. She had tears in her eyes, and she grabbed me by both arms and told us that everything was going to be okay! Chuck was going to make it through all of this. She continued by pointing outside and running to the windows at each side of the building and looking into the sky and repeatedly saying, "The eagle!

The eagle stopped and looked at me. I know, I just know, everything is going to be okay."

When Carly calmed down, she told us that she had been praying for God to give her some kind of sign that everything was going to work out for Chuck and us. She continued in saying that as she was talking to Chris on the phone, she was looking out the window, staring at the cross on top of hospital roof. From out of nowhere, an eagle appeared, and he stopped right there outside the window in front of her and froze. The eagle was huge. His eye met hers, and she knew right then and there that the eagle was the sign from God that she had been praying for. She said she knew deep in her heart that it was the sign; there was no doubt both in her heart and mind that it was God's way of telling her, in His own way, that she could rely on, depend on, and trust in Him. God had Chuck and us in His sight, and there was a hedge of protection around Chuck and us. "No evil weapon formed against us would be allowed to prosper," as reads Isaiah 54:17. We felt it and believed it, even though right at this time, when we looked at Chuck, we could not see even a glimpse of life.

Earlier on, I told you about the eagle flying above and around the cross that is situated on the roof of the hospital. It was at the exact time when Pastor Ernest was sharing the story of the eagle's ability to renew its youth and strength that this eagle was first sighted by Chuck's sister Janice as it was flying over the hospital. Even then we all felt the spine-tingling truth—that this sighting of the eagle was more than just a coincidence. The eagle was sent to us as a sign and wonder of the Lord. Though we were all of different backgrounds and beliefs, every one of us knew and understood that the eagle was a special sign that someone greater was watching over Chuck and all of us.

I want to take a minute to describe the cross that stands on the roof. The cross can be seen from quite a distance, as it's on the highest roof of the hospital. It is very large and is outlined in red-orange neon lighting. It is always on, both day and night. It is like a beacon of hope in the day and even more so in the darkness and still of the night. Its presence on the hospital roof is symbolic to me. I believe, and it reminds me that above every sick person in that hospital is the cross of Christ, and it is above all sickness and disease. This life here on earth is just a passage, and the cross of Christ promises life after death when we leave—eternal life, forever, with no more sickness or disease, no more pain, no more loss, no more tears, and no more goodbyes.

I vividly remember looking at Calvin as we were searching the skies to spot the eagle. Calvin's hands were in the pockets of jeans, and his eyes were filled with tears. Calvin and all of us wanted to see this eagle, the "sign and wonder" that brought the promise of restoration and healing, the promise that life that would fill and live in Chuck's body again.

CHAPTER 11

Day after Day

Well, we never spotted the eagle again that day, but there's no doubt that its appearance was of the supernatural. As time went on and days passed with no signs of positive changes, we had to remind ourselves of the eagle's significance and what the sighting was a sign of.

The doctors ordered tests to be done on Chuck daily. They were watching for a few specific symptoms or side effects from being on ECMO for an extended period of time. The most common complications with ECMO are both blood clots and bleeds. When on ECMO, blood thinners have to be used because clotting can be a complication when the blood travels through the machine. It's truly a science to find the balance, because the blood thinners can also cause bleeding. The bleeding can occur in any part of the body, but the most serious is when the bleeding occurs in the brain, as this can cause brain damage or even death. Even though there were great risks, the benefit outweighed them. ECMO is definitely a life saver. Many lung diseases and heart problems may improve over time with ECMO, which will allow the patient to recover and survive. That is why the doctors had made the decision to put Chuck on ECMO in hopes that his heart would start beating again. We were hoping and praying for the same.

I spent all of my time at the hospital, and Carly was there with me most of the time. She had a job to do, and that was to watch over her dad. I knew God was with us everywhere we were, whether it be in Chuck's room, the family room, at home, or in the car. It didn't matter where we were; God was there. He was everywhere. God is omnipresent and ever present; He is universal. He is the Creator of the universe, the sun, the stars, the oceans, and all of humankind. He is alive; there is no other that compares to His magnificent power and glory. I know He heard our prayers from wherever we were, but I found that in the hardest times, I would always make my way back to the chapel. I guess the reason for me was that this small, still chapel was a familiar, peaceful shelter. In going back to the chapel, it represented the Saviour I was believing in, and it reminded me of how He had got us through Chuck's situation back in 2004. The chapel was my sanctuary; it was my fortress. I was able to go there without having to hear anything else but the promises of God that were written on my heart about Chuck's healing. It brought me strength and was part of the fulfilled promises that manifested twelve years previous. The chapel was in the main hospital, and there usually was no one else there; it was still and quiet. If there was another person or persons in the chapel, they, too, were praying, and there were no other distractions. Then there was that giant cross, front and center, that would draw my attention and help me to focus on the Living Saviour. I would sit there and stare—a lot of the time through blurred, tear-filled eyes—at Jesus on that cross with His outstretched arms, but through my tears I could see the promise on that cross. The peace I found in that small, calm haven was immense—so much so, as I may have mentioned before a few times, that I would lie down and curl up and fall asleep there.

I was praying constantly, though I wasn't always in the chapel on my knees. My prayer seemed to always be in my heart; that promise—the desire, that hope, sealed with faith—dwelled in my heart and was always with me.

The next several days were extremely discouraging. Chuck's

color was even more tawny yellow. More purple bumps seemed to be appearing on his forehead, and when I touched his face, his arms, and his hands, I felt he was cold. Not only did he look lifeless, but to the touch, he felt lifeless. I remember feeling inside of me that this situation was somewhat like being on a tightrope, and it felt very unsteady. It was as though everything that I was seeing in front of my eyes was teetering, with the possibility of Chuck falling off. Very discreetly, hoping that no one would notice me, I slipped the covers up to take a look at Chuck's feet. My heart sank and my body tightened when I noticed that they were discolored. Actually, they were more than just discolored; Chuck's feet were black like death. Fear gripped me, but I didn't say a word. Firstly, I couldn't speak because I was fighting back tears; I was so choked up. Secondly, I didn't want to speak death into this extremely dire situation. And thirdly, I just couldn't talk to Carly and Matthew about this discoloration and what it meant. I felt frozen in my body.

What I saw with my eyes was exactly the farthest from what I was believing for. So you can imagine that in the natural realm, it wasn't a promising or good day for Chuck or us. It was so grievous that Carly, Matthew, and I really didn't want to go in and see Chuck in this condition. We remained in the little family room nearly the entire day, not going in to see Chuck as often as on other days. Family came by as the day drifted on. I always brought my iPad to listen to songs that built us up and brought strength and hope into the room to surround us; this day required immeasurable amounts of both.

I should mention that because Chuck was in such an extremely critical state, I had made the decision that I would not allow anyone other than Carly, Matthew, or me to go in and see Chuck. That decision was intentional. The reason for this was because I didn't want words of death and hopelessness being spoken around Chuck or "out there" in the circles of people who knew Chuck and our family. Words are powerful. Both life and death are in the power of the tongue. Life words were what Chuck needed to be spoken around him—nothing else but life words.

One very valuable point I'd like to take time to mention is that Chuck could at times hear the words being spoken around him. As soon as Chuck had the opportunity to talk again, he asked about a certain night when he was on ECMO. It was that particular night when his feet were discoloring and turning blue. Chuck heard the nurse say that he mostly likely wouldn't make it through the night and they should start getting him ready for when his family came in the morning. Chuck said he tried so hard to give some kind of sign that he was alive in his body and that he was still there. He said he tried to raise an eyebrow, wiggle a toe, or move a finger, but he couldn't; he just didn't have the strength to do any of those things.

When we first heard this from Chuck, we thought that perhaps he had been dreaming or that, because he was under all the sedation and on so many drugs, he had imagined it, but that was not so. To be truthful, we really didn't believe him ourselves. These words were spoken over Chuck in his room, and he did hear them. We told the head nurse of what Chuck had shared with us. The head nurse did a bit of searching and spoke to the nurse who was looking after Chuck that night to see if she had actually said that. With disbelief, she told us it was so. All of us, including all the staff, were shocked to hear that this actually happened. But it truly did. So if you're ever in a situation (and I hope you're not) where you're around a family member or a friend that is critically ill, perhaps on life support, and he or she seems far, far away and gone, he or she *possibly may not be*. If you could have seen Chuck, you would have thought there was absolutely no way he would have been able to hear what was being said around him. But he did. The nurse who was looking after Chuck that evening came in to see him and to apologize for the words she had quietly whispered that night. Not knowing Chuck had been conscious in his unconsciousness, his nurse was totally blown away that he had heard her. The story circulated around the unit, and all staff were reminded formally, and touched personally, that words of a discouraging, downbeat, negative nature that offer no hope should never be spoken around patients by their beds or in their rooms. I'll even go a bit further on this subject, saying that words contrary to life, hope, faith, expectation, confidence, possibility, and promise should never be spoken about any person at all. Whether a person's needs are physical, mental, emotional, or behavioral, only words that are life-building, life-giving, and bring about progress, promise, hope, and positive change should ever be spoken around or about anyone. That's why even today, five years later, every day I look at Chuck in awe and wonder, I know that the only reason Chuck is alive today is because of the goodness and faithfulness of God. We spoke only "life words," and those words reached the heavens and did not return null or void. Those life words validated, certified, and stamp-sealed the promises that are written in His Word. Amen? Amen. (So be it.)

The other day, I looked at a picture I had recently taken of Chuck—as his sister Beth refers to him, the "Amazing Chuck"—with Carly's dogs, Winston and Theo, standing on a little footbridge. I had taken the picture in one of my favorite places in the world, which is Pineridge Hollow in Springfield, Manitoba. I love this picture because Chuck and both doggies look so happy and healthy—so much so that I just had to post it on social media. My caption read, "Chuck (meaning) – living proof of a miracle."

In His infinite power, God saw Chuck through, and He definitely carried me through. During these dark times, I had met a lady whose husband was in the ICCU at the same time as Chuck; I believe her husband had a bypass done. As we began to know each other and shared our circumstances, she became very concerned for Chuck, but even more so for me. I was quite surprised; I mean, when looking at the situation of Chuck and me, I seemed to be the lucky one. But she explained that she herself had had heart surgery five years previous. In her opinion, having been on both sides—previously a patient and now a caregiver—in her situation and her case, being the caregiver was the harder position to be in. Having to make hard decisions and seeing the highs and lows of her husband's recovery, she felt being the patient was an easier state to be in. Furthermore, she did say her husband's situation was definitely not as critical as Chuck's, but she found the ups and downs of his recovery exhausting and had difficulty staying hopeful. As for me, I was okay with being on the side I was on. If I had been able to trade places with Chuck, I wouldn't have found myself in what I would consider to be an easier spot. Chuck was in limbo, somehow clinically alive. There's no other way to describe it; Chuck was going through immense suffering.

I know for a fact I would never survive what Chuck went through. Chuck's great patience, incredible inner and outer strength, and sheer determination, along with God's protection, were keeping him alive.

I understood what my hospital friend was saying, but that wasn't how it was in our situation—not for me anyway. I was able to handle everything solely because the Lord was carrying me through. I'm sure most of you have read the poem "Footprints in the Sand." If you have or haven't, I urge you to look it up and read it again or for the first time. The poem describes the care and steadfast love of God that is ours in the darkest times of our lives.

That was exactly what God did for me. It was His mighty power, wisdom, guidance, and confidence; His all-knowing protection; and His shield, truth, and courage that revealed and made me know things that I shouldn't have ever been able to figure out. He gave me the energy and ideas on how to keep up with all the things that were going on. He gave me courage to talk and speak out, sometimes challenging doctors, which in my own strength would have normally been very intimidating to me. At times, I had to put ideas forth, and some were met with resistance. But with persistence, and with confidence that I was hearing from God—and not in an audible voice, but from within my inner spirit—my ideas were accepted and proved right and better for Chuck's overall well-being. On my own without God, I would have never been able to keep my strength and hope up. But what made it possible was where I was drawing it from, which was the well of living waters that never runs dry—the source of light that never fades or fizzles out. In reading all this, you may think, "Well, that's good for you," and yes, it was. But my whole reason for this book is to share to give whoever reads this strength and hope in times of trouble, whatever they may be. Whether it be financial, relational, emotional, mental, or physical, Jesus Christ is the One who can fix any broken area of your life. He is best and specializes in healing broken hearts of every kind. How does He do this? Well, you have to invite him into your heart. Once you invite Him into your heart, He's there; it's that simple. Does your life change instantly? Simple answer, no. You need to learn about His principles and promises. Do you have to stop smoking, drinking, chewing, and snorting, and change your sexual practices and preference? No. But if you start to listen through your ear gate, read though your eye gate, and feed your mind through reading, listening to messages, and maybe starting with a visit to a Bible-based church, you will begin to change—not because you have to, but because of a heart change. The change occurs from the inside out. All those things that you once desired and fancied seem to lose their appeal and luster. In some circumstances, if you continue with your old desires, they will start making you sick; they won't feel good or right. It's because you are being transformed by the renewing of your mind. Also, the Holy Spirit dwells within you, and there is not enough room for Him and other junk. As these God principles become knowledge to you and you see some positive changes happening in your life, it's as if you want more—more of Him.

The next ten days were long, with no changes in the right direction. In fact, Chuck started having more complications. Carly and I were sitting by Chuck's bedside, when all of a sudden we could hear dripping. We looked down by our feet and saw blood on the floor. We looked at each other, horrified and frightened. Carly lifted Chuck's blanket by his side, and we were both shocked and scared to see the amount of blood that had collected there. As Carly lifted the blankets, the blood fell to the floor, splattering everywhere. We both ran along with Chuck's nurse to the front desk to tell the charge nurse. It's said that timing is everything, and so it was a blessing that Chuck's surgeon, Dr. P——, was there right at this time. Dr. P—— got up and ran to Chuck's room. He took one look at what was happening and looked to find the where the bleeding was occurring. It was from the femoral cannulas, the tubes in Chuck's groin area. He ordered that the blood thinners be stopped, and we would have to hope for the best in this Catch-22 situation between the bleeding and the clotting. Dr. P—— scheduled Chuck to be taken off ECMO and to go back into the OR the following day.

For me to hear that they were taking Chuck off ECMO was depressing and a letdown. The whole reason Chuck was on ECMO was in hope of his heart starting again, but it hadn't. Time was running out, as tomorrow Chuck would be taken off the machine. But having to be on blood thinners while on ECMO was making Chuck bleed, and taking him off the blood thinners meant the development of clots. It was a lot of blood that Chuck had lost through his groin cannulas. They had to give him another bag of blood (which was problematic, as I will explain later), as his red blood count was very low. I guess the perfusionist and Chuck's nurse could see the disappointment and my uncertainty of what was next for Chuck. I mean, Chuck's heart wasn't beating. They explained to Carly and I that Chuck would now be put on a left ventricular assist device (LVAD), which would as act as his heart. They explained that the LVAD would be portable, had the option to be battery operated, and could be carried in a pouch, and that in time, with training about the device and rehabilitation, Chuck would be able to live a pretty normal life. With all that being said, I still felt unsure, and I was not comfortable or knowledgeable on the device or on the process. I really can't say that I wasn't scared for Chuck and us; the truth is that I was scared. But with faith, somehow, I was able to move along with everything taking place. The truth of the matter was that there was no other choice; this was the reality. Chuck couldn't be on ECMO any longer; timing was crucial in every step and every situation. We were entering the next phase of our unexpected journey.

Without my faith, really all our faith, I would have crumbled. When I envision faith in my mind, I see a roll of gauze. Just as one wraps gauze around a wound to secure healing and protect the area from dirt and other debris getting in, that's how I see faith working. You still have all your problems, troubles, and fears, but your faith acts like the gauze, wrapped around you and your personal wounds, not allowing the debris, such as doubt and fear, in. With faith, your hurts seem to be lessened and your troubles easier to manage. This was the truth for me. My faith in God, Jesus, and the help of Holy Spirit was carrying me through.

CHAPTER 12

Drifting

I think that when we updated the family that Chuck would be going back to the OR, we all felt unsure, but we remained as hopeful as we could. Of course, we were all praying and hoping for Chuck's heart to start beating again, but that wasn't in the plan. So, with a new plan in place, Carly and I sat by Chuck's bedside. A doctor came in that we had never seen before. He was dressed in a suit and had a tan leather satchel with him. He introduced himself, took a look at all the monitors, and began to examine Chuck. He looked at Chuck's fingernails, which were blue, and his feet, which were also blue. He checked his reflexes, which there were none of, and then he lifted Chuck's eyelids one at a time and shone his penlight into his eyes. He shut his penlight off, stuffed it back into the breast pocket of his suit jacket, and asked us to step outside Chuck's room.

Carly and I got up and followed him outside Chuck's and room into the hall. He began speaking and reminded us of what a very sick man Chuck was and how much he had already been through. Also, because Chuck had flatlined, he'd had CPR performed on him in the OR and had been without oxygen for a period of time. Because of that, this doctor mentioned the words "brain injury." He kept on by saying that prior to Chuck going through to the next step of being switched over to the LVAD, he wanted to check Chuck's brain function. His plan was for Chuck's sedation to be lifted, and he would ask Chuck a mathematical question, with the expectation that Chuck could answer by holding up the correct number of fingers.

Carly and I could not believe what we were hearing. It was ridiculously bizarre, to say the least! Here was Chuck, who had been out for twelve days with an open chest and hadn't woken up from what he thought was an eight-hour surgery. Chuck would have absolutely no idea where he was when he woke, especially considering the number of machines and medical equipment he was hooked up to. The expectation for Chuck to answer even the simplest mathematical question was completely absurd, and we told the doctor that. He said that if Chuck could not answer the question and he was in a vegetative state, his recommendation would be that they not move forward with the procedure of the LVAD and that there would be an alternative plan (which was not good.) To us this was complete nonsense, unacceptable and downright upsetting, and he wasn't' listening to a word we were saying. This doctor was totally an educated mess, with no belief in the hope of the supernatural or of a miracle. But even so, wherever his beliefs were, push that aside. Anyone with ordinary common sense would have grasped that if Chuck would open his eyes, he'd have a lot more to comprehend and understand than what two and two add up to. I said to him that even I myself was losing track of what day of the week it was with everything that was going on. He had his mind set, and no one was going to change it. He even had the audacity to say that Carly was keeping her dad alive for selfish reasons. The conversation ended, and he went on his way.

Carly was visibly upset, and we were both shaken. We headed straight to the front desk to speak with the head nurse. Once again, timing being everything, Dr. P——, Chuck's surgeon, was there looking at Chuck's CT scan of his head. He came over as soon as he heard us talking and explaining what the neurologist had told us. Dr. P—— was extremely upset in hearing what we were relaying and assured us that no such mathematical test would be going on.

Dr. P—— was moving forward with Chuck and transferring Chuck over to the LVAD tomorrow. We were not to worry about what the neurologist had said. Dr. P—— would be speaking with him and telling him that no tests would be taking place, and that he was moving forward with Chuck.

When I look back at my life, I thank God for his perfect timing in everything and everywhere. Even before I became a practicing believer and it was my choice that God was not involved in every area of my life, He had my back throughout. He was watching over me and protecting me even when I didn't realize it. Now He was doing the same for my family. His perfect timing became so much clearer, so much more evident and transparent, as we were going through this tough season. These situations of perfect timing from beginning to end were not just an endless string of lucky coincidences. It's much greater than that, my friend. It's the protection coming down from heaven, provided by the Source, the Living God, our Creator, the Creator of Humankind, the Creator of heaven and earth, and the Holy, Father of Our Saviour, Jesus Christ.

The day passed, the night passed, and we were back at the hospital before 6:00 a.m. Carly, Matthew, and I were there as Chuck was going back to the OR in a very delicate state. Even though I was aware of everything—all the pumps, monitors, IVs, lines, and tubes—I was taken aback, there is no doubt about it, by the number of people in green scrubs that were there to take Chuck back to the OR. There were at least fourteen. The room was very quiet and somber. There was a lot of beeping and alarming happening as they unplugged the machines and equipment from the wall for them to switch over to battery mode as they transported Chuck to the OR. I had signed the papers for Chuck the day before, and every time I did the signing, I felt that I had taken responsibility for Chuck's life, but I had comfort knowing that in prayer I had sought wisdom and discernment from God.

Each medical person in Chuck's room had concern and compassion for us. There were so many people in the room that

Carly, Matthew, and I huddled in the farthest corner so we wouldn't be in the way. Each person was getting something ready to go, but the room was still very quiet. Dr. M——, one of the anesthesiologists, and one of the perfusionists came and asked how we were doing. We said okay, but I would say all three of us were somewhat overwhelmed. But we also had peace, as we were resting in knowing the protection and power of God.

Well, Chuck and everyone was ready to go. They unlocked the sliding door so it would swing open to allow full clearance to get everything out of the room. Every staff member was pushing something. As soon as Chuck was out of the room, they stopped for us to kiss Chuck and touch him. You could have heard a pin drop. As I'm sure you might imagine, this was a very emotional moment. It was then that the second anesthesiologist invited us to come along right up to the Surgical Ward with them. When we were walking, it felt as if we were drifting or floating. I can still see the surgical coats of the doctors and staff flowing in what seemed like slow motion. We reached the surgical elevators of the Asper Center. When the elevator doors slid open, the elevator was the largest elevator I'd ever seen. I would say it was at least five standard elevators wide, and six deep. To keep Chuck breathing as he was disconnected from the stationary respirator, a respiratory therapist walked alongside Chuck, squeezing a huge balloon-like apparatus. Once everyone managed to get in and the elevator doors closed, all I could hear was the sound of the balloon respirator breathing for Chuck.

The elevator dinged; we had reached the floor. We drifted again in slow motion down a long, wide vacant hallway. We had reached the doors of the Surgical Ward and could go no further with Chuck. Dr. D—— said to let the family have a minute with Chuck. Everyone other than the respiratory therapist stepped back. As I leaned over Chuck, I could feel my tears on my face. I could also hear the swallowing and sniffling of those around us. I straightened myself up and stood close to Carly and Matthew as they kissed and touched their dad and spoke words of affection and encouragement to him. Then I glanced at Dr. M—— and noticed his eyes were wet. The second anesthesiologist, Dr. D——, said to me, "We carefully watch over those who sleep." Then everyone took their places, and they pushed the button to open the door of the OR ward. They wheeled Chuck through the doors, and the doors closed behind them. We watched until Chuck was no longer in our sight. This was a tough moment. Our hearts were heavy, but there was a hope dwelling on the inside with expectation of this portable LVAD they had informed us about. Life was going to get better for Chuck, which was what we wanted more than anything.

We decided to go to the cafeteria before Matthew would head in to work. Going to the cafeteria while Chuck was in the OR brought back a very sad memory for me. The memory crossed my mind, but I didn't let it linger there. It was a memory of my father, who died at Grace Hospital in an OR when he was only fifty-two years of age; I was twenty, and my mother was fifty. It was totally unexpected, and the word I can use to best describe it is "horrific."

My dad had been very sick. He had pushed through a week of work, and finally, on the afternoon of Friday, December 5, 1980, he called me at work to ask me whether I could drive him to his doctor's. I would do anything for my dad. I asked my boss, and he gave me approval to leave early that day. I drove my dad to the Manitoba Clinic around 2:30 p.m. His doctor ran some tests and blood work, and he asked us to wait for the results. Sometime after 7:00 p.m., my dear dad was drifting in and out of sleep. He was so concerned that he was interfering with my Friday night plans. There was no place I would have rather been; I was deeply concerned for him. The doctor came out of his office and called my dad in and closed the door behind him. In a reasonably short time, my dad came out and sat down, and then his doctor called me in and closed the door. He told me that he himself would be driving my dad to Grace Hospital so that he could get my dad admitted promptly. Then he said my dad's tests had come back looking as though he may have leukemia. I was stunned, shocked, and, most of all, sad. I knew leukemia was a serious sickness. I told the doctor I would go home, get my mom and some of my dad's personal items, and meet him at the hospital. Our meeting was done. When I walked into the waiting room, I found that my dad had dozed off. I sat down beside my him and gently nudged him to wake him up. He woke up and asked whether the doctor had told me. I told him that I knew his doctor was driving him to Grace Hospital. I didn't mention the diagnosis of possible leukemia.

This situation with my dad was a mess from the beginning to the end. There were mistakes made, and they cost my dad his life. His parents, my grandparents, didn't see him before his passing, which had an ill effect on my grandmother for the rest of her life; she forever missed her son. My dad went into the hospital on a Friday and passed four days later, on the Tuesday. As I mentioned, sitting in the cafeteria while Chuck went back into the OR reminded me of my dad's calamity. As my mom and I sat in the cafeteria in Grace Hospital as my dad was in the OR, an announcement came over the hospital intercom: "Code blue in OR ..." Again, it came on: "Code blue in OR ..." A code blue is when a patient is in cardio pulmonary arrest, requiring a team of providers to rush to the patient and begin immediate resuscitative efforts. I remember that my mother grabbed and squeezed my arm from across the table and said, "That's your dad." We gathered our things and went back up to my dad's ward. My dad wasn't there. The air was heavy, and my poor mother was distraught and worried. I was beginning to feel dread and fear. A nurse came in and told us we were now to move to the family room on the main floor; the doctor would come and see us there. At this point I can't say I knew what was going on; I was just trying to keep my mom calm.

We made our way down to the family room. It was dark in color, and I noticed tissue boxes on the tables. My sister arrived with my grandparents; the ward had directed them to the family room. There we all waited together for the doctor. My grandparents were very quiet, as they had thought they had come to see my dad for the first time since his admittance into the hospital. My grandmother Mary asked where my dad was, and we explained he was in the OR. Suddenly the door opened, and in came a doctor we had never seen before. He asked who Mrs. Nebozenko was. My mother spoke and acknowledged that she was. He came up to her and leaned over her as she sat and said so very coldly, "Dear, sorry to say, your husband didn't make it through the procedure."

My mother gasped, along with all of us, and, barely able to speak, asked, "What? Pardon me? Doctor, what are you saying? Doctor, please say no; please say this is not true." He said, "Dear, you heard me right; your husband has passed away." At that point, he turned toward the door and left the room. This doctor was abrupt, cold, and uncaring; my father meant absolutely nothing to him. Months later, this despicable man even sent my mother a bill and tried to get paid for the procedure that killed my dad. That killing bill wasn't paid. My mom and I had even gone to see the doctor who had admitted my dad to get some answers. The only thing he said was that this doctor was known for being too quick with his hands. No matter what anybody said, it didn't change things. No words or explanation would bring my loving dad back. Our lives were changed forever. My mother couldn't even walk out of the hospital; we had to put her in a wheelchair. She didn't stop shaking for months, and she cried for years. There was enormous adjustment for my family, but mostly for my mom, as well as for me, being as I still lived at home with her.

As Carly, Matthew, and I sat in the cafeteria, I prayed to the Lord above that I would not hear over the hospital intercom "Code Blue in OR …" I never wanted to hear those words again as the memory of my father's preventable death crossed my mind.

CHAPTER 13

Misunderstood

We finished up in the cafeteria. We said goodbye to Matthew as he headed off to work, and I promised him I'd let him know of any updates. Carly and I walked back to the Asper Center. I'd say it was mid to late afternoon when we were notified that Chuck was back from the OR and we could come in and see him. I called Matthew to let him know Chuck had made it through. I was so comforted to hear he was back in the ward and hopeful to see his portable LVAD. Chuck and our family experienced a huge number of setbacks and disappointments as we made our way through this journey, but this one with the LVAD was huge for me. When I walked into Chuck's room, I guess I was expecting to see this portable LVAD we were told about—the one that would allow Chuck to return to a somewhat normal life. I was totally taken aback by what I did see. All the machines, monitors, and tubes were still everywhere. It didn't seem as if there was any less of anything, and Chuck still looked the same—as if he wasn't there.

The CentriMag LVAD was about the size of two stacked stereo amplifiers and sat on a cart that looked similar to a cafeteria cart. It had two transparent five-foot-long, 2½-inch hoses running from it that went into Chuck's abdomen and up into his heart. The hoses were a crimson red, which I learned later was because they contained

Chuck's blood; the beautiful richness of the red color meant that Chuck's blood was well oxygenated. One hose was for input and the other for output. I remember seeing "4,200" on the screen of the LVAD. In time I asked about that number, because at times it would read lesser. The perfusionist informed me that it was the number of RPMs the pump was spinning at to deliver the right amount of blood into Chuck's body. The entire setup was cumbersome, and there was nothing sleek or portable about it, but it was keeping Chuck alive. So even in my massive disappointment I still was so thankful that Chuck was somehow hanging on, even though it was by a very tiny thread.

Dr. P—— came into Chuck's room shortly after we arrived there. He started explaining that the plan for Chuck changed when he was in the OR. He explained that he felt that there was too much risk for Chuck to be on a portable LVAD. Chuck was just too sick, and it was highly probable that he wouldn't have survived if he had put him on it. Chuck required to be monitored at all times and would need major rehabilitation to get well enough for a possible heart transplant. That was the very first time I heard those words: "heart transplant." Those two words, I have to admit, frightened me. Dr. P—— added that Chuck was a very long way from a possible heart transplant. Regarding the small LVAD, Dr. P—— could not see Chuck getting well to the point of being discharged with it.

Interestingly enough, Chuck has a memory of this consideration taking place while being on the table in the OR. Chuck recalls this major decision, as he seemed to slip in and out of consciousness. Dr P. and other surgeons discussed the best option for Chuck, and it was to be put on the nonportable LVAD and remain in the ICU. If he survived and his condition improved, the likelihood for a transplant was much greater.

So what I was expecting, envisioning, and hoping for was the extreme opposite of where we had landed and what we were experiencing. I had seen Chuck living life at home. Now I heard that Chuck would remain in the hospital and we would continue life in the ICU. But I had been praying all the time, and I really did have to trust God in what He was doing, even though it wasn't what I was wanting or expecting. The Bible states that His plans and ways are much higher than ours and that He gives us more than what we could ever dream or ask for. Even though I knew this, I felt the disillusionment and frustration of what I considered a letdown. There was nothing I could do to change things, and even though I would have preferred Chuck to be able to come home, the truth was that I, we, couldn't look after him there—not in the condition he was in. It was as if he were dead in a body that was still deemed alive. So again, I had to do a swipe and wipe away the way I thought things would go and should be. I had to accept and trust the way things were unfolding, and that's exactly what I did. I had to move forward, and the only way I was able to do so was to trust that I was walking in the Lord's protection and guidance, and trusting in His wisdom. I continued listening to musician and songwriter Jeremy Camp's song "Same Power." That song, those lyrics, resided in my heart and gave me strength to continue walking forward with hope that my prayers would be answered, though just not yet.

I'm not sure if the family's disappointment was as great as mine upon hearing that Chuck would remain in the ICU on the CentriMag. It made me feel that our lives would never be the same. But I convinced myself daily to live one day at a time. For me, who plans every day intentionally regarding when I'll exercise, eat, sleep, walk, shop, and so on, this was an adjustment. There was no other place I wanted to be, so the transition and all that came with it just overtook our lives; nothing else mattered.

Carly made the biggest change to her life. She called into work on Friday, January 8, 2016, to say she would be out because of a family emergency, and she never went back. Carly went back to Calgary only to tie up loose ends with her work and to pack some things up. Being freshly married as of September 5, 2015, she and Chris were really missing each other. Carly made the major decision that she wanted to move back to Winnipeg, and the time was now. It was always in her plan that she would come back to Winnipeg at one point in her life, but this crisis with Chuck made it happen sooner than it otherwise would have. In the few months to come, Chris quit his job in Calgary and found employment in Winnipeg at a company he desired to work for in his field of occupation. In the springtime, Carly also found full-time employment as a sonographer at, of all places, St. Boniface Hospital. Working there had it ups and downs. The upside was that Carly got to see her dad daily before work, on all her breaks, and after work. The negative side was the hospital's code blue pages throughout the hospital hallways, especially when the code blues were taking place at the Asper Center, where Chuck was. Both Carly's and Chris's jobs were direct blessings from heaven. I think Chris's last day of work in Calgary was on a Thursday, and he started work here in Winnipeg on a Monday.

Chuck being put on the CentriMag LVAD was a revised plan not only for us but also for the ICU. The ward arranged to have Chuck moved to the closest room by the front desk, as he was classified as heavy care, critical, and the timeframe of how long he would remain as such was unknown. The move was comforting, as we could see into Chuck's room from the nurses' station. Chuck's doctors were in the ICU daily, and that's where they could be found if they were in the ward. When I say this, I literally mean that having the doctors at the nurses' station and Chuck's room a few steps away was a lifesaver for Chuck on several occasions.

Two weeks had passed since Chuck's first surgery and attempt at a third valve replacement. Now that he was on the CentriMag LVAD, his heart was not working on the left side, and the only way he could ever get out of the ICU was to get well enough to be a candidate for a heart transplant. Dr. S—— didn't want to talk much about the transplant; I think this was because he didn't want to get our hopes up, considering Chuck's depleted condition. I remember Dr. S—— talking to us about Chuck's condition and where it was at. Dr. S—— wanted to make it clear that even though a transplant would be the only option for Chuck, Chuck was tens of thousands of miles away from the possibility. He described it as such. He said it was as if Chuck would have to make it across Canada. Right now Chuck was at the east coast of Canada, and he would have to make it all the way to the west coast before he could even be considered for his name to be put on the transplant list. Then he mentioned that it may happen a year to a year and a half from now, and he didn't know how long it would be or whether Chuck would even make it to that point. I remember looking outside the windows of the family room area, which is situated by the river, when I heard it could take a year to a year and a half. I love the river; its banks are framed by large, magnificent trees with beautiful sprawling, weeping branches. I remember thinking that meant I would see the trees go from being bare-branched as they were now, to sprouting green, to becoming beautifully colored in the fall, to being bare again, and possibly green again, and then returning to their fall color. In measuring time by the trees, Chuck being back home seemed to be a very long time away. But as a believer, I know that what is said here in this world does not always apply to and line up with God's principles and promises. Those promises and principles are what believers operate under. Better said, we live within that holy realm. We hold the keys to the kingdom while we are here on the earth. Jesus said that He gives us the keys and that we will be able to do more than He Himself, with help of the Holy Spirit. I do believe I have those keys in my hand; I believe it in my mind and heart. His promises are yes and amen. I get my confidence not in myself but in Him, Jesus. I get to rest in Him and His mighty holy power. I rest in His promises because He is faithful.

So even though I respected and heard what Dr. S—— said about it taking a year to a year and a half, that was not what I was believing. I knew it wouldn't be an instant progression for Chuck, but I didn't believe in the year-and-a-half time frame.

CHAPTER 14

The Awakening

The time had come. They were going to begin lifting the sedation for Chuck to start waking up. I was anxious and excited that I was going to see Chuck's eyes. He wouldn't be able to talk, because he was still on the respirator, but I could talk to him. I could hardly wait. I remember that as the sedation was lifting, Chuck's body, his arms and his legs, started to stir. It wasn't much, but it was movement. This was a huge deal for me. Chuck had been lying lifeless for over three weeks now, so this was like an awakening from somewhere deep and far away. I was hoping that his eyes would be alive, as the eyes are referred to as the window to the soul. Chuck moved more, and his eyelids started to move. Slowly they started to open and close. I stood right beside his bed. I recall that at first his eyes just focused straight up to the ceiling and were very watery. It didn't seem too long before his eyes started to move around. Carly and I had been talking to him, telling him we were there. Finally, his eyes focused in on me at one side of his bed and then he shut them and opened them to say hi. Then Chuck heard Carly talk to him, and he slowly turned his head to look at her as she was standing on the other side of his bed. Chuck closed and opened his eyes to acknowledge and say hello to her. This awakening might seem small, but in fact, it was enormous.

Chuck slowly began to look around the room; it was obvious it was overwhelming for him as he took everything in. There were at least sixteen IV pumps, four on each pole. There was an art-line, the respirator, the CentriMag LVAD, chest tubes, drainage hoses, and lines everywhere. He looked at me and raised his eyebrows. I knew he was asking me what is going on? I didn't know how much to say, because I didn't want to upset him or cause him more anxiety than he was most likely already experiencing. Chuck was most likely thinking it was the day after surgery, Thursday, January 14, 2016. The thought of the date being the beginning of February would be unbelievable to him. So I started by saying that his recovery was going to be a little different than last time and it was going to take quite a bit longer than 2004. I told him it was now the beginning of February, to which again he raised his eyebrows. I really didn't want to tell Chuck his heart wasn't functioning for a lot of reasons. First and foremost, the reality of a heart not working is something we know we will all face someday, but no one I know is ever looking forward to that time of the end of his or her life. I didn't want Chuck to think or feel that his situation was like a sentence on death row. Chuck was quite coherent for having been "out" for three weeks, and he kept looking over to the LVAD and then to me and raising his eyebrows. Chuck was communicating very well for someone who was unable to talk. As much as I was dreading to tell him what the LVAD was, I knew I had to, so I did my best to tell him with a positive approach.

I told him his surgery had been long and complicated and that many difficulties had arisen in the OR, and I filled him in on the details. I continued to say that they had done everything possible to get his heart to start beating again on its own, but that hadn't happened. I explained that the LVAD he was connected to was acting as the left side of his heart and that the red-colored hoses contained his blood, which was being pumped through his body. Chuck kept looking at the LVAD and all the other machines and monitors, and I could see he was trying to process everything I was saying.

I put myself in Chuck's position and thought that if I were the patient, my next question would be, "So what's next? Am I going to stay like this forever? What's the plan for me?" I knew that was exactly what he was asking of me when I looked at him and he raised his eyebrows. So I told him as best I could, not knowing much about heart transplant. More than anything, though, I wanted Chuck to know there was an out and an option (so I hoped.) As Dr. S——— had explained earlier to us, the family, not with Chuck present, Chuck was on the east coast, and for him to be even considered for a transplant, he would have to make it and reach the west coast. I didn't tell Chuck the time frame or how far away he was from that point; I thought that would be best explained by his doctors. Chuck had just woken up from an induced coma; as it was, I felt as if I had overloaded him with information. Don't forget that Chuck had been through heart surgeries before, the phrase "This isn't his first rodeo" stood true for Chuck when it came to open-heart surgeries. In my heart, I felt that being totally open and transparent was what I would want, and knowing Chuck, I knew that was exactly what he would want too.

I didn't really know what the future had in store for me and both Carly and Matthew. Even with everything I've shared with you to this point, I don't think my words truly describe how extremely sick Chuck was. If I, Carly, Matthew, and especially Chuck didn't have faith in the God of miracles and didn't know that we could access His power, I'm sure that this story would have had a very different ending. The reason for this book is to let you, the reader, know that without our faith in the God of miracles, Chuck would not be alive. There would be no book. There would have been sorrow, devastation, loss, loneliness, despair, and a broken heart, along with a broken life and family. I should say this though: I can confidently say that even if things had gone the other way, I wouldn't have lost my faith. I would have been profoundly disappointed and grieved, but I know that even through my grieving I would have leaned heavily on God. But God is the God of victories.

I know and have witnessed on many occasions and in various circumstances that the person who puts his or her trust in God always fares better when in crisis or in a valley than the one who doesn't. One of Chuck's doctors told me he could attest that he'd found during his years of working in an ICU that patients who had families who prayed around them or with them gained results that were always more optimistic and progressive than those who did not. God will always see us through—always. His promise is that He will do this for us; He will see us through. This promise of God is with me; it dwells within me. I breathe it, know it, and sense it very deep in my soul. I fear nothing: no person, no sickness, no situation. I walk in obedience, and thus His promises are truth and are evident in my life. I'm not saying perfection is what the Lord needs from us; that is totally impossible from anyone. He just needs to see us trying to do our very best to walk in line with His Word. We must also believe in His Son, Jesus Christ, whom He sent to us as Redeemer, Healer, and Saviour. We get forgiveness through Jesus when we acknowledge Him as the Son of God who came to the earth to save humankind. Believing in Christ, (Christianity) is the only religion in which you don't have to do good deeds, in which what you give is not what you get, and in which you don't have to strive to gain acceptance. In our human relationships and in life, there is the law of sowing and reaping. Our horizontal relationships can become damaged, estranged, divided, and ruined through our actions and words, but with God, with whom we have our *only* vertical relationship, it is not that way. Our flaws are overlooked, and we are accepted the way we are. We will always be forgiven for our iniquities and transgressions. The only way we will never be forgiven is if we denounce the Holy Spirit. Christianity is not a "this for that" religion. It's not karma. God's grace is a totally an underserving gift we can access through accepting Christ as Lord and Saviour. Once you do that, you become born again, and you become a new creation. You don't have to stop old habits (sins), but you most likely will. Things will be different somehow. You will see life through different lenses, and you will see situations differently and handle circumstances in a new way. Little victories will start happening in your life. God's greatest gift to us, other than His Son, is His gift of our free will. He will never force anything on you. I hope that, as you continue to read, I ignite a little spark in you to start your faith walk. Or, if you are already a believer, I hope my book causes your faith to grow deeper and urges you to believe in every area of your life, because God cares about it all. Believe for better relationships, healing, finances, career, energy, favor, health—believe for all your needs and wants. I want you to experience your best life possible here on earth. *Your time is now.* You have a purpose! Make the decision on your own to be able to live your best life possible with the wisdom and help of God. Remember: you are loved and wanted by Him just the way you are. God can help and comfort you in every area of your life. With Him you won't just stumble through your life. You will see victory as you become a conqueror of much, with His help and wisdom.

CHAPTER 15

The Journey

So the journey began. For now, the medical objective at this time was to keep Chuck alive. On a daily basis, there were complications that arose that needed to be combatted and conquered. One of the first of many Catch-22 situations was a clot that was sitting in one of the veins leading up to Chuck's heart. The clot formed when they had to ease off the heparin because of Chuck's bleeding from his groin cannulas. It was the next day that Chuck went into the OR and was taken off ECMO and was put on the LVAD. Now there was a clot sitting very close to Chuck's heart. Dr. P—— came and met with Carly and me and explained the method in which they would attempt to remove it. They would have to enter Chuck's body through his groin to access the vein and use a long piece of equipment with a microscopic end on it that resembled a little spider. The microscopic head with the spiderlike legs would be used to attempt to grasp the clot, and it would then be removed from Chuck's vein. The clot was so close to Chuck's heart that they really couldn't even give us the probability of success. All that was said was that it was critical that the clot be removed. If they didn't try to remove the clot, it would either cause Chuck a stroke or it would end up killing him. His medical team said there were no options, and they regretted that they could not promise me success and repeatedly said that the procedure was difficult and complicated, but there was no other choice. So, with a pen in hand, I signed the slate for Chuck to go into the OR.

Being surrounded by family in the family waiting room always made the waiting easier. My sister, her hubby, some of Chuck's sisters, and one of Chuck's nieces, Kristen, were there daily and always came to support us just by being there but also brought some snacks to feed us. Having them around was comforting and a tremendous blessing.

Also having Matthew come every day after work was like a highlight of the day. We worked for the same company at the time (I am now retired), so it was nice to get an update from work and to hear all the well-wishes from my friends and coworkers. The people I was fortunate enough to work with during my entire career with the utility were the best work group anyone could ask for. Throughout the whole journey, I received cards, messages, calls, visits, unexpected financial support, gift cards, and so on. All these acts of reaching out meant so much to Chuck, Carly, Matthew, and me. We were so grateful for everything and will remember their sincere concern and generosity forever.

Then there was Chuck's work with CFB Winnipeg, 17 Wing, and the people he worked with, which made this life-altering transition financially painless. Chuck's immediate co-worker, whom I'll refer to as Mr. R———, looked after us so well and came to visit me frequently at the hospital to find out how Chuck was doing and to let me know that he and all the people at CFB Winnipeg, 17 Wing, were sending well-wishes for Chuck and our family. They, too, sent cards filled with gift cards, offering messages of hope and wishes that Chuck get well.

Then there was the love and support of our personal friends and our present and past church families and pastors. I have to mention it was a huge blessing to have the pastors from Springs Church come and visit with us. The support and love we received from them was nonstop and ongoing. I do have to mention Pastor Ernest again, as he was there every day, sometimes two or three times a day. Pastor Ernest brought hope and reminded us that there were no limits as to what God could and would do.

Chuck's room was full of cards, and I would describe sitting in his room and glancing at them as a spoonful of medicine that that was good for all of our souls and our overall well-being. Knowing that outside these hospital walls, where our normal lives once existed, those people were thinking of us and wanting to help us was of great comfort. We all missed our everyday lives.

Along with all the people we knew, Carly's and Matthew's friends who'd known our family for years also reached out to us and sent well-wishes from themselves and their parents. One of Matthew's friends, J. P. even came down to the hospital to sit and visit with us. I think we can all say that the people in our lives are really the biggest blessing in our lives. We shared a lot of great times with all these groups I have mentioned, and all these people were there for us in our dark time. We will never forget the kindness, generosity, care, and concern they showed us—never.

I must say my daughter Carly made the biggest life change, as she came here to Winnipeg from Calgary to stand beside me through this whole ordeal and eventually moved back to Winnipeg. Carly was with me every day, waiting in the family room, in the chapel, and in Chuck's room, and she sat and waited with me through many procedures when we couldn't be with Chuck. Carly was like a security blanket; she brought me comfort and at times needed to build my hope up, and she did this in part by reminding me of specific scriptures of healing and hope. Carly also lived with me until she and Chris made the decision to move back here; then she found an apartment very close by.

All this support from family and friends and my kids made me stronger. With them I put my faith in God to do the impossible, and He did on so many occasions. Even though I'm trying my best to convey my gratefulness for His faithfulness, awe, and wonder, I feel that I will never be able to reveal His mystery and interpret His greatness and magnificence.

As we were waiting in the family room, we prayed together to the Lord Jesus Christ, the Divine Physician and Healer, to oversee the procedure taking place as Chuck was in the OR. We prayed together, and I can say we all were, and still are, in different places in our believing and faith walks, but it didn't matter; we all believed together and were asking for God to see Chuck through. There is power when people stand in union, believe, and pray together.

I remember it was already dark—I think it was past the supper hour—when I heard the opening of the first heavy door to the family room area and the sound of a single pair of shoes making their way down the short hallway. I heard them stop outside the closed door of "our little room," and there was a light knock on the door, to which we said, "Come in."

It was one of Chuck's doctor's, Dr. B———. He entered the small room in which we gathered every day and closed the door behind him. I could feel my heart in my throat and chest. Finally he spoke, and he shared that they had successfully removed the clot and that Chuck would be returning to the ward and it was a true miracle—a real miracle. When I heard those words come from his mouth, I jumped up and ran over and hugged him. I think he was taken aback by my reaction, but even he could not believe what had taken place with Chuck. He repeated a few times that it really was a miracle.

I'm sure you can imagine the relief and happiness in the room, as well as the tears. Chuck was still with us; there was nothing better than that. Before we would part each other's company, we sat in thankfulness. We waited for Chuck to come back to the ward so Carly, Matthew and I could see him before we made our way home for the night.

Leaving the hospital was never easy; my days averaged fifteen hours. When I needed to pick up some groceries, I would leave just after 10:00 p.m. to make it to Superstore before 11:00 p.m. Every time I left to go home and walked to my Jeep, I so badly wanted to turn around and head straight back up to Chuck's room. I felt this way because Chuck was totally helpless. Chuck had to rely on people for everything, and he couldn't talk, so communication with him was difficult and it took a long time to understand what he needed or what he was asking.

With any job, there are great people and then there is the handful of the not-so-great people. At every business, company, or, in this case, hospital, there are some people you automatically click with, and that's the ideal situation. Then there is the second group of people—the ones you might not perfectly click with, but whom you can talk things over with, whose perspectives you can see and understand (and they yours), and whom you can discuss options with and work together with to come to resolutions that are acceptable to both and get the job done. But then there is that other group of people—those that for whatsoever reason you just don't click with. It's as though there's a standoff before you even get started. Well, those are the ones I would start thinking and worrying about when walking to my Jeep. Again, I'm so thankful I believe and trust in the One who can fight all our battles and who gave us wisdom on how to deal with our problems and the problem people whom we all will encounter.

The days and weeks were passing by with way more downs than ups. During this time, we were building relationships with the medical professionals that were taking care of Chuck. I was really involved in Chuck's care and would always be there for morning rounds to hear Chuck's latest lab numbers and the newest health plans for Chuck. Hearing about Chuck's blood counts, both red and white, was very important to me. A lower white count meant that the infection was being fought off by the antibiotics and they were doing their job. An elevated red count meant that Chuck's blood was producing new hemoglobin. The slightest movement in those numbers in the right direction gave me so much hope and secured the promise of healing even more in my soul. However, it was a total roller-coaster, as one day the count would seem to be going in the right direction and then the next day it would plummet or rise in the wrong direction. On those days I would remember that the One who (Holy Spirit) is in me is greater than he who is in the world (the devil). The words He (Jesus Christ) has spoken are stronger than the curse. The enemy can't take what I have, because I belong to Him and His power flows right through me as it does all believers; the keys are in our hands. So on the days of the unhealthy blood counts, I refused to let them shake my faith.

As we all are aware, medicines, antibiotics, painkillers, and life-saving drugs—any kind of drug you want or need—are in-house commodities in hospitals, including narcotics. There is no denying that drugs can do great things in keeping people alive just by daily managing their conditions. Drugs save lives and are amazing in helping people get better; they help people get through their sickness and disease. I'm thankful for the drugs that manage my asthma and for the antirejection drugs that Chuck now takes. But there is also the other end of the spectrum, and that is drug abuse with both prescription drugs and street drugs. I'm sure you can think of some famous people who died of overdoses of prescription drugs. While I was spending all my time at the hospital, I witnessed with Chuck and other patients the use of narcotics that was detrimental to their progress and, in fact, caused them to regress. In one case, (actually out of province, not In St. Boniface Hospital) I saw one patient that did not recover from a dose of something that put him into a very deep sleep. The patient never woke up, and the family was devastated. Again out of province, another similar incident happened in the same ward. There again was a middle-aged man who was very aware of what was going on with him and his body, and he kept wanting to talk to the nurse. I could see and hear that she was getting very inpatient with him. She would go back and sit down at the front desk, and he would soon use his call button. She would go in and quickly say a few words; she pretty much brushed him off. I could see whether they were busy, but they weren't; there was a gab session taking place. After several times of this taking place, she went to the drug drawer and pulled out some drug. She went into his room, opened his IV line, and injected the drug that was in the syringe, and in under a minute he was out. I remember that she had left the head of his bed up so he was slumped right over; he looked dead. I can honestly say I heard her tell the other nurses at the desk, that he would now be good and out until at least midnight. I am not embellishing any of this incident at all, and I honestly thought that what had happened to the first man was possibly going to happen to this man.

Even at St Boniface Hospital, I got to know which nurses would administer more drugs (sedatives and narcotics), thinking that Chuck would be knocked out for a few hours. The bad thing about this was these drugs had a huge ill affect on Chuck and made him harder to handle.

At one point Chuck was hallucinating and had one of the most terrifying, devastating nights in the hospital, thinking there was a man with a gun in the corner of his room. Chuck's only method of communication at this point was writing down words on paper, which were not always easily legible. Chuck kept on writing down the words "son," "call," and "gun," along with Matthew's name. After work, Matthew came directly to the hospital. Chuck wrote down words to Matthew, such as "man," "trouble," "gun," "help," and "stay." So that was exactly what Matthew did; he stayed with Chuck throughout the night. Matthew comforted Chuck by holding his hand and reassuring him that no one was there and everything was going to be okay. It wasn't a good night for either of them, especially Chuck, as this scenario was very real to him.

I had mentioned to Chuck's doctors that the drugs were making matters worse for Chuck physically, emotionally, and mentally. Even though I kept saying this at morning rounds, I felt that I really wasn't being heard. Our relationship with the doctors and medical staff was growing positively; it was mutually respectful. An in-house hospital social worker had been assigned to us, as there were so many aspects in Chuck's care and because of the additional stress on our family managing this life change. We were told that when we wanted to discuss things, we could tell the social worker and she would set up a meeting with all Chuck's caregivers, doctors, nurses, and several different kinds of therapists, including respiratory, physiological, and occupational. Those who could make the meeting would be there to resolve any issues that were involved with Chuck's care. Well, the time had come to gather to discuss the amounts and kinds of drugs that they were pumping into Chuck. The narcotic drugs were making matters worse for Chuck than they already were. ICU psychosis was definitely not what Chuck was suffering from. Chuck was experiencing an overdose of drug cocktails that were playing havoc with his mind, and I knew it. I know they thought all these sedatives would calm him and make him sleep, but they did the exact opposite. The drugs made him hallucinate, keeping him uncomfortable and restless. As he was stuck on a rubber mattress with hoses and lines and wires and monitors everywhere in all parts of his body, the last thing Chuck needed was induced agitation and to see things that were not there. I requested our social worker call a meeting to discuss what was going on with Chuck. She told me she would set the meeting up to do just that.

The meeting would take place in the next few days, and I felt that choosing my words carefully was of extreme importance so that I could get my point across without sounding unappreciative of the care Chuck was getting. I was well aware that those around me were very well educated and experienced in their work, but no one knew Chuck better than I did. Plus I was constantly praying for wisdom, discernment, and guidance from the Holy Spirit on just about everything.

It was my lucky day; the meeting fell on my birthday. The room was full, and Matthew and Carly attended the meeting with me. I felt fortunate to have so many of Chuck's caregivers in attendance, especially two of his surgeons, the ICU doctor, his cardiologists, the pharmacist, and the physiotherapist, along with others. The atmosphere in the room was light; I felt a deep sense of calm and confidence, and I felt that those in the room were open to hearing what I had to say.

I think Carly mentioned it was my birthday, so everyone wished me a happy birthday, and the joke that I was turning thirty-nine was made with a few laughs. After that, the real meeting started. I thanked everyone for their genuine care for Chuck and our family. I also thanked them for coming to the meeting and making time for us. Then I spoke, saying that we had all seen Chuck's mental state lately and how he was going through distortion and hallucinations. While sitting at Chuck's bedside, what I had been witnessing was that to combat this, another drug was used to try to alleviate the situation. The end result of this only heightened the confusion and paranoia and caused Chuck to get extremely restless. The drug cocktails were now causing Chuck to attempt getting out of bed, which was life-threatening to him because of all the lines, especially the LVAD lines. If the LVAD lines were pulled from his heart, it would be all over for Chuck in less than thirty seconds. In response, ICU psychosis was explained even further to us. I flat-out had to say that I didn't think or believe that was the cause. I continued by saying that every time sedatives or narcotics were used, the drugs would send Chuck into a complete tailspin. When Chuck was heavily drugged, he was now trying to pull out his lines. I had also overheard the idea of restraints being tossed around, which I definitely did not want to hear of or see for Chuck. I believe it was Dr. S—— who spoke and said that they could try an approach of fewer heavy sedatives and painkillers and see whether things would improve. Dr. S—— said he would give the order immediately. We were so relieved and pleased to hear agreement that there would be no more heavy drugs for Chuck. I knew that the drugs were definitely causing him to act as if he had lost his mind, as I was with him about sixteen hours a day. I could see the ill effect they had on him shortly after they were administered. I felt as though we had won the war on drugs in the hospital.

Then, unexpectedly, the meeting's agenda changed to a brief

discussion of what the team envisioned for Chuck. I'll never forget the feeling I felt when I heard the tremendous news that it may be possible for Chuck to undergo a heart transplant if, and only if, he could get well enough to survive the surgery. When I heard those words, it felt as if Chuck and us were being let out of a corner and there was hope being given for a new lease of life. Again Dr. S—— cautiously reminded me of his analogy of Chuck being at the east coast and having to make it all the way to the west coast to even be considered a candidate for a heart transplant. Also, Dr. S—— reminded us that Chuck was eons away from the goal, but for now that was the objective for Chuck and his team. One of Chuck's cardiologists, Dr. Z——, added that Chuck would also have to be in an excellent frame of mind. Chuck would have to be able to sit down and have the ability to complete a crossword with her. With that being said, the meeting was adjourned. I really have to stress this one point to you: if you yourself could have seen Chuck with your own eyes, the possibility of Chuck working up to a heart transplant in the natural realm would have looked completely impossible. But with God, all things are possible. That is what we chose to believe, and this is the promise we stood on from beginning to end.

Over the next forty-eight hours, we did see positive changes in Chuck's mental state. The hallucinations subsided, and Chuck was able to commutate what he needed in writing a little better. His writing even became more legible. However, it seemed throughout this journey that when one problem was resolved, another would develop. There was never a time of smooth sailing or calm. Even now, as I sit here and write this, it reminds me of actually how hard it was. It was our faith and divine intervention that got all of us through. Every time we saw a smidgen of success of positive change, we would always stop and make time to give praise and offer our thankfulness to God. It didn't matter who was there; we would all pray together and listen to songs that made us stronger and made our belief system indestructible, and we were getting and seeing the results of doing so.

Chuck was completely bedridden without the help of others. In fact, for Chuck to sit in a chair to make sure his lungs stayed clear, he would have to be mechanically lifted from his bed to the chair in his room. It was a huge undertaking, and it took two health-care aides and a nurse for the transfer to take place. Chuck was enormously uncomfortable in the chair, and honestly, he was also uncomfortable in his bed. Chuck was losing all his muscle, and his body was weak from being immobilized for so long. Chuck had a physiotherapist and a physiotherapy aide assigned to him to help build some strength back into his body. The first assignment was for Chuck to start sitting in the chair daily. It took supports, pillows, and props to make Chuck somewhat comfortable to sit at least fifteen minutes in the chair. Also, it took time for Chuck to work up to those fifteen-minute periods, and it was very tiring on him. Sometimes it took coaxing, but Chuck would always end up sitting up in the recliner. Later a wheelchair was used, as it was less cumbersome and a tiny bit more comfortable. I knew all this was hard for Chuck, but a heart transplant was the only option for Chuck to have his life return to normal, and we all wanted for that to happen. Little by little, Chuck got stronger and worked up to having the ability to sit for forty-five minutes. It may not seem like much or like anything spectacular, but believe me; it was.

Chuck had been on the respirator since the beginning of January 2016. It was now the end of February; he was almost reaching the two-month mark. The longer a patient is on a respirator, the more difficult it is for him or her to come off and breathe on his or her own. Breathing on one's own is a requirement to be considered a candidate for a heart transplant. So Chuck's team began the process of weaning Chuck off the respirator. The process began with the respiratory therapists beginning to turn down the level of oxygen. It was hard on Chuck; he felt that he wasn't getting enough air. It took about a week before Chuck was able to be extubated. Even after the breathing tubes came out, Chuck still needed assisted oxygen. Nose prongs were first tried, but they didn't give Chuck the support he required, so to make it easier, Chuck was put on a face mask. With the respirator tubes now out, it was a blessing and a gift to hear Chuck's voice. Chuck was able to talk. His voice was weak and a bit different, but it was just so good to be able to communicate with him in a normal way.

Oddly enough, the first thing Chuck spoke about was of the time he was on ECMO and his feet and hands were beginning to discolor, and he heard the nurse speak over him about getting him ready for his family in the morning because he most likely wouldn't make it through the night. To me, the words we speak are like the rudders of a ship; they steer in the direction in which our lives will go.

I'm going to veer off here briefly to pause from the story to quickly share what is really being burned in my heart as of late. It is the power of words. Since the start of my "new" Christian journey, in which my entire life was affected by my relationship with Jesus Christ, I kept hearing about the words we speak. The new teachings I was listening to from several different evangelists was the importance of us not speaking of what we see but instead speaking of what we hope for. So during some of the more serious situations of my life, that was what I, or at times we, began to do. With no word of exaggeration in those unfavorable situations, I began to see things change and move in the direction of healing and restoration. I especially saw this in the area of physical sickness both in my own life and those of friends and family, and even acquaintances. We would pray for and request healing directly from heaven through Jesus Christ.

We are now in the end of January 2019, and I have been doing daily devotions and declarations over my life since the beginning of January, written by one of my favorite pastors, Joel Osteen. Every day has been inspiring and faith building. All the declarations have resounded deeply with me and truly have been amazing. The one on January 24 really struck me and reminded me that we are in total control of shaping our lives by the words we speak. It reads as follows: "I declare that I will speak only words of faith and victory over myself, my family and my future. I will not use my words to describe the situation. <u>I will use my words to change the situation.</u> I will call in favor, good breaks, healing and restoration. This is my declaration." The line that speaks to me the most, and that I feel is going to deepen my faith walk and lead me into my next level of relationship with Jesus Christ, is "I will use my words to change the situation." It seems easy enough to do, right? Well, to do it we must consciously begin to do it every day, in every situation. It must become the new way in which we speak and choose our words. Our words we speak are so important.

Having Chuck off the respirator definitely made the circumstances better, although Chuck never felt that he was able to get enough air, so the oxygen mask was a must. I don't know what I thought when the respirator tubes came out; I guess what I really thought was that things were going to move along a lot faster than they did. Also, Chuck was so very sick and weak that any small glimpse of recovery was a tiny pinch of hope. When it looked as if things were moving ahead, there was always another issue, some kind of problem that arose, and they all were critical. If we were not people of faith, all the issues that constantly developed would have slapped the hope right out of us and would have knocked us to the ground.

Chuck wasn't doing well at all being off the respirator. In fact, the doctors had talked to me about allowing them to do a bronchoscopy on Chuck. A bronchoscopy is a test that allows the doctors to examine your airways by threading a bronchoscope through your nose or mouth and down your throat to reach your lungs. That idea instantly triggered a red flag for me, because back in 1980 my dear dad died in an OR while a bronchoscopy was being performed on him. I told Chuck's doctors why I was both hesitant and very apprehensive about Chuck having one done on him. Dr. S—— took time to explain to me that Chuck's would be different than my dad's. For Chuck, no biopsy would be taken, as there was for my dad, who then hemorrhaged in his lungs because of it. Still, I told them I needed some time to think it over.

As much as I didn't want Chuck to have the test, I could see that his breathing condition was worsening. I certainly didn't want Chuck to have to be intubated again, so with fear gripping me somewhat, I did sign off for Chuck to have the procedure done. The procedure was going to be done in Chuck's room, and they would allow me to stay in the room while the test was taking place if it would be easier on me. I couldn't, but I asked Carly if she would, and she agreed to. I really couldn't help the anxiety I felt, and through the next month or so Chuck had at least two more bronchoscopies done. I never felt comfortable enough to stay and watch while Chuck had them done, but I thank God that Carly stayed and oversaw what was taking place with her dad.

The test determined there wasn't anything obstructing Chuck's airways, but there was a lot of fluid around his lungs. The plan was to drain that fluid, which they did. They extracted something like 375 milliliters of fluid. It was almost instantly that Chuck felt relief. He continued to use the face mask and nose prongs for additional support. It was good to see that nose prongs were enough at times; it was just one of those small pinches of hope.

As I said before, smooth sailing was really never something we experienced. Even though the fluid was removed from around Chuck's lungs, he was falling back into difficulties breathing. He was back to using the face mask, and now he was coughing, and it was coming from deep down in his chest; he was constantly trying to clear and cough up whatever was in his lungs. To my complete disappointment and shock, Chuck started coughing up blood. To be honest, no one really had a solid reason as to why this was happening. There could have been a few reasons, such as a chest infection or being on the LVAD for two and a half months thus far. Chuck would actually start choking if his nurse wasn't in his room to suction him. It was getting so frequent that some of the nurses asked me whether I was okay to suction Chuck should they be out of the room when Chuck needed help to get rid of the blood, which I was. On the wall on both sides behind Chuck's bed were cannisters with measurement lines on them. The suction hose and wand emptied the blood from Chuck's lungs into the cannisters, which were filling up way too fast. The doctors were keeping close attention to how much blood was coming from Chuck's lungs. I could feel the deflation of hope within myself and all those around me.

Pastor Ernest was always a beacon of hope, and his timing was perfect. He showed up daily, and it seemed he was there right when we needed him most. Chuck was always so contented to see him. I guess that was because he always gave Chuck hope and offered encouragement and reminded us of God's promises. I know Pastor Ernest, too, was taken aback by the blood from Chuck's lungs. He prayed over Chuck, and we stood with him, agreeing that this too would pass and that God knew the plan for Chuck and we had to trust Him.

Chuck was getting weaker, and the amount of blood coming up from his lungs was increasing. The clots were getting larger and more frequent. Chuck needed to be suctioned constantly. The ward had ordered Constant Care for Chuck, which meant that there would be a health-care worker in Chuck's room at all times. Chuck had a feeding tube placed in his nostril that ran down into his stomach, because he was losing weight rapidly. The specialty bed they had ordered for Chuck had many extra features, and one of them was a scale mechanism built right into it. Chuck was weighed daily, and his weight kept going down, as he had no appetite and was experiencing acute nausea. Chuck found the feeding tube intensely annoying and uncomfortable; in fact, everything was starting to bother him. His body was getting tremendously hypersensitive. Chuck had pulled the feeding tube out twice now and was starting to tug at the other lines. I could see that everything was getting to him, and I completely understood why. It was very hard for me to see Chuck in this state of suffering, but we couldn't give up. We had to make it the best we possibly could for Chuck so that he could be considered a candidate for heart transplant. It was then that I heard God speak to me in my heart and mind. I felt very strongly that I was to stay with Chuck in the hospital for seven nights. I can't say that I knew why, but I was being led to do so. Was it because it was Chuck's last seven days? In a way that's how I felt, because Chuck was in a very deep valley. Or was it the opposite? Did I need to be there for a miracle to take place? Whichever it was, I listened to that still, small voice. I packed a bag and brought my own blanket, and a recliner was brought into Chuck's room for me, and I started my overnight stays with Chuck.

The days and nights were long, and no matter what anybody did for Chuck, he was past the point of anyone being able to make him comfortable. Chuck's entire body was weakening, and Chuck winced at every touch. It broke my heart, as Chuck was one strong, tough guy. I was noticing that Chuck was getting even more fragile. His skin was paper thin, and he was bleeding from his PICC line site in his right arm so much so that his bed and gown stained with blood. His veins were collapsing, and his PICC line kept sliding out, so they had taped his arm up tightly and wrapped the tape a few times around his arm. I remember that one of my overnight stays was a really rough night for Chuck. Actually, all the nights I stayed over were very rough nights for Chuck. On this occasion, Chuck's nurse needed to unbandage his arm to see what was going on underneath all the bandages and taping. I remember that the nurse started taking off the tape aggressively. The tape was about three inches wide and wrapped around Chuck's arm three times. Chuck never complained or objected to being poked or prodded, but the ripping off of this tape was extremely painful. This nurse was reckless and careless in the way in which he was pulling the tape off Chuck's arm. This removal of the tape was unacceptable; I saw the pain on Chuck's face and in his eyes. There had to be a better way of doing this, at least slower and with more care and compassion. I couldn't stand to see Chuck wincing, because Chuck never winced at anything. I told the nurse to stop. He looked at me, appearing rather shocked, but I didn't care; he knew that Chuck was in a delicate state and needed to be looked after with the utmost care. He heard what I said, and he started taking the tape off slower and holding Chuck's skin with his other hand so he wouldn't be pulling the skin three inches up. Once he removed the tape, he could see that the PICC line site was bleeding and that the PICC line was almost completely out of Chuck's arm. The nurse pulled it out and said he would have to try to put the PICC line back in. The reason why Chuck was bleeding so heavily was because he was still on heparin (a blood thinner). The nurse continued to clean up Chuck's arm and changed Chuck's gown. Changing Chuck's bed was a huge undertaking because of all the lines and his LVAD tubes, so that had to be left to do until the morning. For now, he placed a towel sort of half underneath Chuck so he would not be lying in his blood.

Now the nurse began attempting to reposition the PICC line, which meant he was poking, jabbing, and rolling the needle underneath Chuck's skin. This was tremendously painful for Chuck, and his attempt was unsuccessful. He said he was going to see whether there was another nurse who could try to place the PICC line back in. Again I spoke out and said there were to be no more attempts. It was time to get someone, whoever it was, that could get the PICC line in as effortlessly as possible. As I have said many times before, God's timing was perfect throughout, and this was no exception, as just then one of Chuck's surgeons walked into the room. Dr. S—— was a gentle man and very soft-spoken, and he asked how things were. I told him what was taking place. Dr. S—— said to the nurse that Chuck couldn't be poked anymore and that he himself hated the thought of poking him again. He would place the PICC line that night, but from then on his order was that when they needed to poke Chuck for anything, the lab team or the PICC line team must be called up. What a relief it was for me to hear that order. I made one more request of Dr. S——, and that was that before any tape was placed on Chuck's arm to secure the site, they please shave his arm. Dr. S—— said he certainly could do that. Dr. S. called in the nurse to get water and a razor, and Dr. S—— himself shaved Chuck's bruised, thin, pale, limp arm. My heart was crying in my chest. The whole situation was pretty hard for me to take in, never mind the undue agony for Chuck on top of everything else he had to endure.

The nights were very long for Chuck, and he hated them. It didn't matter at this point; either day or night, it was a struggle to get through. Chuck was hanging on by a very thin thread. Chuck was also retaining a lot of fluid. They had to put electric compression boots on his legs that went from his thighs right down to his toes. The boots would squeeze his legs and then deflate in hopes of getting the fluid to move so that Chuck's skin would not split because of the swelling. If Chuck's skin did split, he would be very susceptible to a cellulitis infection. Chuck was in such a grave state and so hypersensitive that he kept asking if they could stop the treatment boots, which they could not. They did agree to let him have rest periods from them from time to time, but it couldn't for very long. In a few days even the compression boots were not enough to move the fluid. Chuck did have to go on dialysis because his kidney function was declining and they needed to get the fluid off.

We kept praying in hope of the light at the end of the tunnel. I am speaking not of death itself but of getting through this deep, dark valley. Chuck's Constant Care workers were helpful. One night at shift change, a middle-aged man was on to watch Chuck for the next twelve hours. His demeanour seemed very gentle and caring, and he immediately had compassion when he saw the condition Chuck was in. Chuck was lifeless, pale, very thin, and totally uncomfortable. Every spot on his body was painful, and the wires and lines were weighing heavy on him. Within the first few hours of the Constant Care aide being there, the aide totally sympathized with the agony Chuck was in. He tried everything possible to make things better for Chuck.

Chuck was so uncomfortable in his own skin; he was itchy, sore, bumpy, and bruised, and his skin was paper thin. He was constantly cold because of his blood circulating outside his body to the CentriMag LVAD, but yet at times he looked like he was sweating. This Constant Care aide wanted to help Chuck get restful and peaceful in any which way he possibly could. Around 2:00 a.m., this man with a gentle demeanor offered Chuck a sponge bath. Chuck slowly nodded his head, saying yes. This man would fall into the profile of an angel. At the hospitals they use wipes to freshen up patients, but this was a real bath with a huge basin of very warm water and soft white terry cloths. As he washed Chuck's face, neck, and chest and held up each arm and washed and dried his entire body, I tried to hold back my tears and tried to keep my heart together as I heard the water falling in the basin as he wrung the washcloth out. Even as I write this, I'm crying, as I can't explain how close to death Chuck was; Chuck barely moved. I could see Chuck was beginning to relax and find peace, and near the end, Chuck fell asleep. I couldn't thank this man angel enough. No one was able to comfort Chuck as much as he. I made it a part of my day to wash Chuck's face and hair daily with warm water; it did make him somewhat restful.

This morning as I finished writing about my seven-day-and-seven-night stay at the hospital, I went to do my daily devotion. Today's daily devotion was titled "Too Great for Words." This truly was another one of those God moments for me. The devotion verse came from Job 2:13, which reads as follows: "Then they sat on the ground with him for seven days and seven nights. No one said a word to Job, for they saw that his suffering was too great for words." Before today I didn't even know of this scripture; I believe it is more than a coincidence that even today, two and a half years later, God reveals more to me about His plan and protection He provided us through our affliction. Having that nudge to stay at the hospital for seven days and seven nights so fiercely within my whole being confirms to me the fact that it was God who put it in my heart and mind, and this scripture seals it as so. Exactly as it reads is exactly how it was.

Chuck didn't sleep much through the nights, and neither did I; I was too worried about, and very concerned for, Chuck. With Chuck no longer being pumped with narcotics, his mind was alert, and he was coherent and aware of everything going on around him. Chuck was no longer hallucinating or talking about imaginary things, but he was still in intense physical suffering and agony. He was so very weak, and there were new issues popping up seemingly hour to hour.

Chuck was still having difficulty breathing and coughing up blood chunks. I am not at all exaggerating when I say the blood chunks were the size of pickled beets and were coming up more often and getting larger. I kept on suctioning as I had been taught to do to help Chuck clear his throat passage. On one particular evening, Chuck had a nurse assigned to him that had never looked after Chuck before. She was very efficient at her job and was constantly checking, changing, and straightening. Each patient's room in the ICCS was private, with one person to one room and one nurse to each patient. Each room had a station right outside the patient's room with windows at the desk area so the nurse could see the patient at all times. I remember that Chuck's nurse was outside of the room at the station when Chuck began to cough up blood. So I automatically went for the suction wand and starting suctioning Chuck's throat. No sooner had I started than his nurse flew in the room and aggressively grabbed the suction wand from my hand. She scolded me for daring to do this. I explained that I had been asked and shown how to do it for the reason that I was constantly in the room with Chuck. She told me she was not comfortable with me doing the suctioning, to which I replied that I respected her wishes but would not let Chuck choke if, for some reason, she was not around when Chuck started coughing and gagging, not being able to breathe. I also told her I had been given approval to do so from other nurses and the charge nurses. She told me she was trained to care for Chuck and that was how she wanted it to remain, so she would do the suctioning. Again, I told her I would not allow Chuck to choke, but I said I would call her in before I took the initiative to help Chuck out.

Through the night, the blood chunks became more frequent and were getting larger. It was around 4:00 a.m., when I requested that the charge nurse come in to assess the situation. He immediately came in and was taken aback by the size of them and the amount of blood Chuck was coughing up. The charge nurse looked at his watch and said that first thing in the morning, when all staff were in, they would call a doctor to come and assess what was going on with Chuck. The charge nurse took the suction wand and suctioned as much blood as he could from Chuck's lungs. With the divine protection of our Good God, Chuck made it through the dark hours until the doctor came in the early morning to see him. Doctor S——— said they would need to take Chuck back into the OR later that day. He said that he would come find me to sign the OR authorization papers for Chuck to have yet another procedure. At this point I wasn't sure whether signing for Chuck to go back into the OR yet another time was even the right thing to do. It was weighing heavy on me. There was so much going on daily to keep Chuck alive; at times it was unconceivable, but it was also very stressful, painful, and hard on him. Chuck was in a very unsteady place. It felt as if some of the lyrics from the song "Unsteady" by the X Ambassadors were written about Chuck. This song was on the radio at the time of this ordeal and it seemed as though I heard it everywhere. Carly had told me that she had once heard the song playing in Dollarama and she'd had to leave the store because it just made her weep and become so sad thinking of her dad.

I felt that maybe I was being selfish in always allowing Chuck to have yet another procedure, something else tried on him. Maybe allowing all of these things wasn't right anymore. But I knew how much Chuck loved life and our family. Chuck himself would choose to fight to the bitter end, and that was the deciding factor I based all my decisions on. Every time Chuck went into the OR, I was uneasy because of Chuck's fragile state but also because my father had died in an OR when I was just twenty years old. That time of my life and that situation haunts me to this day, and that was over forty years ago.

Dr. S—— came and found me and some family in the family room with the OR papers for me to sign. I explained to him that I was feeling uncertain and questioning whether allowing Chuck to undergo procedures that were uncomfortable, risky, and, at times, painful maybe was no longer right anymore. Chuck had been in the hospital for almost three months now, and I had witnessed his great suffering. Dr. S—— explained that to leave Chuck as he was, with his lungs filling up with blood, would be the means to the end. He said that there was always a risk with Chuck going into the OR, but there was also the chance that they could establish the cause and hopefully resolve the issue, and Chuck could get better. Dr. S—— highly recommended I sign for Chuck go to the OR. Being that I respected, valued, and appreciated all the doctors and what they had done for Chuck and our family to this point, once again I signed the papers for Chuck to go back into the OR. The only way we were going to get through this was to keep moving forward. Even though the steps we were taking were the smallest, tiniest baby steps, we were still moving ahead, and that's what I had to keep my mind frame and focus on.

Chuck was scheduled to go to the OR at 4:00 p.m. I was very worried—and very tired, as I hadn't slept much; I'd had maybe a total of two hours in ten- to fifteen-minute intervals. I didn't go home this day to shower, because I was thinking that Chuck could die while I went home, and I didn't want to be away should that happen.

Four o'clock could not come fast enough, but it had finally arrived. There were at least ten people dressed in scrubs, gowns, and caps to take Chuck up to the OR. Dr. S—— said that Chuck wouldn't be gone too long and that he should be back in his room in about two hours or so. We said our goodbyes to Chuck, I kissed him, and we went to wait in the family room. After the two-hour mark had passed, I started to get antsy and began to wonder what could be going on with Chuck. Truthfully, I was thinking that something must have gone wrong. I was anxious about him going into the OR because of his very fragile state, and now that the time had passed the two-hour mark, I was uneasy. My niece Kristen picked up on my nervousness and reminded all of us that maybe we needed to pray again like we had at the beginning and listen to the songs that gave us strength. Kristen was right; through all the twists and turns, and amid the arising issues, our group prayer somehow had slipped away. We all agreed that was exactly what we needed and should do, and so we did. We immediately started to pray and listen to the songs that lifted us and lifted Chuck to the strength and power of the Lord. That was the best idea, and in minutes peace rolled in like a wave and took over and pushed away all the fear and doubt. It's a mystery to me how prayer can be the answer to everything, whether you are in abundance or in a scarce time of your life.

It was past 7:00 p.m. now, and so we decided to order some pizza for supper. No sooner had Matthew and Chris come back from picking up the food and we were about to begin to eat than there was a knock on the family room door. It was the doctors. They joked by saying that their timing was perfect for pizza. The best news was that Chuck had made it through the procedure, which had actually turned into a surgery. Dr. A—— explained that they had called in the thoracic team from the Health Sciences Centre Winnipeg and that as they went down into Chuck's lungs, they found a small cut in his left lung. They were able to patch it, and they believed that would be the end of Chuck coughing up blood. Again they said it seemed that it was one thing after the other with Chuck, and yet all these successful procedures and surgeries concerning Chuck were really beyond explanation. But that was not so for us. We knew exactly who was the author and finisher of all these successful procedures and surgeries. He had trampled over death over two thousand years ago, and He was overseeing theses victories one at a time, and He was not going to fail us now or in the future. Jesus Christ was and is the Divine Physician; He was and is the miracle worker that we entrusted Chuck to. To this day I entrust Him with my entire life. Even when things don't go as I planned or wished they would, I yield to Him and trust Him completely; it's a very easy way to live.

When I went in to see Chuck after he was back in his room, he was feeling the instant relief of being able to breathe again. I was taken back to find that they had performed a tracheotomy on Chuck's throat to help him transition easier to breathing on his own. Honestly, it was overwhelming to see it. I did get somewhat used to it but was never 100 percent comfortable with it. On the positive side, it was a huge relief that there were no blood chunks to suction. We had definitely passed through another dark valley unscathed. We may have been bruised, but we weren't defeated. Gratitude was overflowing for the grace and protection we had been covered with. God had us under His wings.

I was on day six of my overnight stays, and even though Chuck's breathing had improved, the narcotics were no longer being administered, and any pokes to Chuck were being done by the PICC team or lab. I still really felt that seven days was the time I was to stay at the hospital overnight with Chuck, and I was not going to budge from it. As I mentioned before, I didn't even know why this was; it was just there in my heart, so I was obedient to the nudge.

I thank God that the day was somehow uneventful. What I mean is that there were no new problems arising on top of the issues that had been around for some time now. I just wanted to stay in the moment of "urgent free" for a day or two, or even several. So, the day passed, night fell, Chuck settled as best he could, and I stayed in the recliner at the foot of his bed. Chuck didn't sleep much, and nor did I, but at least Chuck was no longer coughing up and choking on blood, and suctioning was no longer required. Morning took its sweet time rolling around, as it always did, but it finally arrived. At the break of dawn, just before 7:00 a.m. on my seventh day there, Chuck called my name and said it was okay for me to go home now. I'll never forget him saying those words that morning, because I never told Chuck about the leading in my heart to stay seven days. I felt it would be fruitless, because had I needed to stay longer, I simply would have done so, but that wasn't the case. This was one of those times when I knew that what I heard from my heart was not of my own thoughts or ideas but was from God. I heard Him and obeyed. I followed that nudge, and now it was as though a veil had been lifted. I wanted to go out into the hallway and shout, "I heard from the Lord, and He was right!" But I couldn't, because most of the people and staff would have thought I was unstable and batty. I needed the staff, doctors, and nurses to keep listening to me, so I held back my overjoy and resided in a contemporary spirit. All that mattered was that I knew and that I shared it with those close to me who believed alongside me. But now I want to share it with the world! We were spared time and time again, not only in this life-and-death crisis but also through many different times in our lives, as a family and individually. As time goes on and I journey down the line of my life, I see God's leading and protection over me and those around me. I guess it could be said that I see His handiwork, and as time goes on it becomes clearer and more obvious in my life.

On this morning on the seventh day at 7:00 a.m., I knew that Chuck was clear-minded and at peace. Chuck was calm, cool, and collected, as he always had been in his normal everyday life before all this happened. It was about 7:30 a.m., and when I was leaving for home, I had to walk past the front where the nurses' station was and where all the staff, including some doctors, would huddle at shift changes. Dr. S—— saw me and asked whether I was finally going home. I explained to him that yes, I was, because it was now day seven and Chuck had said it was okay for me to go home and that he would be all right now. I again said to Dr. S—— that I couldn't explain the seven days, but it was definitely what I had heard from within my heart. He was looking at me right in my eyes, and he smiled and nodded, and his eyes watched me as I left the ward feeling confident that Chuck would be okay. I knew that this time, nothing bad would happen while I stepped away from the hospital.

CHAPTER 16

Blue

For the first time since the beginning of this ordeal, everything was going okay. Things seemed good and steady, which hadn't been the case since we had stepped foot into the hospital back in January. It was comforting and encouraging at the same time to see some progress being made. I also was more at ease to leave to go home at night, as Chuck had been extubated and, with the tracheotomy, could now speak for himself.

One night we had a great evening together. We had watched a Winnipeg Jets hockey game on TV. I had soaked Chuck's feet in an Epsom salt solution, in hopes of healing the bedsores on Chuck's heels, as he was not allowed to have any open sores whatsoever as a candidate for a heart transplant.

It was getting close to 10:00 p.m., and I started getting ready to leave and helping Chuck get settled for the night. Chuck was always extremely cold because the LVAD was circulating Chuck's blood out of his body at 4,200 RPMs through the pump, which meant his blood was outside his body more than it was inside. To try to keep him warm, I had bought two rice bags and warmed them up in the ICCS unit's microwave. To up the ante, I also used to heat up a couple of saline bags (under the radar.) Every time I warmed the bags, Chuck would ask whether they could be a little warmer.

So this time I thought, *Okay, I'll put the saline bags in thirty or so seconds longer than usual and I'll run to the bathroom.* Well, on my return, when I buzzed into the unit and opened the big steel doors, I saw that the unit was hazy, and I could smell burnt rubber, and to top it off Chuck's nurse and a few others were wearing masks. I was horrified, as my first thought was, *It's the bags!* As I walked through the unit to Chuck's room, I felt that the staff were shunning me, as not one person looked at me. Maybe that was my perception, but no, the staff weren't happy. I asked Chuck's masked nurse whether it was the saline bags that had caused the smell and haze, and she nodded. I went over to the microwave, and when I opened the door, oh my, the smell! I quickly shut the door. I couldn't believe I had caused this ghastly stench, and the worst part was that this was where the staff heated their meals! I filled the sink with water and dish soap and washed the microwave out a few times over and left the door open. Eventually the smell faded, thank goodness! It is not one of those memories that I reminisce about and later find funny, although at this time I'm smiling and I'm a bit amused by it all. Actually, truth be told, I just chuckled.

It was close to 11:00 p.m. now, so I finished up with Chuck's bedtime routine, kissed him good night, and drove myself home. I quickly washed up and finally crawled into my bed. Just before I fell asleep, I thought, *We're in a good place right now; things are on track and going well.*

I guess it was about 3:30 a.m. when I was woken up by the phone ringing. I'm sure you have experienced a phone call in the middle of the night that startles you and you know it's either a prank or bad news. I ran to the phone in the loft and said hello. Just as I dreaded, it was a nurse from St. Boniface Hospital. Of course, I thought the worst, and reality was really not far from it. The nurse explained that there had been an incident with Chuck. The few seconds it took her to speak seemed like hours. She told me they'd just had a code blue with Chuck. I couldn't' believe what I was hearing or what she was saying, as we had just come to a place of progress. No new issues, and now this. I asked what happened. She explained that Chuck was on the bedpan and he had tried to lift himself or shift his weight, and his arm leaned on the line, and in doing so he squeezed off the flow. She explained further, saying it had happened an hour or so ago and Chuck was doing okay now and that he was now stable. My heart was pounding in my chest. I asked whether I should come down, but she assured me that Chuck was stable, so there would be no reason for me to come in the middle of the night. She said she was sorry that she called at this time, but hospital protocol was that in a situation like this, they had to notify the contact person. She told me to try to go back to sleep, and she said goodbye. I hung up the phone, sat in the dark, and went over in my mind what I had just been told. I started praying, thanking the Trinity, God, Jesus, and the Holy Spirit, who had saved Chuck from death again. I went back to bed and probably fell asleep around 6:00 a.m. My clock rang at 7:00 a.m. so I could make it back to the hospital for 8:30 a.m. rounds.

I made it to the hospital for the 8:30 a.m. rounds. I was tired, and when driving there I had still a sick, knotted feeling in my stomach and uneasiness in my spirit, wondering how Chuck really was. After I parked my car and made my way up to the unit, was buzzed in, and walked through the big steel doors, I felt all eyes on me. I washed my hands at the sink in front of the receptionist and she asked me whether I was okay, to which I said, "Yes, I think so."

As I walked into Chuck's room, I was so happy and relieved to see his shiny, moving, blinking eyes. I think he was just as happy to see me as I was to see him. I told him they had called me and informed me of the code blue and asked him more about it. He told me it was absolutely dreadful. He said he was on the bed commode and was getting sore and uncomfortable waiting for the nurse to get back. So he shifted his weight, and as he leaned on his arm where the line was underneath, he accidently cut off the flow. The last thing Chuck remembered was the sound of alarms and the room spinning, and he was out, done. Chuck described the feeling as being like a "dog chasing his tail." This incident was frightening, shocking, disturbing, and upsetting, and it also raised a red flag for the unit. No one wanted to see an accidental death with Chuck or any other patient. Chuck was the only patient in the ward on the LVAD, though, so he had "special needs." So many people had invested in Chuck. Now they were investing more, as they changed the procedure and protocol. There would now have to be a perfusionist in the hospital 24-7 while Chuck remained on the LVAD. A perfusionist would be paged or called to the ward anytime Chuck had to be lifted or moved. Chuck's life was on the line. Literally speaking, Chuck's life was on those LVAD lines. We were more than pleased and considered ourselves extremely fortunate for this decision and change in procedure to be established. We all felt a little more comfortable, especially Chuck, in knowing the perfusionists would be there when they were needed. After the dust settled, Chuck went back to his routine and schedule of rehabilitation, trying to meet the requirements of becoming a heart transplant candidate.

CHAPTER 17

Not Now

Chuck had been going through so many dark valleys and coming out alive that I think everyone thought that his luck would eventually run out. I knew who was saving him—none other than God Himself. But living on the edge all the time was causing unease for everyone, staff included; everyone was feeling the same way. That being the situation, Dr. Sch—— came in late Sunday evening and told Chuck that he would be finishing up his case and along with the heart failure team and they'd be sending it off and presenting it to the Ottawa Heart Institute first thing Monday morning, March 21, 2016. Again we played the waiting game. The line "The waiting is the hardest part," from the song "The Waiting," by Tom Petty and the Heartbreakers, describes exactly how we all feel as we have to wait on things in this life, and it definitely was the way things were in this very situation. Through it, though, we learned how to be patient. For now that was all we could do. So we waited, and the waiting was the hardest part.

It was late Thursday afternoon, March 25, 2016, when we were told that Chuck's team had heard back form the Ottawa Heart Institute and they wanted to hold a meeting with us in Chuck's room at 9:00 a.m. on Good Friday morning. To say the least, we were ecstatic! As believers, we thought a meeting on Good Friday was automatically going to be good news! Our faith made us think this way. We should have thought a bit further about what took place on Good Friday, but we didn't. We updated the rest of the family to let them know we were going to hear what the decision of the Ottawa Heart Institute was. Friday morning couldn't come fast enough, but it finally did arrive.

I remember that when we reached the hospital, most of Chuck's doctors and specialists were standing outside Chuck's room. It was 8:57 a.m., and everyone started gathering into Chuck's room. Chuck's nurse had Chuck sitting in the wheelchair, and the meeting was ready to commence. Dr. S—— spoke first, thanking everybody for coming, and basically went over the history of Chuck and all the things that had taken place since he had entered the hospital. It was hard to listen to the lengthy list of life-threatening events no one would ever want to go through, to say the least. Then he spoke the words we had all been waiting to hear, which were, "We've heard back from the Ottawa Heart Institute, and it's not the response we were hoping for. They have denied Chuck as a candidate for a heart transplant."

I remember looking at Chuck's face and him looking at me. I don't know why, but I was standing across the room from Chuck, right near Dr. P—— and Dr. Z——. Then I looked at Carly, and she put her hands to her mouth and immediately started crying. As my heart was pounding in my chest and I was trying to manage my denial of what I had just heard, my eyes found Matthew fighting back tears.

I don't think I said a word; I was at a loss for words. Dr. S—— started to list the reasons why Ottawa had denied Chuck, and the reasons were many. First and foremost, Chuck was overall just too sick, and they felt that he would not survive the surgery. The list of people waiting for heart donations was in the hundreds, and as a heart is a highly sought commodity, they want to make sure that the patient receiving the heart will survive the surgery. At this time, they felt Chuck would not be able to do that. The candidate also had to be able to walk a fair distance, and Chuck had stood and managed only maybe ten steps at most by this time. The candidate also had to be breathing on his or her own, which Chuck wasn't; he had a tracheal tube in his throat, helping him breathe. The candidate had to have proper kidney function, and that was not the case for Chuck; he was having to be put on dialysis every other day. The candidate could not have any open sores. Chuck had pressure sores on both his heels, and the back of his head had been split since after surgery and the wound was taking a very long time to heal and was still open. The candidate also had to be mentally alert and sharp to process everything exactly like a healthy person, but Chuck was slower than his normal.

Dr. Z—— asked Chuck what he thought of the decision from Ottawa. Chuck answered, "What did you expect? I failed five of the five requirements. Of course they denied me, what choice did Ottawa have?" In Chuck's mind, he felt this was a death sentence, and so did everyone else in the room. Chuck decided right then that he would trust God to keep him in His hands and help him to overcome this decision.

Dr. Z—— looked to me, and as I write this, I can still see the look on her face after she had said Chuck would have to sit down with her and complete a crossword. Maybe she wanted to see whether I was understanding everything that was being said. Maybe she was checking to see whether I realized and understood that Chuck had failed in meeting all the transplant requirements. Oh, believe me, I understood. I wasn't happy, and yes, my heart sunk into the pit of my stomach. But I wasn't panicked; nor did I think this was the end. How could it be? We believed in the One who could do the impossible—the One who could raise people from the dead. Not only was that the case in the past, but His promises are the same for today and for the future; His Word says so. He can make a way when there is no way. I believe that wholeheartedly. This belief even overrules the thoughts in my head. Through reading His Word (the Bible), I have trained myself to let my spirit be led by the wisdom of the Holy Spirit. By doing this I know His Word has the power to overrule the thoughts that come from this world, such as science, medicine, and just being a mere mortal.

I still couldn't speak, maybe because the Holy Spirit was holding my words back. But then suddenly Dr. P—— spoke. He said, "This is disappointing, I know, but we won't stop here. I think we jumped the gate and presented Chuck too soon. We're in a tender spot, and we went ahead and were refused. We will try again. If Ottawa won't accept Chuck, then we'll try Edmonton or Toronto. For now, we will work toward getting Chuck to meet all those areas that Ottawa listed and stroke them off the list."

Hearing what Dr. P—— said, I felt the weight of bad news lifted off me. We would fight, no doubt about it, but not by arguing and debating and challenging what Ottawa said. We would fight from a place of victory, with spiritual warfare, such as prayer and speaking what we hoped for, definitely not from what we were hearing and seeing. Doing this is far more powerful than fighting the way the world does. We do our best in applying God's principles and let God do the rest. We hold the keys that have been given to us so that we can do the same as Jesus, if not more.

Matthew 16:19 in the NIV reads as follows: "I will give you the keys of the kingdom of heaven; whatever you bind on earth will be bound in heaven, and whatever you loose on earth will be loosed in heaven." I fixed my thoughts on the positive remarks Dr. P—— spoke, including "We will try again." The meeting ended, everyone parted, and left in the room were Chuck, Carly, Matthew, and me. We all did our best to hold our heads and hearts up, and somehow we managed.

CHAPTER 18

Goals

The push to get Chuck started on a road to rehabilitation was now turned on high. We all wanted nothing more than for Chuck to have his life back. We had heard what Ottawa said was required to get Chuck considered for a heart transplant. Chuck had to be walking, breathing without a tracheal tube, free of bed sores, stable minded, and pretty much normal other than being hooked up to the machines that were keeping him alive. The vision was big. In fact, the vision was huge. But it was not impossible. There were some doubters in the midst, but the hope was contagious in the majority; everyone wanted the transplant to happen. Without a transplant, the future was determined; actually, the truth was that there would be no future.

The first major assignment was to get Chuck up walking. His once very buff muscular body had diminished, and his arms and legs had shrunk to nothing. Being on the LVAD depleted his muscle and body mass three times faster than the normal rate would be for anyone who was bedridden. So the physiotherapy started, with exercises and a plan and visit from the physiotherapist daily. Chuck was also assigned a physiotherapy assistant that also did exercises with Chuck daily. The physiotherapy assistant not only brought expertise with her but also brought humor and light when she entered the room. I think I heard her count reps in at least ten different languages. Zee, as I'll refer to her, always ended her counting with some kind of jingle and a joke as she lifted Chuck's leg up and down. Sometimes I would watch the clock, as I always looked forward to 3:00 p.m., when she would come up to Chuck's room. Zee had the most wonderful accent, and her pronunciation and annunciation were crisp and clear. We had the longest standing joke about how she said she loved my nice booty. What she meant to refer to were the short boots that I was wearing on my feet, but that's not how it came out. Her comment made everyone laugh, and for months afterward we laughed every time we referred to it. Zee has gone on to be a very talented and gifted public speaker, and she sometimes uses that "booty memory" in some of her speaking engagements. It truly was that funny.

Chuck still required mechanical lifting, but that soon would come to an end. The process of getting Chuck mobile again would start with Chuck getting from the bed to the wheelchair by himself. Well, not quite by himself, as he would have people to support him and equipment to aid him to do so. It was hard to watch Chuck struggle, and the struggle was real. Chuck was still hooked up to all that equipment. To get Chuck to stand took a team of people. Plus the half-inch LVAD lines were life-threatening if they weren't cared for properly. Because the lines were placed in Chuck's heart through his abdomen and held in by just a few stitches, watching Chuck move was very nerve-racking for everyone. The perfusionists had to be in the room and handle the lines when Chuck was moved the slightest bit. If either of the two lines was tugged at and dislodged, it would be over for Chuck in less than a minute. Knowing that information was frightening. That possibility sat in the deep hollows of all our minds, and absolutely no one wanted to be witness to that.

The day came for Chuck to try standing and remain standing for ten seconds with the aid of a walker. It's hard to think that Chuck, who formerly had been able to do everything independently, was now challenged by standing up on his own. Chuck had placed in the top four at his lunchtime boot camp challenges at the Air Force Base where he worked as a safety officer. It was now hard to believe that standing for ten seconds would be difficult and demanding on him. As minor as the challenge seemed, it would be a trophy moment for Chuck if he could do it. The physiotherapist, two perfusionists Chuck's nurse, the charge nurse, Carly, Matthew, and I, were present for his first stand. Chuck's face displayed both determination and doubt, as though he was ready to do it but wasn't sure if he'd be able to do it. With the physiotherapist 's one arm around Chuck's waist and her other arm under his arm, she asked Chuck to be ready to stand on the count of three. She counted, and Chuck was out of the gate; up he went. Chuck stood, started to shake, and wobbled. He watched the second hand on the clock, and those ten seconds seemed to last hours, but he was successful! Everyone in the room went wild, cheering and praising Chuck for having done it. Chuck's face showed so many emotions, including both victory and disappointment—victory because he had accomplished the goal set before him this day, but disappointment because it had taken all his strength and energy to do it. After everyone had finished celebrating Chuck's triumph and left the room, Chuck and I talked about it a little longer. Chuck felt disappointed that it was so hard for him to stand for the ten seconds; he described it as being pretty pitiful. I assured him that it was just the beginning of the road to be able to do the things he once did. I told him I didn't know of anyone else who could stand without a working heart.

Standing became a daily exercise for Chuck, and his times increased bit by bit. As Chuck's standing times became a bit longer, the next steps would be just that—Chuck would be trying to take his first steps walking since he had come to the hospital back in January.

I was so proud of Chuck and was happy that Chuck was getting physiotherapy, standing, and now attempting to walk. It took a team of people just to get Chuck up to get him ready to walk. These people that served us faithfully every day were more than medical professionals or mere employees. These people were investing in

Chuck's wellness, and I could sense and see their compassion and concern and their boundless care for him and for Carly, Matthew, and me.

Following is part of my acknowledgments from the beginning of the book, which I just want to mention again because it is so true. "This book is for all the people who were a part of our family's victory and who stood beside us as health professionals. Some of you became like friends, some like family, some like coaches, and some, I testify, were heaven-sent angels. We know that without you alongside us through this journey, I would not be writing this book."

So daily Chuck would receive his physiotherapy and exercise with the physiotherapy assistant, and within a week of his first stand, he was moving toward taking his first steps, which was an event, to say the least. I think "major event" would better describe what needed to be coordinated just to get Chuck prepared for the walk. It took at least twenty minutes to get everything and everyone organized. Chuck needed the perfusionists, the physiotherapist, two health-care aides, and his nurse to get him out of bed. On some days, Chuck would finally be ready to go and, because the perfusionists worked mostly in the ORs, their pagers would go off and they would have to leave and head back to an OR. Without the perfusionists, Chuck couldn't be walked, so when they got called away, all the effort seemed wasted. But the day that Chuck took his first steps will live in my memory halls forever.

I personally was expecting a little more from Chuck than those first few steps, but I didn't let the small number or teeny distance steal away from the incredible feat. I got into the habit of bringing to mind that Chuck was doing all of this without having his own beating heart. Chuck's first steps were under the number of ten; actually, they were probably closer to five. I recall the morning that all the people resources were there as Chuck was going to attempt his first walk. He was holding on to his walker very tightly, looking very unsure but focused at the same time. He stood up with support and then said he had to sit down. My heart sank, especially when one of the others would say, "If you're not up for it, Chuck, it's okay; you can wait until tomorrow." I would think to myself, *Wait till tomorrow? We can't wait till tomorrow; Chuck has to start walking now if he is going to get on the transplant list to get a heart.* So I would speak out and really encourage Chuck to try again, and it was more than a couple of words. It sounded urgent, as though walking wasn't optional but mandatory—and really it was. I know that some of the staff would say I was bossy and pushy. I called it assertive and insistent, and it seemed to work positively for me, especially in this situation. I had to be confident. Don't forget that it wasn't coming from me. Even though it was coming from within me, I was being guided from the Holy Spirit (that small, still voice inside of me). I was praying every chance I could. I was praying for His guidance, wisdom, and confidence, and I was receiving what I was asking for.

So Chuck was still sitting down when I told him he needed at least to try again. I felt a few eyes on me, but I didn't care, because Chuck agreed and tried again, and this time he was successful. As I said, it was under ten steps, but he did it! I can compare those small steps to filling up your gas tank with a small amount of fuel. It may not get you completely to your destination, but it will get you to the next place, where you can fill up again. Chuck's steps were exactly like that. Those first few steps didn't get him far, but they filled him up with the confidence that he could still walk. Those first steps gave him the courage to try over and over again. Chuck would try until he could walk far enough so he could be presented to the Ottawa Heart Institute for a second time. There was nothing that we wanted more than for Chuck to be accepted as a candidate for a heart transplant. That's what we *all* wanted; it was what we all were praying and hoping for.

The walks needed some tweaks so the resources wouldn't be standing around too long while they waited for Chuck to be ready to go. To prevent this, specific times were set up in the morning and afternoon. This allowed for Chuck's nurse to get him prepped as much as she could on her own before all the specialists arrived. In doing so, it helped in cutting down the time of resources standing around; it was much more efficient.

Chuck was now walking pretty well. The goal was to make two laps around the unit without stopping. It took about a month or more to attain this goal, but it happened! When Chuck crossed the finish line of those two laps, the whole unit, including us, were cheering and clapping; it was as if he had won an Olympic Gold Medal, and really, didn't he?

One afternoon when Chuck was doing his midafternoon walk, we had just rounded the second corner when all of a sudden Chuck asked what the date was. It was right then and there that he realized my birthday had passed on February 19. He said he couldn't believe he missed my birthday, and he wished me a happy birthday. My heart welled up, and I choked up a bit. Our family have always made birthdays a big deal and have celebrated them to the nines. On my birthday, the kids and I and some other family members had celebrated by having chicken wings in the family room outside the ward. I was given beautiful thoughtful gifts, but for some reason we didn't tell Chuck. I guess my birthday fell on one of Chuck's harder days, and telling him would have just made him feel worse. Chuck said that he felt bad that he hadn't bought me a gift. I told him not to worry because actually he had gotten me a gift. I went on further, saying I had picked up a beautiful baby-pink Calvin Klein purse when I had been doing the Christmas shopping a few months back. All kidding aside, that was the last thing I cared about, but Chuck really did surprise me the following week.

On the following Sunday, Carly had told me that there would be a surprise for me but didn't elaborate on any details. All she did say was that she, Matthew, and I should plan to eat at the hospital, which was unusual for me. I didn't question this but got ready to go see Chuck. When I arrived at the hospital and entered the ward, Chuck's nurse had an extra-bright smile, and the staff kept on looking our way. It was as though there were a small buzz or a quiet rumbling in the air. It was about 3:00 p.m. when Chuck's nurse said she would call the perfusionists for someone to come up to Chuck's room and we would get ready to go for "our walk." Chuck had a look on his face that conveyed to me he was up to something; he looked happy. The perfusionist came, and we were ready to go. Dr. M—— and Dr. A—— were sort of hanging in the wing, and when we left Chuck's room, we turned right and began leaving the ward. Both doctors came with us, and Dr. A——had his camera. Chuck had me wondering.

We walked through the big steel doors and down the straight, short hall, and this time we turned left and entered what I'll refer to as the IZZY Room. As the perfusionist opened the doors, my eyes were opened to this large, beautiful room. At the very end was a table set with a white tablecloth, lit white pillar candles, two vases of red roses, and a baby-pink rosebud-iced red velvet cake. Also, the table was surrounded by both a ceiling and walls of windows overlooking the river. But this wasn't all; dinner was coming in from Moxies, with my favorite meal of baby back ribs with a double baked potato and seasonal veggies. I just couldn't believe this surprise and what Chuck had thought of and made happen with his nurse and Carly, Chris, and Matthew. The five of us had a beautiful dinner together. The doctors and nurse said they would leave us by ourselves to eat our meals together. The perfusionist said he would be close by so we could call him if we needed him anything. There we were, the five of us alone, with candles burning, flowers, a view, and a delicious meal set before us. It had been a very long time since the five of us had eaten a meal around a table together. I will never forget this birthday celebration, as I felt so blessed that even in Chuck's terrible sickness, my sweet husband, the love of my life, cared and did so much to celebrate my birthday. There was nothing more we needed, other than for Chuck to get well enough to be accepted by one of the transplant centers and to be put on the transplant list.

CHAPTER 19

Expectations

After Chuck was extubated, he had needed a tracheotomy to assist him in transitioning to breathe on his own, which was another requirement for transplant eligibility. The patient had to be breathing completely on his or her own and could have no open wounds, abscesses, or infections. The next step was the removal of the tracheal tube from Chuck's throat. but the tube left a hole that was not healing fast enough. So, for the first time ever, the St. Boniface Respiratory Team, with Dr. Sch——'s, agreement, called in a specialist to stitch Chuck's tracheal abyss closed.

For the next little while, I was relieved and happy just to wake up and realize the night had passed with no phone calls from the hospital and no more code blues. For the state Chuck was in, he was doing exceptionally well with his walking. From where Chuck had been in January and February, he had come a long way, and he was doing amazingly well. Chuck's situation was similar to the change of seasons. In fall, when the weather begins to change, the cooler temperatures really feel cold. Then, on the other hand, when winter is closing and spring is arriving, that exact same temperature that in fall was thought of as cold is now thought of as warm and is welcomed. That very same temperature is now seen from a different perspective, and that is how it was with Chuck. Those of us who had been around Chuck since January saw him as winter coming into spring, knowing that from what he had been through and where he was coming from, he had made leaps and bounds of progress. But for those who didn't know what Chuck had gone through, they saw him as fall going into winter. To those sets of eyes, it was as if he were in a downward spiral, close to his last stretch. As Chuck got stronger, the perfusionists thought it would be beneficial and a treat for Chuck to walk down to the Tim Hortons in the main entrance of the hospital. This was quite a walk; the distance was probably close to half a kilometre or even a little further. Chuck required an entourage, which would consist of two perfusionists and his nurse, and I would be pushing the wheelchair so he could have rests along the way. When we would reach the elevator and front entrance area, there would be lots of people; it was similar to the parting of the Red Sea or walking through automatically opening double doors. The crowds would see Chuck and make a way for him; it seemed like they gave him a clearance of ten feet on either side. It seemed as though this parting would take place in slow motion and Chuck would flow on through.

These little kaffeeklatsch gatherings didn't last long, though; they were pretty much nipped in the bud. We were all sitting at Tim's one time when my name came over the intercom asking me to call the ICCS Unit at the Asper Center. I was a bit surprised but not shocked or panicked. My heart didn't jump out of my chest because Chuck was with me, living, breathing, drinking coffee, and eating a muffin, so this definitely was not about him being in a code blue state. I called up to the unit as requested to find out that they wanted Chuck back immediately. I didn't ask why; I just relayed the message to the entourage. Everyone quickly finished up, and we began to make our way back to ICCS.

When we reached the unit, I went straight to the nurses' station to see what was up. Chuck's nurse came with me while the perfusionists took Chuck back to lie down. The charge nurse told us that Chuck was no longer permitted to go off of the unit, the reason being that Chuck was at a high enough risk even being in the ward. Confidentially, someone had brought forward the concern that taking Chuck such a far distance to a public place with people, kids, and furniture was elevating the risk to a whole new level. With that being said, once again, it confirmed everything I already knew regarding the fragility of Chuck's condition. To be honest, leaving the unit did raise my stress level when we were in the unfamiliar surroundings. I thought it was good for Chuck's mental state to have a break from the same four walls, but not if it would cost him his life; that was too high a price to pay for a change of scenery.

So I went back into Chuck's room and delivered the news. Truthfully, we were all okay with the new restriction. There was no doubt that taking Chuck off the unit was a greater risk to him. But on the same hand, it was extremely important to keep Chuck's well-being healthy. Because Chuck was in the ICU so long, he was susceptible to experiencing ICU psychosis. So there was a trade-off to balance this new restriction. With temperatures getting warmer as we headed into spring, Chuck was allowed to go to the IZZY part of the Asper Building, where he could be taken onto the patio deck to get some fresh air and feel sunshine on his face. I will never forget the look on Chuck's face as we opened the doors and the breeze and sun touched Chuck's face. It was an expression of a fond memory, something that is valued and treasured. When all resources could be pooled, and if Chuck was feeling up to it, he was taken outside as much as possible.

CHAPTER 20

Seriously?

There is something I should have mentioned earlier, but there's a lot to remember—most of it things that I'd really rather forget. About six weeks after Chuck had been living off the CentriMag LVAD, the machine started beeping and flashing the message "MAINTENANCE REQUIRED." This was alarming and another nerve intensifier. When this started happening, we asked the perfusionists what it meant. The answer was almost as alarming as the LVAD flashing itself; the perfusionists didn't know. Actually, no one did.

The perfusionists were in contact with the manufacturer of the LVAD, and the answer was distressing. The company said the flashing "Maintenance Required" message meant the machine needed to have a tune-up. The machine was to be used on a patient for a maximum of four weeks—maybe six, but that was pushing it. The hospital only had the one CentriMag, and to change it out was not recommended regardless because it needed to be done in under a minute. Also, the procedure had never been attempted before. The CentriMag had been designed and placed on the market only fourteen months prior to our situation. We considered ourselves blessed that this did not happen fourteen months prior, as Chuck would not have survived.

So the continuation of the loud beeping and the flashing "Maintenance Required" message was upsetting and frightening. The feeling that the machine could possibly break down at any given moment never went away. To stop the machine beeping, the perfusionists would hit a reset button This new circumstance was yet another worry we needed to lay down at the foot of the cross and trust Jesus, our Source, to see us through. All the staff, including Chuck's doctors, were very uncomfortable with the situation. We all had to learn to cope with it, as there was nothing that could be done to change it.

Chuck was getting stronger and had more stamina to walk. Walking was never easy for him, and he did not enjoy the process of getting ready to walk; but he knew what he had to do, and he did it. Chuck was slowly meeting the requirements and checking them off the denial list from Ottawa.

1. Chuck no longer had a tracheal tube, as they had removed it and stitched up the hole, and he was now breathing on his own.
2. Chuck had accomplished walking the two laps around the unit, though not without stopping for a rest, but he could go a little farther every day before needing a break.
3. The wound at the back of his head was slowing healing up.
4. To try to heal the bedsores on Chuck's heels, they elevated his calves with pillows so his heels would be off the sheets. The term for this is "floating."

The only thing that would still be a reason for refusal was that Chuck was still requiring dialysis three times a week. At one time, Chuck had come off dialysis because his kidneys started functioning better. But then Chuck again started to get puffy in his hands, legs, and feet, so they decided to put him back on dialysis in hopes that things would turn around.

When I arrived to the hospital one morning, Chuck seemed

very solemn and quiet. I didn't think anything of it at first; I just thought everything was getting to him and he was having a down day. In fact, it was amazing that Chuck's spirits were so even-keeled and his outlook was hopeful. But as the day went on, even normal responses from Chuck were hesitant. Even when he turned his head on the pillow, it seemed so much slower than usual. His eyed looked hollowed, and as the day went on his demeanor really started to concern me and had me wondering what could be going on in his body. I mentioned this to his nurse, and she looked at his vitals and said that everything was the same and nothing had changed. But I knew that something was off, and I couldn't stop thinking about it. It was bothering me, and God knew it was. The day passed, and Chuck's spirits and energy level stayed low. I asked Chuck how he was feeling, but he had so much going on that he didn't know himself. I mentioned it to the charge nurse in the daytime, and she, too, didn't think too much of it. She was probably thinking to herself, along with everyone else, "Girl, be happy he's alive!" I was definitely happy Chuck was alive, and I wanted him to stay that way, so I wouldn't and couldn't let this go. The day passed very uneventfully, and it came time for me to go home, and I was thinking that maybe I shouldn't leave. I stayed later than my usual time that I headed for home, but I did have to go home, as we were now into month four, and at night I needed to sleep in my bed.

As I was driving home, I kept on going over it in my mind and praying for God to protect Chuck from whatever was happening with him, and then suddenly it came to me. Right then I realized what was going on with him; I knew Chuck was dehydrated! Chuck was lifeless; he was exactly how Carly had been when she was sick as a baby. I'll never forget that, and his symptoms were identical to hers. I quickly pulled over, stopped right in front of our Costco, and called up to the unit. There had been a shift change at 7:30 p.m., and the charge nurse that was working answered my call. Let's put it this way: I annoyed this person, and this person felt that our family was getting special treatment, and he didn't like it. As soon as he knew it was me, his voice changed; it sounded both cold and annoyed. I asked to speak with Dr. A——, as I knew he was there. He asked me why I wanted to speak to him. So I told him about my day with Chuck and how Chuck was listless and dispirited and his eyes looked sunken to me. We all knew Chuck's whole body was overtaxed and drained, but this hefty wave of weariness was something new. I proceeded to tell him I felt that Chuck was dehydrated. He had been on dialysis, and I thought maybe that had taken too much fluid out of him. Perhaps Chuck required an IV to put some fluid back in him. This charge nurse at the other end of the phone snapped at me, saying that he had no time for me and that he took orders only from doctors, not me. That's all he said, and he quickly hung up. I was totally floored and ticked off because I knew I was right on with my diagnosis. My prayer had been answered to help resolve this issue, but now I had this charge nurse to deal with.

I really couldn't to go back to the hospital, so I continued to drive home upset. As soon as I got home, I went upstairs to the loft, sat myself down on the floor, and called back up to the unit. The same person answered the phone and asked "What do you want now?"

I told him I was very concerned and that I knew that Chuck was dehydrated and that was the problem. I said to him, "If you aren't going to let me talk to the doctor, could you please at least relay the message to him?"

He answered, "No."

I kept on explaining that I felt there was an urgency that Chuck be looked at regarding the information I had shared with him, and finally he said, "If I see the doctor, I'll tell him to go in and see Chuck, and he'll assess the situation." He asked whether I was happy, and that I was. My heart relaxed, and I had faith that Dr. A—— would see Chuck and would know exactly what to do. I got up from the loft floor, washed my face, and went to bed and fell sound asleep.

In the morning, when I arrived at the hospital and walked into Chuck's room, the dialysis machine was unplugged and had been pushed into the far corner. There were two empty IV bags hanging from the IV pole; one was a bottle of albumin, and the other a bag of saline. Most importantly, Chuck was improved, his eyes alive, his skin not so thin and ghostly. Chuck being better was the only thing that mattered, all the time. Chuck was alert, and his living spirit was peeking through all the illness that was trying to take over his body. I let out a big sigh and thanked and praised the Mighty and Powerful One, our Good and Gracious God. He was the One who revealed to me what was going on and gave me the courage to follow through with His leading. His goodness and faithfulness once again calmed the winds and stilled the waves.

CHAPTER 21

Dreadful Blue

Chuck was doing well with his rehabilitation, and slowly things were getting checked off the to-do list. The rumor was that the heart failure team was going to present Chuck's case for the second time to Ottawa in the very near future. The one problem that couldn't be fixed by either Chuck or his team was the alarm and the flashing "MAINTENANCE REQUIRED" alert on the CentriMag LVAD. That alarm never became a sound that we got used to, or one we could ignore, or one that did not invoke fear. All we could do was hope that the machine was not going to fail and that reset button would work just one more time. What we really desired was for that reset button to work one thousand more times, or until Chuck no longer needed the LVAD to be alive.

So, with the second presentation lurking in the background Chuck's rehab was turned up to yet another level. Not only was Chuck walking two laps around the unit, but the physiotherapist and his perfusionist were taking him to a small rehab room that contained a set of stairs that he would climb and come back down, and a bench with weights. Chuck didn't lift any weights because of his LVAD lines and the frailty of his sternum and heart, but it was amazing to see what he could do. To capture his success, Dr. A—— would video him climbing the five stairs and also sitting on the bench and standing up, which was very difficult for Chuck, as he had no muscle left in his legs whatsoever, plus the weighty LVAD lines were cumbersome. This video was being made to send to Ottawa for the second presentation.

When a heart transplant was first being talked about for Chuck, I came home one night and googled both the Edmonton and Ottawa Transplant Centers. My desire was for Edmonton to accept Chuck for a few reasons. Firstly, I have a sister that lives in Calgary, so that gave me comfort in knowing that I had a family member in Alberta; In Ottawa I knew no one. Secondly, Edmonton would give short notice and fly patients out just before the surgery. And thirdly, the Ottawa Transplant Center, in some cases, required the patient to reside in Ottawa while waiting for a heart. The living costs would be one's own responsibility. But I didn't want to leave my kids, my extended family and church family, and our friends. So with those few reasons being the main ones, I was hoping for Edmonton over Ottawa. More importantly, though, Dr. P—— (Chuck's primary surgeon) preferred Ottawa for Chuck's case; therefore, he was presenting Chuck again to Ottawa for the second time before approaching Edmonton for a first time. All that mattered, though, was that Chuck would be at the right place at the right time and be at the best place possible. I would manage somehow; I always had. Even though I was a bit anxious, I wasn't going it alone; I had Jesus right there with me. I have to say it here and right now, thank you, God, for your great plan, Your great big plan from the very beginning.

The word was out; the team was going to present Chuck to Ottawa at the end of week, on Friday, April 29, and Ottawa had requested a video conference, with Chuck and me present. I was so glad that the time had come, as I hated the maintenance alarm on the LVAD going off all the time, progressively more frequently. For the video conference, I was planning that Chuck would get dressed in his normal clothes and wear a Winnipeg Jets jersey since it was the time of hockey playoffs and the Jets were in them. I thought that maybe Chuck should wear an Ottawa Senators jersey, as they were in the hockey playoffs as well, and since we were trying to win over the Ottawa Heart Institute just maybe the Senators jersey would somehow benefit the cause. But we are unwavering Jets fans and stuck with the plan of Chuck wearing his Jets jersey proudly. For Chuck to be able to wear his normal clothes, some alterations had to be made. I had cut some of his T-shirts and undershirts to accommodate the LVAD lines so he could wear them under his hospital gown, hoping that they would give him some warmth. So, for the video conference, I picked clothes that he would be able to put on and wear.

I believe it was Wednesday, April 27, in the afternoon, and I was sitting beside Chuck as he was in bed, and I remember looking at him and thinking how good he looked. Chuck's skin was well hydrated, and he had great color, plus I had arranged for the hospital hairstylist to come and give Chuck a haircut, as the video conference was a couple of days away, so he was looking good for the state he was in.

I was really grateful and thankful for how far Chuck had come. We were coming up to month five, and I think the only way we had made it thus far, had not lost hope, and could still smile from time to time was just by living and taking it one day at a time. With the almighty power of God, we were blessed, protected, and highly favored.

Nature was calling for both Chuck and me, so Chuck notified his nurse, and I stepped out to use the bathroom outside the unit by the family room. The entire time I was gone, I couldn't stop thinking and thanking God for how good Chuck was both looking and doing. I finished up and was heading back to the unit, and I called in. To my surprise, the clerk put me on hold for quite some time. She had me wondering. She finally came back to the phone and said it was now okay for me to come in. When I walked into the unit, I was utterly shocked and couldn't believe what my eyes were seeing. The light above Chuck's doorway was flashing blue, and I could see from the bottom of the curtain that there were at least ten people in Chuck's room. Yes, Chuck had had another code blue! The sliding door to his room was shut, so I remained outside his room with my heart in my throat and waited for someone to come out. My mind was racing, trying to figure out what could have happened. *Did the machine go into alarm mode and quit working?* That was my first thought; I just didn't know, and I stood outside the room praying. The minutes seemed like hours.

Finally, Dr. S—— opened the sliding door to Chuck's room and came to speak with me. Firstly, he said Chuck was okay. He explained that what had happened was that the lines were underneath Chuck as the nurse and the aide had rolled Chuck over, and therefore Chuck's blood flow was cut off and he went into cardiac arrest. Dr. S—— assured me again that Chuck was okay, though, and motioned that we could go in. When I walked in and looked at Chuck, he looked so different than when I had left to go to the bathroom. Chuck looked so well twenty minutes prior, and now he looked drawn, gray in color, and exhausted, to say the least. Chuck's nurse looked extremely upset and stressed, and within a few minutes he grabbed his knapsack and went for his break, and he never did come back. The charge nurse came in and told Chuck and me that Chuck's nurse had left for the day and that she would be looking after Chuck until the nurse they had called in would arrive.

More discussion took place about the incident, and what was realized and admitted was that the nurse had taken direction from the aide, whereas what really should have taken place was that the aide should have been taking directions from the nurse. The nurse knew this and was severely affected by the code blue, to the point that he ended up on leave, and when he did return to work, he never returned to working in the ICCS ward. The truth of the matter is that it could have cost Chuck his life, but faithfully the protection of God's mighty power somehow kept Chuck alive once again.

I sat next to Chuck, tremendously relieved and thankful that he was actually still alive to sit beside. The atmosphere was thick as the smoke cleared from the realization of what just had happened. Everyone, especially Chuck, Carly, Matthew, and I, just wanted this over and done with already. Little did I know we still had a long way to go, as we weren't even halfway.

CHAPTER 22

Good Friday

Do you know the feeling you get when you have vacation coming or a special weekend planned and you can't wait for Friday to roll around? That's exactly what it was like waiting for what I will call "Presentation Friday," the day of the second presentation of Chuck's case to the Ottawa Heart Institute. But Presentation Friday finally did come, and we were anxious, to say the least.

Chuck was looking sharp; on this day the statement "The clothes make the man" was really true. Even though Chuck's clothes were hanging on him because Chuck had now lost close to forty pounds, Chuck still looked better in his normal street clothes than the blue hospital gown. Seeing Chuck dressed made a mega difference to me and all of those who had seen him over the past four months.

The video conference was scheduled for 1:00 p.m. Winnipeg time, and everyone was starting to gather. Chuck's surgeons and various other key players and heavy hitters were there, such as Dr. Z—— from the transplant team. Dr. Z—— was the doctor that had told me back in March that Chuck would have to be able to do a crossword with her before they would present him again. Chuck was not quite at that point, but he was as close to it as he would ever be, and the incidents going on around him were pushing the envelope to the very dark side. The time to present was now or it would be never.

Everything and everyone, especially Chuck, was ready to get started, so we all shuffled into the room. I was so happy and relieved that Carly and Matthew were able to attend and be there. Having both of them there was not only a comfort and support; there was a chance that maybe, just maybe, they would say something that would influence Ottawa, or that just seeing their great love they had for Chuck would somehow impact Ottawa's decision. Chuck and I sat at the head of the table, where the camera was pointed. Dr. Z—— sat to the right of us, so she was also in direct line of the camera's lens. The transplant coordinator, whom I'll refer to as Ms. S——, was in attendance; she was highly efficient at dotting the *i*'s and crossing the *t*'s. Ms. S—— coordinated with the doctors from Manitoba and the doctors from out of province at the transplant centers. Chuck's surgeons, doctors, physiotherapist, perfusionist, and nurse were all in attendance. On the screen in the conference room, the camera was focused on a small, empty office in Ottawa; we were patiently waiting for someone to walk through the door and appear. Dr. Z—— looked at her watch, as it was a few minutes after the starting time. Finally the door opened, and there appeared a silver-haired doctor, small in stature, whom I'll refer to as Dr. S. H. (for "silver hair," as I can't remember his last name.) He greeted us with a friendly hello and apologized for being late. He said that there was another person we were waiting for and excused himself from the camera and left the room. So there we sat again, staring at an empty room, wondering where this meeting was going. I knew that everyone in the room had time commitments with other appointments and meetings, so I said a prayer in my heart asking for the meeting to commence before everyone started to leave.

We watched the empty little room on the screen as for what seemed to be an eternity. Then once again the door opened, and it was the silver-haired doctor with another person, this one female, whom he introduced as their transplant coordinator. The meeting started, everyone introduced themselves, and then the focus was on Chuck.

Just as I had thought might be the case, the first thing mentioned was the Jets jersey. I shared that we had tossed around the idea of Chuck wearing an Ottawa Senators Jersey but would have felt like traitors had he done so, and everyone laughed. Now it was time to get down to business. They opened Chuck's files. The silver-haired doctor had two files sitting in front of him. I gather one was from the first presentation and the other was for this presentation. Dr S. H. acknowledged that Chuck had come a far way in five weeks based on what he had read. He said that Chuck's progress was almost unbelievable (and there were many in that awestruck camp). Dr. S. H. said he had seen the video of Chuck walking and doing the stairs at the gym. But even through Dr. S. H. acknowledged all of Chuck's accomplishments, his skepticism was seeping through his words and his body language. Everyone in our room was very aware of Dr. S. H.'s uncertainty. But then Dr. Z—— stood up and spoke to Dr. S. H. in Ottawa and their transplant coordinator. Dr. Z—— took over the meeting, and it was brilliant that she did, because I believe that if she hadn't, the meeting—and, more notably, Chuck's destiny—would have turned out a whole lot different.

Dr. Z—— acknowledged she could understand the reason for their doubt, but Chuck had achieved the items on their checklist. To deny or not believe it was totally unfair to him. Dr. Z—— read several of Chuck's favorable test results, which Dr. S. H. from Ottawa kept nodding his head to. After that, she asked, "Do we need to send Chuck over there for you to get him on the list?"

Dr. S. H. answered, "Well, it would be good if we could see him for ourselves."

As Dr. S. H. was still nodding his head, Dr. Z—— clearly and loudly said, "Fantastic! When should we send him there?"

Dr. S. H. stopped shaking his head and looked up and over to his transplant coordinator, not sure how we had reached the point of Chuck coming to Ottawa. Actually, everyone in both the Winnipeg and Ottawa meeting rooms was thinking the exact same thing, but no one verbalized it. Ottawa hadn't said it, but Dr. Z—— had implied it, and Ottawa believed it and bought it! Everyone in the Winnipeg conference room stood up and closed their files and thanked Ottawa for their acceptance of Chuck. Ottawa kept on going along with Dr. Z——'s leading. Dr. Z—— knew exactly when to close and fold 'em; it was complete mastery on her part. Had she not been there, there would have a totally different outcome for Chuck; that I'm sure of.

With that being said, we were to leave for Ottawa on Tuesday, May 3, 2016. My heart was in my throat, and the fear of going to live in Ottawa with no return date was real. But underneath that fear lay something greater—the treasure with the precious gem that lay inside. This precious gem, the one thing that would save Chuck's life, was the possibility of Chuck receiving a new heart. To Chuck and our entire family, this would be the greatest gift of all—the gift of life for Chuck, and for us to have Chuck healthy and whole! Nothing, absolutely nothing, could be better than that!

The meeting adjourned, and everyone congratulated Chuck and me. Dr. Z—— and Ms. S——, the transplant coordinator, stayed back to discuss with us what had just taken place. There was no doubt this was great news, but there was also a definite uncertainty in the room. The unanswered question that needed to be cleared up was, Is Chuck on the transplant list or not?

Dr. Z—— and Ms. S—— didn't discuss whether Chuck was on the list or not; they only focused and spoke on what needed to be done and arranged to get Chuck to Ottawa. They told me I would have to take a commercial flight, as there would be no room in the plane with Chuck, because a doctor and perfusionist/nurse and another nurse would be required to fly with him. The plane was only a four-seater, and they needed to lay Chuck in the stretcher area. Believe me; this was more than fine with me, as I have a fear of small planes. Ms. S—— told me that the social worker assigned to me from within the hospital would be up to inform me of a few options of where I could stay in Ottawa. Basically, that was all we discussed. Our family thanked Dr. Z—— again, and we parted and went our own ways to do what was needed to be ready to leave for Ottawa on the morning of Tuesday, May 3, 2016.

Chuck, Carly, Matthew, and I, along with Chuck's nurse and perfusionist, headed back to Chuck's room. Not long after we were there, so many people came to the room to congratulate Chuck. There was an undeniable buzz in the air that something good was happening. In between staff popping in to come and congratulate and gently hug Chuck, I made calls to family. Everyone was ecstatic and joyful about the news, but that gray area of whether Chuck was on the list or not was clearly out there, because everyone asked, "So is Chuck on the list?" The only answer I could give was the only thing I knew, and that was that we were going to Ottawa on Tuesday morning, which meant we were one step closer to the possibility of Chuck getting a new heart.

My mind was racing because there were so many things I needed to do before Tuesday morning. Chuck and I were so happy but shocked at the same time; it was completely surreal. I couldn't imagine how Chuck felt. Of course he was joyful, as this could be the lotto ticket for his life, but what lay ahead of him was massive, and those thoughts crossed Chuck's mind. But greater than that, Chuck was looking forward to the change, even just the simple change of scenery, and to moving forward in this situation. Being in the same hospital room for the past five months had been taxing on Chuck. But he stayed mentally strong through his faith and his faith only. Chuck's faith offered him hope that no one else could. Pastor Ernest visited every day and always spoke life and miracles with Chuck. He said things to Chuck to help build him up. But the most important part was that Chuck had to believe what Pastor Ernest was saying, not just hear it through his ears and in his head. Chuck had to believe it in his heart, and he did. Chuck's belief in Jesus Christ and His supernatural power to heal was Chuck's saving grace mentally, emotionally, physically, and spiritually. Chuck's belief system was key in giving Chuck what he needed to stay positive and endure the course. Simply said, Chuck's belief in Christ Jesus, in who He is and what He can do, saved his life time and time again. Chuck didn't receive only one miracle; he received a stream of ongoing miracles; that is the only reason Chuck is here with us today. Jesus Christ brought supernatural peace, wholeness, and healing to Chuck exactly when he needed it most.

The support that we received was amazing and appreciated and oh, so helpful. We were and still are beyond grateful. When I think back, I realize I definitely could not have handled the load without all those angels (people) around me, helping and planning Chuck's transportation and my residency in Ottawa. These people and God himself carried us through all of this. My fears were drowned out by the love and support I felt from the people that God sent to cross our path. It actually scares me when I look back, because I definitely know I could never have handled this all on my own. It definitely was not in my own strength that I was able to keep moving forward; it was all because of Him, the King of my heart, who is so good and will never let me down.

The weekend passed, and I looked after everything I could think of. My flight was booked; I hoped to arrive at the same time as or before Chuck. I had called my work. Actually, I called into my work regularly. The people whom I worked with were just not coworkers; they were friends. And really we were like a family in some ways. They were great supporters and wished us well in Ottawa. I told them I would check in and call should the "big day" happen. Most importantly, I was packed.

Everything Chuck required also was in place and ready to go. The ambulance to transport him to the airport had been arranged. The medical jet was booked, and the doctor, nurse, and perfusionists were ready to go on the long-awaited Tuesday morning.

To my complete surprise Sunday evening, Chuck's nurse came in to tell me not to pack my meals for Monday. She told me that they had planned to have a send-off party for us, and we weren't to bring anything. I couldn't believe they were doing this for Chuck, Carly, Matthew, and me. I was so surprised and felt very privileged and honoured. Also, I was so appreciative, as we had been treated beyond excellent during our time in the ICCS. They certainly did not owe us anything. In fact, I felt we owed them everything. They had kept Chuck alive and had gone way beyond the normal expected care. The entire staff did everything to make this fragile situation as safe and comfortable as it could possibly be. Not only did they care for Chuck, but they truly cared for the well-being of Carly, Matthew, and me, and they tried in every way to ease the frailty of the situation we were presently living in.

CHAPTER 23

The Send-Off

Monday came, and with it came a strange feeling. I have to say it was a bit scary, too, knowing that this would be our last day in the care of St. Boniface Hospital. Manitoba Hydro allowed Matthew some time off during the day so he could spend time with Chuck on his last day in Winnipeg. Carly was working that day at the hospital. Her department had scheduled a lighter day of patients, giving her more time to be with Chuck.

I looked around the house before I left for my last day at St Boniface hospital. I had cleaned the house to freshen it up, although it stayed pretty clean, as Matthew and I were not really living in it much. I have to mention yet another unexpected blessing that came my way. I'm only mentioning these things to prove the words that Jesus said about going through trouble: "My burden is light and my yolk is easy." I know all these circumstances may seem like coincidences, but they aren't; they are all direct blessings of God's favor. In this situation, my vacuum had broken down several times since January and had been in the repair shop three times and had broken down again. One night as I came into the dark house, I could see something sitting in the middle of our family room floor. Here sat this beautiful, shiny bright yellow vacuum. I couldn't believe it! I was completely surprised and found out that it was from Matthew!

A lady had randomly asked him whether he had any use for this vacuum she had never used! Of course, the answer was yes! Matthew gifted it to me, and he was so happy about it, and so was I! This was not another lucky coincidence. Believe me; I'm not that lucky. My stream of good luck would have run out long before this blessing.

Anyway, I took one last look around the house. My suitcase was lying in the middle of the loft floor, open, all packed and ready to go. The house was so still. Some negative thoughts ran through my head, but I pushed them right out as fast as they came in. I grabbed my coffee and keys, and away I went to see Chuck.

When I arrived at the ward, there was a buzz in the air. The atmosphere reminded me of Christmas "Goodie Day" at work, where everyone brought in a treat to share through out the day. All the staff, doctors, nurse, specialists, health-care aides, and other patients' families dropped by with hugs, and well wishes to say goodbye. The realization of leaving what had become our security blanket and safe haven was real and sad. All these people kept us safe and kept our family count at four. That is why faith in the One True God is so vital for life. If I believed that it was only the people that got us this far, I would have never had the courage or faith to move forward. But I knew that God had put these people across our path and that He would continue to be faithful in His goodness. I can't say enough that this kind of favour wasn't and isn't available only to me. This kind of love and protection and never-ending and never-failing love is for everyone—yes, you and me. Not only in heaven, but while we are here on earth, we can have a little bit of heaven on earth. But we have to do our part and do some searching to know God and His Son, Jesus. It's up to us to seek and decide to enter a relationship with Him. I do have a relationship with Him, but I can't have one for Chuck or Carly or Matthew or their partners or even my "Granddaughter Swayzie" they all have to have their own. I can pray for them, which I do, but each of us has to have his or her own personal relationship with Christ. Without it, we would have never made it through this. Never. The entire journey was all supernatural; every last part of it was beyond human capability or understanding. The doctors and nurses, even they proclaim the miracles they saw take place in Chuck's journey. Chuck still has follow-up appointments and will his entire life, and to this day his doctors are still awed that Chuck survived all that he had to go through.

Around 11:00 a.m., the perfusionist came by to Chuck's room to get him ready to go to our farewell lunch; both Carly and Matthew were also there. We were ready to go, and there were staff hanging outside Chuck's room, cheering us on. Chuck walked through the big steel "ABSOLUTELY NO ADMITTANCE / AUTHORIZED PERSONNEL ONLY" doors for his last time. We walked down the short hall, turned left, reached the Izzy Room, and opened the doors to probably around thirty people smiling and welcoming us in. The aroma of three long tables of delicious food filled the room. As much as the lunch was a celebration feast, it was happy but sad too; I'd describe it as being bittersweet. Really, no one knew what the future had in store for us. So many people had invested in Chuck. Keeping Chuck well had become a team effort that required care, skill, knowledge, and, above all, hard work. All these people in this room had invested enormously in Chuck. As we were sad to leave, they were sad to see us go. But we all knew that for there to be a future for Chuck and our family, there was no other choice than to keep moving forward. The only way we were able to step into the unknown was by moving in faith one step at a time. In doing so, we were able to boldly face every circumstance and challenge that came our way. We knew that we were protected and covered by the One who could and would do the impossible. Jesus Christ was the peace amid the chaos and madness.

The lunch was scrumptious, but more than the goodness of the food, I felt the goodness of people's hearts. I felt completely humbled and couldn't believe that all these people, pretty much the entire unit, gave us such a treasured and memorable send-off. I will never forget this lunch, as it was one of those full-sized, completely unexpected moments of my lifetime. On top of all this thoughtfulness and kindness, a presentation was made to Chuck. Chuck was gifted a red T-shirt with the ICCS logo printed on it, with the signatures of everyone who had cared and looked after him. Every doctor, specialist, nurse, health-care aide, and building staff member had all signed his or her name. As I'm sure you can imagine, tears filled many eyes in the room. We were beyond fortunate to be treated so exceptionally well. Blessed and forever grateful are we.

I have to mention one particular building employee I'll refer to as Ms. T——. One day she came looking for me and found me in the family room. Ms. T—— was carrying a bag with her and passed it to me and said it was for me. Ms. T—— had told her husband about me and what Chuck was going through. Her husband, who did most of the cooking in their home, had cooked extra food for her to give to me, and they did this several times. All I can say is that I was awed and humbled by their goodness toward me. I appreciated the food so much, and this gesture filled my heart beyond full. All my needs were being filled and met in ways I could never have even dreamed of. I attribute it all to the goodness of the Lord and the good people He directed to cross my path.

The day flew by and went faster than I wanted it to. So many people came and said goodbye. I can only say I had an unexplainable calmness over me throughout this entire trial, even at this point, where we were transitioning from one hospital and our home province that we had grown to feel completely comfortable in, to a totally different hospital in another province, where we knew no one and no one knew us. Believe me; in the natural realm I should have been completely anxious, but I wasn't. Instead, I had an unwavering trust that things would turn out well. Over me I had the peace of God that surpasses all understanding, just as is written and promised in the scriptures.

Even now, if things make me anxious, I have disciplined myself to stop fretting about whatever situation is bothering me and zone into the promises of God. I believe this is the best and most powerful thing I can do. The outcome of trusting and leaning on God is that our lives and the problems that come our way become easier for us to manage and handle. This doesn't result in a problem free life, but the problems don't weigh us down so much. The only reason I'm bold and confident in saying this is because of years of "hands-on problems" that I have overcome and conquered with more ease than expected. I can't emphasize enough that it is not because of my own strength or wisdom but only because of God's wisdom and strength that I've been able to overcome many difficult situations.

I remember sitting in Chuck's room and hearing the supper carts arriving outside his room for the last time. Chuck didn't eat much; he never did, as all the drugs he was on made him feel extremely nauseated. That's why he was down to weighing 135 pounds. I didn't stay late, as I wanted to return in the morning at 6:30 a.m. to make sure Chuck would be loaded and transported in the ambulance to the airport successfully. Carly, Matthew, and I stayed at the hospital until around 7:30 p.m. We said good night to Chuck. I encouraged Chuck to try to get some sleep, which he probably wouldn't, as he hated the nights in the hospital, never mind the anticipation of the following day's trip to Ottawa. A few kisses goodbye, and away I went to try to catch some winks myself. I, too, would probably not have the soundest sleep either, as tomorrow was a really big day for us.

CHAPTER 24

Up and Far Away

The night passed quickly, and I was up early. I can't say I was well rested, but I had adrenal energy. I just wanted to get to the hospital before Chuck would be leaving. Luckily Matthew was able to drive me both to the hospital and to the airport. As I mentioned before, Manitoba Hydro was very supportive to our family; it is a company composed of many good people.

When we arrived to the ward, the process of getting Chuck ready to transport had begun. The sliding double doors to his room had been unhinged so that the staff could get Chuck and all the equipment through into the hallway. So many people were there to ensure Chuck would get away without incident in a safe and timely fashion. Plus people were there for mere support and to say goodbye for the last time. Chuck was in a good frame of mind. The perfusionist, the perfusionist/nurse, and the doctor who would be flying with Chuck to Ottawa were all there and greeted us with smiles and kind words. Carly was already there, as she was working on the second floor of the hospital doing ultrasound, and her department greatly supported her and had booked her off from patients for an hour or so to be able to say goodbye to Chuck. Supposedly an ambulance had already been to the hospital to pick up Chuck, but it was sent back for exchange of another ambulance that had enough auxiliary power outlets to be able to support all of Chuck's life support equipment and systems.

Everything was ready for Chuck to go they were now waiting for the second ambulance to arrive. Chuck's nurse came over, gently touched my back, and asked whether we wanted some alone time with Chuck. The answer was yes. Carly, Matthew, and I surrounded Chuck, and the nurse drew the privacy curtains and closed the doors as much as she could. So much was going on in my heart and head; there was a definite battle going on. But every negative thought was pushed out by knowing the promises in His Word, the Bible. As is it written, He said He'd be there in our darkest hour and through the deepest valleys. I believed it; I felt bulletproof. Somehow He was keeping me stable in a very unstable situation. At times, the kids and I felt that people thought we were naive about Chuck's condition, but we weren't. We were experiencing the promise of peace that He keeps; He was the peace amid the chaos.

So there we stood around Chuck, saying that this was his lottery ticket, and Chuck agreed; it truly was. There's no doubt about it; we all had lumps in our throats. We spoke words of promise and of a good outcome. Then we all prayed out loud and agreed with each other that Jesus would protect, provide for, guide, and bless every part of this journey. He could and would do the impossible; He would make the impossible possible. Then, from under the curtain, I heard the footsteps of the paramedics come from down the hall. Chuck's nurse told them we were just having a moment together. With that, we quickly finished our confessions of faith and prayers. We put our four fists together and pounded them, saying that Chuck had this and would get a new heart. Carly took a picture of our four fists together. Now when we look at the picture, just by looking at Chuck's fist, we can see how truly sick he was. His skin was translucent and had a khaki tinge to it. Looking at the picture now, is frightening to me. It's a definite reminder that the miracle is real!

I slid open the curtain, and everyone was waiting to load Chuck into the ambulance to get him to the airport. The process went into

fast-forward, and before I knew it Chuck was getting wheeled down
the hallway with Carly walking by his side. As he passed staff in
the hallway, everyone wished him good luck, saying they would be
thinking of him and to keep in touch. I promised we would. I was
given more hugs as I made my way to exit the ward. I hit the open
button to engage the big, heavy steel ICCS doors for the final time.
Standing in the open doorway, I turned around one more time and
gave a loud goodbye and waved to all the staff. I heard the doors shut
behind us as I pushed the down arrow for the elevator. Matthew and
I hurried to his Jeep, as my flight would be leaving in an hour and
a half. All I can say is "peace." Peace resided within. We arrived at
the airport, and Matthew lifted my bags out and put them on a cart
for me. He gave me one of his big, burly bear hugs and a kiss on the
cheek. That was it; I was by myself but not alone. Christ was with
me; He was with me every step of the way.

I checked myself in, went through security, located my gate,
and found myself by the windows above the tarmac, looking to see
whether I could spot an ambulance. I didn't see one. It was time
to board the plane. Once I was onboard and seated, I leaned over
to look out my window, hoping to catch just a glimpse of Chuck,
but I didn't. Before I knew it, we were taking off, and we were soon
landing in Ottawa. I unfastened my seatbelt and looked out the
plane window again, and this time, at a small hangar in the distance,
there was an ambulance. I knew it had to be Chuck! I was content
to know that even though we were far away from home, Chuck and
I were in the same place at the same time. I departed the plane and
went to pick up my bag. I made my way outside the airport to catch
a cab, hoping to get one more glimpse of the ambulance Chuck was
in. I flagged down a driver, hopped in, and gave him the address
of where I was staying. He said he knew right where it was. As we
were talking, he asked a few questions about why I had come to
Ottawa; right then Chuck's ambulance came up from behind us.
The cabdriver pulled to the side of the road to let it by. I told him
that it was my husband who was in there. At first he was taken

aback and he thought I was joking, I further explained the story. He extended his compassion and best wishes for Chuck and me. He then turned off the main road we were on, and there it was—the medical residence where I would be staying. The building was about twenty stories high and on spacious treed grounds. I paid the driver, he wished me well again, and I got out of the cab and pulled my bags up the ramp. I entered the first set of doors of the building and had to buzz to get through the second. I was relieved someone answered. The voice on the other end gave me directions to the office so they could check me in. I thanked her and made my way there. The girl sitting behind the counter looked as nice and friendly as she had sounded over the intercom. She gave me the building details and a tiny brown envelope containing the keys to my room. I was on the sixteenth floor. She answered all my questions, and I thanked her and gathered my bags. I made my way to the suite that for now I'd call home, without a clue as to how long that might be. All I wanted to do was to drop off my bags and make my way to the Ottawa Heart Institute and find Chuck and know where he would be staying.

I went into to elevator, pressed the button labeled "16," and went straight up to my floor. The elevator doors opened, and I turned right, right, and right again, and I found my room. My room was facing east. I put the key in the door and turned the knob. When I walked into the small suite, I experienced instant déjà vu. As I turned on the kitchen light, I was taken back to our very first little apartment we shared together thirty-three years prior. This suite was identical; it was just a reverse plan. I stood there in awe, experiencing memories of how we had loved our first little place. Starting off together was such a great chapter in our lives. Back then we were so excited just to have a place to call our own. Because of the sameness of the suites, it didn't feel as strange as I had first thought it would. Anyway, I put my bag in the bedroom and was ready to find the Ottawa Heart Institute, which was somewhere among the sea of buildings on campus that I could see outside my window. I grabbed the little map the receptionist had given me and made my way to find my one true love.

CHAPTER 25

Uncertainty

It was around 2:00 p.m. when I started walking to find my way to the Ottawa Heart Institute. It was located in a nice, mature residential area, so I felt quite comfortable walking in the neighbourhood, but I was always aware of my surroundings. On my way, I passed a chip truck offering homemade French fries and burgers, which smelled yummy. As I looked in the serving window, the owner of the truck gave me the biggest smile and wave, which felt so good and welcoming. I knew I'd be trying his chips sometime in the very near future. I must say I found it ironic that this type of food truck would be right outside the Heart Institute. I would have imagined something more like a salad or veggie truck. Anyway, before I knew it, there I was, standing in front of the doors of the Ottawa Heart Institute. I took a picture of the name "Ottawa Heart Institute" above the door and the sign on the front lawn. I walked into the building for the very first time, took a quick look around, and then went directly to the hospital reception and gave the woman Chuck's name. She gave me directions on where to find Chuck. Chuck was somewhere in the basement level.

Of course, the hospital was very different from the one in Winnipeg. There was a lot of hospital equipment in the hallway, such as stretchers, carts, and wheelchairs. Then I noticed the portable stretcher board leaning up against the wall; it looked like a spine board, and perhaps that's what it was. This board was right outside the doors of the unit where I thought Chuck might be; I just knew it had to be his! I opened the doors to the unit, looked to my right and through the window into a small room, and there he was; I had found Chuck! Chuck's eyes locked with mine. The woman talking to Chuck turned around to see who Chuck was looking at. I saw Chuck tell her that I was his wife. She motioned for me to come into the room, so I did.

As soon as I walked into the room, I instantly noticed that the way the LVAD was set up would not have been acceptable at St. Boniface Hospital or even allowed for one minute. Chuck's LVAD was so far away from the bed that the lines were stretched to their max, and they were bouncing around everywhere. Also, the lines weren't secured to the bedsheet, which was bunched up and had fallen behind Chuck's shoulders and waistline. The LVAD lines always had to be clamped to the bed so that there would be no kinking or movement of any kind. The head of Chuck's bed was raised to the sitting position, which was also not allowed, because that would cause the lines to be bent and block straight blood flow to Chuck's heart. I wasn't in the room for a minute before I had to say something! All these oversights and casual approaches meant death for Chuck, and that's no exaggeration. As you know, I'd seen Chuck experience code blues caused by kinked lines; I never wanted my heart in my throat again because of negligence about the sensitivity of the LVAD.

The head nurse and I introduced ourselves to each other. The nurse immediately asked how I thought things looked. The question couldn't have been any more perfect for me to lead in to all the concerns I saw. I didn't want to come across as unappreciative and bossy or as though I had two guns blazing. So I gently said things weren't what they had been like at home. She asked me to explain. The first thing I mentioned was that the LVAD was too far away from the bed. I mentioned I had never seen the lines jump around as they were doing now. She immediately left the room to call for Perfusion to come down and access the situation. I was so relieved! I myself lowered the head of Chuck's bed to flatten out Chuck's torso. I explained to her why it was important for Chuck's stomach be somewhat flat. Honestly, she herself seemed overwhelmed; in fact, she said that Chuck and all his stuff was quite a bit more than they were expecting.

It wasn't too long until the Perfusionist (I'll refer to him as G——) came to Chuck's room. G—— was different; that's all I'll say, his demeanor seemed nonchalant. I told G—— that back in Winnipeg the lines were never allowed to jump around as they were now and the lines were always clamped to the sheet or bed so that they would never slide under Chuck's body or get caught in the bed. G—— gave me a nonchalant shoulder shrug. I didn't want to perceive his body language as it seemed to come across. He slowly did move the LVAD closer to the bed, and he asked me how I wanted the lines. How I wanted the lines? Ah, it wasn't how I wanted the lines; it was how the lines were supposed to be. I had been watching the great care given to these lines for five months now and had experienced the result of kinked lines. The result was Chuck instantly passing out and a code blue being called and all the staff running into the room with the crash cart. The correct positioning of the lines had nothing to do with my preference; it had to do with keeping Chuck safe and alive. To say the least, I felt as though we were labelled as the "out-of-towners" by this first experience. Maybe it was just I who felt this way. Regardless, G—— did move the LVAD closer to Chuck, and he also clamped the lines to the bed. The lines instantly stopped jumping around. I thanked G——, and he nodded and left the room.

I told the nurse that I appreciated her calling Perfusion and that both Chuck and I were much more comfortable with the placement of the lines. Even she noted that the lines looked better as they were now hanging still. The nurse told us that because it was getting so late in the day, the doctors would most likely not come down to meet Chuck today but would be in tomorrow morning. With that, she said she would be at the desk outside Chuck's room should we need anything. As the nurse was leaving Chuck's room, she noticed there was no place for me to sit, so she brought in a very small office chair on wheels that didn't lock. Chuck and I sat and talked about how different everything was and felt in comparison to home. We knew that things would be different, and we agreed that we would just stay chill as we got to know the people and the workings of the hospital. We made a promise with each other that we would take every situation on with our faith in Jesus Christ. We knew He would never fail us and would continue to be our strong tower.

I stayed with Chuck a bit longer, and I could see he was very tired. The morning had started extremely early with very little sleep, if any at all. The travel was exhausting for Chuck. During my taxi ride from the airport, I had noticed a Shoppers Drug Mart en route to the residence. Chuck kept nodding off, so I thought this would be a good time for me to slip away and go get some groceries. I had never really had done a grocery shopping at a Shoppers before, but today seemed like a good time to start. I'd get milk, coffee, and some frozen meals and whatever else I could find for me to bring for lunches and dinners at the hospital. With that in my mind, I kissed Chuck goodbye, and off I went to put some food in the fridge and cupboards. Shoppers didn't seem to be that far away, and I felt that a good walk might be exactly what I needed. It ended up being farther than I first anticipated, but the time outside gave me a fresh perspective and cleared the air. I bought quite a few groceries and was happy that tomorrow morning I would be able to have early morning coffee out of the coffeemaker that was in the apartment. I had way too many bags to walk home, so I called a cab. It wasn't too long before my ride arrived. He and I loaded the groceries, and I was back at the residence in no time. I paid him and hauled the groceries up to the apartment, where I quickly unpacked my food and put everything away. I hung up some of my clothes and turned on a couple of lights, as I was unsure of what time I'd be back. I was really never sure when each night would end; it depended on what the evening would have in store for Chuck and me. Anyway, I thought this time I would try walking in the underground tunnel the residence receptionist had told me about when I had first arrived and checked in. The tunnel started somewhere off the underground parkade. I found it and had to use my pass card to get both in and out of the big steel doors that were in the tunnel. To say the least, it was beyond creepy; I was very tensed up. The tunnel seemed miles long, it had an extremely low ceiling, and there were pooling puddles in some areas. The worst part was that there was not another person in sight. There were hallways and doors coming off the main tunnel. It was spooky and empty, and I couldn't wait to get out of there. I was relieved to see what looked like a speck of people way down at the end of the hallway. As I got closer to a bank of elevators with more people around, I felt safer. The directions in the tunnel to the various buildings were confusing, but I did make my way back to Chuck's room. Chuck had rested most of the time I was gone.

I know that I have mentioned this before, but I have to mention it again. For Chuck to even be considered for a heart transplant, he had to be able to walk a fair distance, which was measured as two laps around the unit back at home. It took at least three months and a team of people to get to that point, but most of all it took Chuck's determination and hard work.

It was already early evening, and no one had been down to take Chuck for his evening walk. At home, Chuck walked at least three times a day. We decided to buzz the call button and ask the nurse what the plan was for Chuck's walks. The nurse that I had met earlier that afternoon was still working, and when she came in the room, we asked whether Chuck could expect to go or a walk sometime soon. Needless to say, she was taken aback by the question. I explained to her the walking requirements Chuck had to meet to be accepted by Ottawa. She said no one had given any instructions or directives whatsoever on walking Chuck. Because it was so late in the day, most of the perfusionists had gone home, so she would have to inquire about Chuck walking tomorrow. She was able to guarantee us, though, that there'd be no walk for Chuck tonight. With that, her shift had come to end, and we agreed we'd start fresh tomorrow. I stayed with Chuck until about 10:00 p.m., and we said our good nights. It was harder than usual to leave Chuck this night, as I didn't feel the security I had felt at St. Boniface, but I needed some rest as well. I would have liked to stay overnight with Chuck, but I had only the small chair and I needed some sleep desperately. As hard as it was, I gathered my things and put my faith in the idea that things would go well overnight and my walk home would be incident-free and safe. I really wasn't sure what way to take home, but I did make it back to the apartment and dropped my stuff at the door, washed my face, prayed, and pretty much fell into bed and was out like a light.

CHAPTER 26

The Right Place

I fell asleep immediately, but my sleep was very broken. Even though we had made it to Ottawa safely, I still wondered whether we were in the right place. What I mean is that there was the option of going to Edmonton, and someone I knew had just been there and undergone a successful surgery. Plus Ottawa had rejected Chuck the first time when the team from St. Boniface had presented him. There is no doubt about it; I woke up feeling uncertain. I got up from bed, walked to the kitchen, and made some coffee. I decided to hop in the shower while the coffee was brewing. I quickly showered, and I couldn't wait to have my first coffee of the morning, it smelled delicious. I opened the cupboard, found the cups, poured the coffee, and went to get my flavored creamer out from the fridge. I couldn't see it where I should have placed it, so I moved a few things around. Still no creamer. I looked on both the table and counters. I even went to the front door and checked by the apartment door just in case it had rolled out of the bag. No creamer for my coffee anywhere. So on to plan B I went.

I had noticed there were salt and pepper shakers in the cupboard, so I thought there was probably sugar somewhere in the cupboard. But I couldn't see any sugar anywhere. I stood on my tiptoes, running my fingers and hand along the highest shelf in the cupboards. Ah, I had found a bowl with what felt like packets in it. I brought it down. I looked at the packets and I couldn't believe my eyes! I immediately fell to my knees with my face in my hands and started crying. I remember kneeling in the center of the kitchen floor, thanking God over and over again for this miraculous sign! In this small, white bowl lay packets of sugar with *my* name on them. "Tannis" was written on every packet of sugar, and to top it off, it was spelled just as I spell my name. I was sure that someone must have personalized my sugar. They had to have! I got up, walked over to the phone, and called down to the office and told them who I was and what suite number I was in. The sweet young lady with the sweet young voice answered the phone. I asked whether someone had personalized my sugar. Her reply was a simple "Pardon me?" I explained to her what had happened—that my very name was on my sugar packets in my suite. She giggled and told me there was a sugar company named Tannis in Ottawa. I thanked her for her time and said goodbye.

In the Bible, it is written that God gives us signs and wonders. This time and moment in my life was exactly that: a sign and wonder from God. I was putting all my trust and faith in the one true God who knew I was distraught, wondering, and questioning so many things. But this incident made me know deep within my heart of hearts, with my whole being, that I was precisely in the right place at the exact right time. Even the fact that the apartment was exactly like the one we lived in when we were first married spoke to me deeply and sparked good memories even in this uncertain time. Now this, the Tannis sugar, just sealed the deal. God had chosen this journey for me at this place and this time. Not only did this sign make my faith grow, but it also made clearer the truth in my life and confirmed yet another promise out of His Word. 2 Corinthians 12:9 NIV reads, "My grace is sufficient for you, for my power is made perfect in weakness."

I know that there have been critical times in my life that have been solely executed by God himself. If He hadn't been in the center of these circumstances, I would have never been able to go through any of them. Within my own self, with my own strength, and with my DNA, it would have been impossible. I was able to walk through situations that in the natural realm I shouldn't have been able to walk through. In my own abilities and strength, I would have stopped in the middle of them all and drowned. One thing about God is that He is known only by the evidence of what He does, because He is not visible to our human eye. God made certain "happenings" happen for me to have the ability to go through the most difficult dark valleys. How do I know God is real? I can't point to His nose or His ears; nor have I ever heard His audible voice. But there are just some things in my life that in the natural realm don't make sense. How about you? It's like wind; you can't see wind, but you can see the effects of wind. That's what it's like with God; you can't see God, but you can see the effects of God in your life. When I look back over my life, I soon realize I've had too many experiences that should have pushed me down and pulled me under, but they haven't. I've experienced victory, and I seem to walk out unscathed, not even smelling like smoke—but only because of God.

I know that me forgetting the creamer was a planned intentional "happening" planned by someone other than me. It might have been an angel that simply directed my steps away from the cooler where the creamer was. Had I purchased the flavored creamer, I would have never found the Tannis sugar, as when I have flavored creamer, I do not use sugar. Forgetting the creamer was an answer to my prayer that revealed the confirmation that we were to be exactly where we were—in Ottawa. It was the miraculous sign and wonder that I had been praying for. I thanked God and Jesus a thousand times over for His unique communication and relationship with me. I took a picture of the Tannis sugar bowl and posted it on social media. This was completely a divine moment between God and me. He knew how much I needed a sign to show me that we were exactly where we were needed to be!

I pulled myself together and finished getting ready to go see Chuck. It wasn't long before the phone rang, and it was him. Chuck heard the joy in my voice and asked why I sounded so happy. I told him I'd tell him as soon I'd see him. We hung up, and I continued to get ready and was filled with joy, comfort, and peace. I couldn't wait to share my sugar story with Chuck.

CHAPTER 27

Is He, or Isn't He?

When I got to the Heart Institute, I told Chuck my Tannis sugar story. Chuck smiled and believed with me that this was evidence of God's supernatural power and orchestrated plan. It was the answer to my prayer, confirming we were exactly where we needed to be.

Chuck looked good to me—and probably only me, but that was because I had seen what Chuck looked like when he was hanging on by a thread, as close to death as one could possibly be without dying. Chuck was on the edge for a long time, and more than once. So to me Chuck was doing well and looked healthier than he had looked for the past five months. But to those who hadn't met Chuck and were meeting him for the first time, he looked deathly sick. Most were shocked by what they saw, and I am speaking about medical people who were used to seeing critically sick people. It was the same at home in Winnipeg, and it was no different here in Ottawa for anyone coming in and meeting Chuck for the first time. The funny thing was that everyone in Ottawa seemed intimidated by the CentriMag LVAD. Most of the staff hadn't seen this large, cumbersome LVAD; they were used to working with the small, portable LVADs that could be toted in a knapsack. But as I mentioned before, Chuck was so sick and had so many issues that Dr. P—— decided that Chuck needed to stay in the ICU. that would be the safest and only way

Chuck would remain alive and possibly get strong enough to work up to a transplant. That's why the CentriMag LVAD was used. Also, being in the ICU would put Chuck at the top of the list in Canada and nearby surrounding states if he could get strong enough to get on the transplant list.

Back to the story. Chuck had an okay night, but again he didn't get much sleep. Being in a new place, with a different bed and different sounds, it was all a bit unsettling. Chuck hated all the nights in the hospital. In fact, Chuck told me he would sometimes pretend to be sleeping, after an incident of being given a cocktail of drugs to get help him relax. This cocktail caused all Chuck's vitals to spiral down extremely fast, so much so that all Chuck's life support machines went into alarm mode and Chuck had to put back on a respirator. So Chuck, with the little power he had, would do what he needed to do to protect himself and stay alert of those few nurses who preferred sleeping patients. Chuck pretending to sleep was fine with me; I never wanted to see that situation happen to him again! It was an enormous setback, and it took a month or more for him to ween himself off the respirator and breathe on his own again.

We patiently waited for the team of Ottawa doctors to come by and meet Chuck, and they arrived just before lunchtime. There were three doctors, and I had the feeling that they may have skimmed over Chuck's file but were not deeply knowledgeable about his situation. They introduced themselves, and then one of doctors casually asked the room whether Chuck was on the list. No one could answer that question, including Chuck and me. We wondered the same question—"Is he or isn't he on the list?" Back in Winnipeg, at the end of video conference with Ottawa that resulted in Chuck coming to Ottawa, that critical question was left hanging in the air. The answer to that important question was still unknown. The doctors excused themselves and left the room to see whether they could come back with an answer. The answer they came back with was the one we were dreading—a hugely disappointing no. Chuck was not on the transplant list. My heart fell to the floor.

This news was so upsetting because Chuck had worked so hard to meet all of Ottawa's requirements, most of which he exceeded, and I stated this fact to the doctors again. They looked at me but really didn't acknowledge what I had said. They discussed the next step, which was to run tests on Chuck and try to get him on the list as soon as possible. I didn't understand why all these tests had to be run again! Even back in Winnipeg, Dr. Z—— thought that Ottawa hadn't gone through Chuck's file and test results, based on some of the questions being asked during the video conference. At this point, I couldn't have agreed with her more. Dr. Z—— was 100 percent right; Chuck's file had only been skimmed.

The sooner Chuck could have his name at the top of the transplant list, the better. It would take time to find a heart to match Chuck's blood type. Chuck had so many blood transfusions, and because of that Chuck had a large count of antibodies in his blood. Every day that Chuck's name was not on the transplant list, he could possibly miss an opportunity of a heart. For Chuck it meant missing an opportunity of a life-time, literally.

I kept reminding myself that this was not Winnipeg; we were now in Ottawa, and Ottawa was going to approach Chuck the way they thought was best. I transitioned myself to finding the positives in most of Ottawa's procedures, methods, and practices. At times, I did have to speak up and speak out; I quickly learned to pick my battles.

I changed my mindset to think, *It's good they're running all the tests again; at least they're not sending us back home.* To be honest, their decisions were based on unbelief that Chuck could do all he was doing. In addition to that, it was hard to believe that Chuck could have successful test results after what they had seen at Chuck's first presentation. So it was what it was, but don't forget we had favor on our side—something way bigger than just ourselves. We had God in the midst of everything, He was there in absolutely everything. God was the only reason Chuck was still alive.

For the next two days they ran the same tests that were done in Winnipeg that lay in Chuck's file. They were well aware of the urgency of completing the tests as quickly as possible; they hoped to have everything done before the weekend. I focused on the fact that things were moving forward and prayed that all the tests would be successful and we would patiently wait again.

The next item on the list was getting Chuck up for a walk. Chuck wanted to keep up the little strength he had built for himself. It was already Thursday; the weekend was nearing, and I wasn't sure what that would mean for staffing, specifically regarding the perfusionists, because they were the only ones that could walk Chuck. I asked a nurse whether Perfusion had been contacted about Chuck's walking, which prompted her to call up and check into it. My inquiry paid off, because a perfusionist came down later in the day. It wasn't G——; this man was burly in stature (I'll call him Mr. Burly) and somewhat more friendly. Mr. Burly took Chuck for three laps around the unit. All eyes were on Chuck as he walked with his lifelines around the unit and down the hall. When the walk was finished, I asked about the next time a walk would be scheduled. The perfusionist guaranteed me one thing: he didn't know. I quickly thought to myself, *Baby steps. We'll get a schedule for Chuck by taking baby steps toward the best routine possible.* The rest of the day was pretty much uneventful, and in Chuck's case, that meant it was a good day.

I usually stayed until around 10:00 p.m. Saying good night was always hard; I felt that part of the reason Chuck had made it this far was because of me being there sixteen hours a day; I was a big part of that reality. But I remembered that my responsibility was to do my best and that God would do the rest. Remembering that simple phrase put me at ease regarding most things. Yes, there were times when I felt anxious, but I had to make time to meditate on God's Word and really focus on it, keep rolling it over in my mind, and let it sink into my bones and my heart. The truth of His Word was so alive in me during this time; I felt that no matter what, God would not fail me.

As I sit here and write this, it makes me think that going through crisis and trials is instrumental in drawing us closer to God. Could it be? We are all God's creation, but only do we become His sons and daughters when we give our lives and hearts to Him. Chuck and I have wonderful families and friends who support us with love in many different ways; we are abundantly blessed. But no one can do the impossible, and not one of them could be with us all of the time. But God could. God could be with us, Chuck and me, all of the time, even when we were apart. God was with Chuck in the hospital bed, and God was with me wherever I was, even in the underground tunnel I hated, which I had to take from time to time because of stormy weather. That's because God is omnipresent. "Omnipresence" refers to presence everywhere at the same time and the state of being widespread or constantly encountered. This is how God can be with everyone everywhere at the same time. I knew deep down inside that when I left Chuck, Chuck was not alone. More importantly, Chuck knew that too; Chuck really never feared his days or the days ahead. We both lived with unwavering faith; that was the only way we would get through this long and winding road.

So here it was, 10:00 p.m. on Thursday, May 5, 2016. Chuck and I said our good nights, and I left Chuck with faith in his room, and I left with a little faith in my pocket.

CHAPTER 28

Closer

Friday morning rolled around, and I got out of bed and put the coffee on. I glanced at the bowl of Tannis sugar on the table, the sign that kept reminding me that we were exactly where we were supposed to be. I showered and got ready for the day. During that time, the suite phone rang, and it was Chuck. I loved hearing his voice. Chuck had had a good night, thank goodness. I told him I'd be there shortly. I did my daily routine, packed myself my lunch and dinner, cleaned up, and made my way to the hospital. On the nice days, I enjoyed the walk with the clear blue spring sky and the buds of cherry blossoms coming out on the trees.

When I arrived at the hospital, it was like any other place of work; there was that universal "Friday buzz" in the air. You know, "the Friday buzz," where everyone seems a little a bit happier and has a spring in his or her step. People have the "Let's do this" vibe. Chuck was doing okay. He didn't have the Friday vibe, and really neither did I, but at least we were both at peace.

Chuck didn't eat much of his breakfast; in fact, he didn't eat much of anything at all. Chuck had lost close to forty pounds. Chuck didn't say much at the time about his deteriorating frame, but later he said it bothered him immensely. Chuck himself was shocked the first time he saw his legs. When Chuck was well enough to move his legs and he looked at them for the first time after being in bed for three months, he couldn't believe eyes. His once strong, powerful legs and dwindled down to nothing. Chuck wished he could eat better and more, but the nausea was so bad he couldn't. Chuck looked frail and pale, but that was on the outside. On the inside, underneath his shell, Chuck had a fierce fighting spirit. Chuck's own nature of a strong will, stubbornness, and faith, mixed with the Holy Spirit's supernatural nature, was the perfect blend for triumph and victory, but to the human eye it was invisible and undetectable. Chuck's life at this time was the living example of Hebrews 11:1 (NIV), which reads, "Now faith is confidence in what we hope for and assurance about what we do not see."

It was around 11:30 a.m. when I noticed two of the doctors that had ordered all the tests to be run on Chuck standing outside of Chuck's room. They deliberated a bit longer, and then they opened the door and came in. I was expecting they were there to share the test results, and that was exactly the reason they had come to see Chuck and me. My heart moved up into my throat, and I could feel my body tighten slightly. Then the female doctor spoke the words that we'd all been waiting to hear. Chuck had passed all the tests! Hearing those words released so much anxiety from within me. Her words were made of gold. This meant the magnificent news that Chuck's name would be going on the transplant list; with hope, it would happen that same day! I remember my eyes welling up; I was overwhelmed with joy and disbelief at the same time. It had taken six long weeks since the previous denial to get to this point with this transplant center. Now here we were; we had finally reached this high and lofty goal, which at times had looked unattainable. Chuck and I were beyond jubilant; it was all very surreal.

Chuck and I thanked them so much for this great news. The doctor continued to say that Chuck would be on the list as a category 4, which was the very highest priority of urgency. Chuck's name would be at the top of the list. With that, the doctors left the room, and to be honest, Chuck and I sat there in amazement. These five months had been a long road, but through all the darkness there had seemed to be a light that never stopped flickering, and now with this news the light had just gotten much brighter.

But behind this awesome news, we also knew that this meant another intense, massive surgery for Chuck—if he lived long enough as he waited for a matching heart. We also acknowledged the bittersweetness of receiving a heart. Chuck receiving a heart meant joy and a longer lifetime for Chuck and our family. But on the other side of the circumstance, it meant loss and sorrow for the donor and their family. We talked about it frequently, and it made us feel sorrow and compassion for them. Organ donation is bittersweet, and is a personal choice. But we know our death is certain, and if we can give life to another human being when our life has come to its end, is there a more beautiful precious gift than the gift of life?

I really was hoping Chuck would get on the list that day, and he did! Now we would wait, and we tried to wait patiently, but it was hard—very hard. The CentriMag LVAD was sounding its alarm more frequently every day; it was making Chuck, me, and all the staff extremely nervous.

The basement ICU we were in was very dark and very secluded. There were no windows, so it could become very depressing. The other patients in the ward had come out from their cardiac surgeries, so most of the people were unconscious. The procedure was that once patients woke up, they would be moved up to the ICU on the main floor. The head nurse could see that Chuck needed some daylight and the ability to look outside from time to time, so she had put in a priority request to get Chuck moved upstairs.

It was my mistake to think that because Chuck was on the transplant list it was going to happen quickly. Even though Chuck was on the list, the waiting was still the dangerous game we had to play. Every time I would see a doctor coming to Chuck's room, an expectant spirit would arise within me, soon to be let down. It took about a week before the expecting and being let down settled and fell dormant in my spirit.

In the meantime, we were moved up to the main floor. Chuck now had a window, which brought in some natural daylight and gave him the ability to see the sky and some waving leaves on the trees. At that time in our lives, that window room was a breath of fresh air, and the window wasn't even that big. We were so grateful to be moved up into that room. It makes me realize how much the ordinary things in life are really blessings, but because of their commonality we all take them for granted from time to time.

This reminds me of a short narrative I once read; I'll try to capture it as best I remember. It goes as follows:

There were two men that shared a hospital room. Every day, the man by the window would tell the other man what he could see outside from the window. He would describe the park with the fountain, the children playing and carrying balloons, and dogs playing fetch with their owners. Sometimes he would describe the flowers and blooms on the trees. The man closer to the door of the room enjoyed and appreciated his roommate sharing what he saw, sometimes several times a day.

One morning when the man by the door woke up, he looked over to his roommate's bed to see that it was freshly made up and the man was no longer there. Shortly a nurse came in to explain that the man by the window had passed during the night.

The man was very sad to hear about the news about his roommate. He asked the nurse whether he could now be moved to the window. The nurse readily agreed and had the man moved and placed by the window. The man was so excited to be able to look out the window and see all the things his friend had told him about.

The man lifted himself up to peek out the window. He couldn't believe what he saw. There was nothing there, other than a flat, gray brick wall. The man then realized that his friend had told him all those fabricated wonderful things to build up his hope of getting well, as he knew how his words brought him life and made him much happier.

Isn't that what we should all do with the words we speak—especially to those who need encouragement? Words have the ability to build or break down. Choose words that build. Words also speak life or death; always choose life.

CHAPTER 29

May 11, 2016

There's no doubt about it; the days were challenging. Chuck's walking time was very sporadic, and he could feel whatever strength he had built start to diminish. His LVAD lines were still a point of contention, as not all the nurses were trained on how to care for them. I think the icing on the cake concerning the lines and the inconsistent exercise came to the forefront when they brought an exercise bike into Chuck's room.

The concept was good, but the procedures weren't; it was totally unsafe. I remember the day the nurse put Chuck on the bike and left the room. Chuck was pedaling away, and the lines were swinging like bungee cords, too close to his feet for comfort, and the LVAD kept sounding its alarm every few minutes. I guess it was about the third time the nurse came into room to hit the reset button on the CentriMag LVAD that I said something. I know I was a bother to him, but he did listen, and he clamped the lines onto the stationary bike. The lines were still dangling, which left Chuck and me very uneasy. At times I think the Ottawa staff were relying on me to share how things were done back in Winnipeg. There came a point when every nurse on shift asked me to provide instruction on how the lines were to be clamped. Then, when there was a shift change, the nurse that was leaving would demonstrate the line placement to the nurse starting the next shift. That meant a huge improvement in the care and safety of Chuck's lifelines. Chuck's bike riding continued only when there was no perfusionist to walk him, but a nurse or physiotherapist had to stay in the room while Chuck was on the bike. That raised our comfort level slightly.

There was one day when a perfusionist we had never met before came up early in the afternoon to walk Chuck. I call him Brad. Brad was soft-spoken, and his demeanor was gentle. After we introduced ourselves, I'll never forget the first thing he said to Chuck: "Chuck, you've been on death's doorstep a few times." The funny thing was that we knew that Chuck had been on death's doorstep a few times—actually several times. But to hear a complete stranger say it was a revelation of the truth that death had been lingering around Chuck for some time, but somehow Chuck had continued to beat the odds. That "somehow" was the grace, protection, and the continuum of miracles streamed to us by Jesus Christ. Chuck surviving all the potentially lethal trials was a living testimony to those who surrounded us, both in Winnipeg and in Ottawa. All these miracles were miraculous and left us thankful and grateful, and deepened our beliefs.

Brad was definitely a breath of fresh air in this time of transition. He went beyond his job as a perfusionist; he was personable along with his professionalism. Brad made Chuck and I feel that he enjoyed his time spent with us when he walked with Chuck, and we enjoyed this. In fact, when Sunday, May 8, 2016, rolled around, which was Mother's Day, Brad arrived to walk Chuck with a bouquet of flowers for me, explaining that he knew I wasn't at home to celebrate with Carly and Matthew. I was totally surprised and deeply touched by his kindness and his sensitivity to our situation, especially mine on this Mother's Day.

May 11 was approaching very fast, and that date marks Chuck's birthday. Chuck would be turning fifty-nine years old, and I didn't want the day to pass without celebrating it somehow. There was another person that went beyond her job duties, and that was a female physiotherapist. Every time she looked at Chuck or me, I could feel her compassion and concern for us. I had mentioned to her that I was planning to get a cake for Chuck, and she had offered to pick up a cake for me. Dairy Queen's ice cream cakes have always been a family tradition for birthdays in our family, and because of this physiotherapist's kindness, the tradition continued even here in Ottawa.

So, on May 11, we had and ice-cream cake with candles, and a huge group of staff came in to sing "Happy Birthday to You" to Chuck to celebrate and have cake with us. Plus, there was another surprise for Chuck. A woman Chuck had worked with back in Winnipeg with was in Ottawa for a training course. This co-worker had contacted me to ask if she could come see Chuck, and it just happened to be the same day Chuck's birthday celebration was going to take place. When she found us in the hospital and walked into Chuck's room, I knew she was totally taken aback and shocked by Chuck's appearance and condition. Chuck was very happy to see her; he only wished he felt better so he could visit with her. It was so nice for Chuck to see someone familiar from back home, she also enjoyed seeing Chuck, and she visited him twice when she was in Ottawa. I think she feared she wouldn't see Chuck again, and that's why she came to see him for a second time before she left back to Winnipeg. May 13 also marked Matthew's birthday, so between Carly and me, we made birthday arrangements, and Carly celebrated Matthew's birthday back in Winnipeg. Of course, part of the plan was that Matthew also had the family traditional DQ ice-cream birthday cake. Because of Carly's goodness, the tradition lived on.

The days were passing by, and there was still no heart for Chuck. Chuck was getting thinner; he was sallower in color and looking more exhausted. The plan was for Carly and Matthew to come and see Chuck at the time of the transplant, but I wasn't sure whether we should wait that long. So I made arrangements for Carly and Matthew to come out on the May long weekend; seeing them would be medicine to both Chuck's soul and mine. Chuck missed seeing them, as they visited every day when we were back home.

Another welcoming surprise was when a perfusionist from Winnipeg came to visit Chuck on one of her visits home to Ottawa. Ottawa is where she is originally from. She came in with many hellos and well-wishes from everyone back at St. Boniface Hospital. I wished I could have hired her to be Chuck's private perfusionist here in Ottawa, but that wasn't possible. When she saw how Chuck's lines were being treated, she became very tense and worried. I could see by the expressions on her face that it was difficult for her to watch and not to say anything, but she couldn't. Chuck and I appreciated that she visited a few times before she left back to Winnipeg. On her departure, we sent our hellos back to Chuck's team in Winnipeg, along with our gratitude and indebtedness to everyone.

I was deeply longing for home. I felt far away, and I was. I missed everyone and everything; I even missed driving my Jeep. I missed my home. I missed my bed. I missed the daily visits from our pastors and missed my church family. I missed my friends and family. I missed everything! I was really looking forward to seeing Carly and Matthew, and Chuck was even more so. I made sure the residency where I was staying brought up extra bedding and extra pillows for the sofa bed.

When either Carly or Matthew texted me to tell me they had landed, I couldn't wait to see them. My heart popped as I went over to meet them on a street that was lined with many cafés and restaurants. It was so good to see them, and their hugs were even better. We had a quick lunch, made our way back to the residency, dropped off their bags, and made our way over to see Chuck.

Both Carly's and Matthew's presences brought so much more light into the next few days. I truly believe that their being with Chuck was the "shot in the arm" that Chuck needed to keep fighting and going through this deep wide valley. That longing desire to have more time with the ones we love and the life we love, has tremendous power over us and can benefit us and assist us in reaching our desired outcomes. Chuck appreciated every minute we spent together as a family on the weekend. The time brought smiles and fresh conversation to the weekend. The weird thing about the Ottawa Heart Institute was that the cafeteria was closed on the weekend, which made eating something other than microwave dinners very inconvenient. There was a Tim's, but it was way at the other end of the campus, which meant walking through that spooky, eerie tunnel. It wasn't an issue to go down there with Carly and Matthew, but it was something I avoided when I was on my own.

Back in the good old days, when things were normal, the weekends always flew by, and this weekend was exactly like that. I wished I could have clicked the restart button, but that wasn't an option. If I could have, I would have done it five months prior. It was Sunday, May 22, and Carly and Matthew would be leaving for home on Monday. It was a nice day, and Chuck usually needed an afternoon rest, so we decided to take a walk to one of the main streets in Ottawa that hosted many restaurants and outdoor patios. We picked a restaurant that someone had recommended and had a great lunch outside. We all got a little too much sun in that hour and a half; that's how nice it was outside. We finished up and made our way back to Chuck. It was a great afternoon, and as the day went by I realized that sooner than I wanted, Carly and Matthew would be leaving for home.

Chuck had slept the entire time we were gone. We all spent the rest of the day together. I could see that Carly and Matthew were very worried for Chuck and were extremely anxious when it came to the difference in care for the lines and the LVAD alarm sounding so frequently. Chuck and I prayed every night before we said good night, praising, thanking, and asking—praising God for His magnificent power, thanking Him for getting us this far, and asking Him to get us through one more day, every day. This weekend we prayed as a family for all these things, and we believed we would see them. The evening passed by quickly. Before we knew it, the time had come to say good night to Chuck, and it was a hard experience, as the kids were leaving the next morning. The plan was that they would come over and say a last quick goodbye to Chuck before they left for the airport. That's exactly what they did, and before I knew it, it was 11:00 a.m. Monday and they were gone back home and Chuck and I were alone again.

Hope Threads

After Carly and Matthew left Ottawa, I was feeling both a little down and a little anxious. My yearning for home was getting greater, and I was at a point of something good needing to happen. The LVAD alarm sounding frequently was a constant reminder that time was of the essence. My hope was hanging on by tiny fragmented threads. I was now praying for much-needed patience myself. I wanted the ability to wait in peace, and I was praying for endurance for Chuck. Chuck was missing his regular walks that he had become accustomed to back home so much so that he strongly requested (just shy of demanded) to speak to someone who had the power and would manage making improvements to the sporadic schedule that was now in place. The reduced walking was making Chuck weaker. Chuck had worked so hard to get up and start walking; he didn't want to go back to being bedridden. Chuck also lost all interest in food; already extremely thin, he was losing even more weight. Even the smell of food coming from down the hallway made him nauseated, and sometimes he would start heaving and gagging; no food appealed to him. So, the Heart Institute assigned a nutritionist to Chuck. This nutritionist was exceptional. She was sympathetic and very considerate toward Chuck. She actually asked Chuck to make her a shopping list of anything he might want to eat, anything, and she would do a special grocery shopping trip for him. She told him to put whatever he might want to eat on the list; even some junk food on the list would be acceptable. The desire was for Chuck to be able to eat, keep the food down, and not get any more frail than he already was.

Chuck's room was small and had a lot of equipment in it, but we did appreciate the window that allowed the light in. I noticed that they had started cleaning the room in the opposite corner of the ward, as the patient in there had been discharged to go home, the lucky man. This room was quite a bit larger and had an entire wall of windows, so I inquired to see whether it was possible for Chuck to get moved over there. The nurse looked over to the room and agreed that it would be a better fit for Chuck. Before we knew it, we had moved and settled in. Again, on the bulletin board I pinned up my beautiful picture of Jesus that my friend had given me years ago. It was Jesus Himself that was directing my steps, He was saving us and sparing us from loss and tragedy time and time again. I knew He was with us whether the picture was on the wall or not, but having the picture up in Chuck's room was a visual reminder He was there, in the mix of everything that was going on and taking place. Jesus Christ was and is the *only* One who could do the impossible. He did so in history, He does so in the present, and He will do so in the future. When I glanced at His picture, all the promises of following Him would saturate my spirit and strengthen me to keep hoping and believing in what seemed impossible. Seeing Jesus's picture strengthened my faith, even though in front of my eyes was a different picture of reality. What was I going to believe?

I chose to believe what Hebrews 11:1 (NIV) reads: "Now faith is confidence in what we hope for and assurance about what we do not see".

The day after we had moved into the new room, the director of the ward came to see Chuck, as the message had been passed on to her that Chuck wanted to speak with someone about his lack of walking. She was friendly, caring, personable, and open to what we were saying about the need for Chuck to be walking more. She openly admitted that she herself could not make any promises on a certain number of walks daily, but she would be in contact with the Perfusion Department and would see what improvements, if any, could possibly be made. As she was meeting with us, she experienced the LVAD alarm sounding. I noticed her distress as the alarm sounded more than once. She inquired as to what was happening, so I explained what had taken place with the machine over the past five months. She then asked Chuck's nurse to call up Perfusion. G—— (the head of Perfusion) was up In Chuck's room in a short time. G—— explained that there was nothing they could really do to stop the LVAD alarming. Changing the head of the LVAD would have to be done under forty-five seconds, and it was way too risky. One of the hoses had developed a permanent line or fold in it, allowing the line to be bent more than forty-five degrees all the time. Dreadfully, the plastic material was weakening. G—— said that a support like a coated metal weave would have to be fitted over the line. He said that he would have to craft something, but for now he would change the position of the head, which looked exactly like an oil filter. He slowly moved the head so that it was pointing down toward the floor. Chuck and I really couldn't handle the LVAD head in that position, pointing downward, as that was where Chuck's blood was spun at 4,500 RPM, and we communicated that to G——. He told us that it was not possible for the head to disengage, but he would not leave us in fear of that, so he turned the LVAD head back up, pointing toward the ceiling. G—— left and said he would be back as soon as possible to install the coated protective sleeve to aid in supporting the line so it would not kink or, worse, possibly crack. Gee returned and placed the sleeve over the line that held Chuck's precious blood. The line support helped somewhat, but not as much as I had hoped for.

The nutritionist delivered the food she had bought from Chuck's wish list. I was hoping either the cookies or maybe the cashews, just something, would stimulate Chuck's palate so he would to want to eat more, but unfortunately it didn't. Chuck would try hard to force a few bites down, but he was struggling even with that.

Chuck's walking schedule picked up a bit. He usually had two walks daily, which helped him not to totally stiffen up. The walks were also beneficial for his mental health; they were something he could look forward to, and they gave him a short glimpse of a change of scenery. When the ward doors opened and a Perfusionist walked through those doors, it lifted our spirits. All these extra things— the bigger room, added walks, and special food—were above and beyond what was expected, and we were enormously appreciative for them all. We felt and we were extremely blessed.

As the days passed, the LVAD took a turn for the worse and began sounding its alarm frequently, and now the RPMs were slowing down from 4,500 RPM to 3,200 RPM, and at times even as low as 2,700 RPMs. Seeing the machine slowing down was completely nerve-racking; it was causing panic to my soul, and I feared that one day it would keep going down, right down to zero. Between Chuck's medical team and the Perfusion team, they decided to put Chuck on bed rest—no more walks. They set the machine at 3,200 RPM which made Chuck feel even more tired than he already was, but in doing so, the LVAD functioned a little bit better; at least it was not plummeting into a downward spiral. Chuck was allowed to sit in a wheelchair once a day just so he wouldn't develop anymore bedsores. His skin was breaking down from being in bed for the past five months, soon to be six.

On one particular afternoon, Chuck wanted some time to sit in the wheelchair. Having to move Chuck anywhere was a process, and it now seemed that the lines were getting tangled more often, exactly as garden hoses do. So we buzzed the nurse, and she came in, very carefully untangled the lines, and did all the steps required to transfer Chuck into the wheelchair. I was seeing Chuck every day, and even with my eyes I could notice a big change in him. Chuck's color was—well, I'll put it this way: indescribable. Chuck was beyond pale. There's no color I can write here that would accurately capture Chuck's skin tone. I can best describe it as tawny green.

Chuck needed something to help pass time, so when he was sitting and feeling up to it, he would have a shave. I would get him warm water in the little aqua-blue kidney basin, and he'd open the tray table to find the little mirror within, and he'd shave.

This day I watched Chuck shaving, and I knew that he needed a pick-me-up. We mostly listened to Christian songs from our iPad, because they offer so much hope. Especially in our darkest times, when it seems there is no hope, Christian recording artists' songs always offer hope. Christianity even offers life after death. Isn't that the biggest parcel of hope one can believe in? I think so.

Anyway, today I thought we'd listen to some of Chuck's favorite artists, so first up on the playlist was Bob Dylan. I think we listened all of Dylan's greatest hits, and as usual, Chuck sang along, knowing every word. I sat there looking at Chuck, feeling a bit downhearted and wondering how much longer Chuck could keep going. And to be truthful, I wondered the same for myself. The LVAD was now sounding the alarm even when Chuck was sitting or lying down. The nurse would come in and hit reset; nothing much was said. After Chuck finished shaving, he sat in the chair for a while, but then he wanted to go back in to bed. His entire body was sore, and it was hard for him to sit. The rest of the day was very low-key and quiet. I straightened his room, as there was just so much stuff and I needed something normal to do. Sometimes I would straighten a few times a day. The day ended, and both Chuck and I were tired, both of us wondering when God would move and when His timing would arrive. Really, I think we were both wondering whether God's timing would arrive on time, but neither of us spoke of this. God had brought us through so much and this far; not making it all the way to the finish line was a thought we never entertained.

Evening rolled around, and Chuck was having a very difficult time getting comfortable. Everything was bothering him. He was hypersensitive to everything, especially his senses of touch and smell.

Is it any wonder? It was getting late, and it was time to say good night to Chuck. I did the regular routine: heated the rice bag and ensured his tray table was close to his bed with water, a gingerade, and his cell phone all in reach. I could tell that Chuck really didn't want me to go, as it seemed that every time I started to gather my things, Chuck wanted or needed something else, or wanted something changed or straightened. I think it was a combination of the hypersensitivity and the failing of the LVAD. Everything Chuck was dealing with was a heavy load, and I was amazed at how well he was holding up and managing his crisis. He was totally awe-inspiring. His sister Beth had coined his nickname "Amazing Chuck," and my son-in-law's sister Victoria called him a rockstar. Everyone was amazed at Chuck's strength, stamina, never-ending hope, determination, and all his other positive attributes that kept him going. But inside Chuck lives the Holy Spirit, and He was dwelling in Chuck's spirit and body, keeping Chuck alive. Chuck indeed was ill; he almost died several times. As Pastor Ernest says, Chuck was dead three times. But God had mercy on him—and not on him only, but also on me, to spare me sorrow upon sorrow. That sentence is a paraphrase of Philippians 2:27. As it is written, so it was and is with me.

I got Chuck comfortable and made him feel secure as I possibly could. It was time for me to go, as it was close to 9:30 p.m.; it had been a long day, and we were both tired. We prayed and kissed good night, and I was off for my walk back to the residency. As I got closer to the building, I knew which apartment was mine, and I could see in my window up on the fifteenth floor the light from the lamp I had left on. I knew it was from my suite, but looking at it made me feel even farther away from home. I was really hoping Chuck was going to make it though the night. Any confidence I had in the LVAD had dived below and surpassed zero; it was in the negatives. When I reached my suite, I dropped my things, got ready for bed, and prayed fervently for Chuck to make it through just one more night. I didn't want to receive "the dreaded phone call." I climbed into bed, and before my head hit the pillow, I was fast asleep.

CHAPTER 31

The Phone Call

Before I knew it, the night had passed and morning had arrived. I was up earlier than usual, and I thought I'd get ready and wait to hear from Chuck or walk over and surprise him. Chuck always called between 8:30 and 9:30 a.m. I got out of the shower, and the phone rang. I think it was just before 6:30 a.m. To be truthful, my heart froze. Fear gripped me for those few seconds. I picked up the phone and said "Hello?" After what seemed like an eternity, Chuck answered, and my heart instantly relaxed. I was so relieved to hear his voice. He said, "Hello, guess what? It's today. It's here." Chuck sounded excited and calm at the same time.

I answered with "What's today? Are you telling me what I think you're telling me?"

Chuck said, "Yes, I am. They have a heart for me!"

I'm sure I asked ten times or more whether he was kidding me, but he wasn't. I can't even describe my emotion. All I know is that I was loud and excited and went into overjoy times ten. I could hear Chuck's nurse and whoever else was in his room laughing as they listened to my response. I literally could not believe it; nor could I contain myself. I'm sure I woke up every person on my floor, and maybe even those above and beneath me. I continued, laughing, crying, and asking, "You're not kidding me, right Chuck?"

Chuck answered, "No, I'm not. It's today."

I'll never forget that date: Wednesday, June 1, 2016.

Chuck told me the plan was that he would be going up to the OR around 11:30 a.m. I told Chuck I would be there as soon as I possibly could, but I was going to call the kids and make arrangements for them to come to Ottawa. I told Chuck that God's promises were coming true and His timing had come. We said goodbye, and I started making my calls. I felt a bit scattered, as I wanted to get over to see Chuck as soon as possible, but yet I wanted Carly and Matthew to be in Ottawa as soon as possible too, so I gained composure and started to make my calls.

I looked at the time. Winnipeg was an hour behind Ottawa, but I wasn't waiting to tell Carly and Matthew the news. So I called each of them. They both knew something was up when they saw my number come up on their phones at such an early time. Going in the order of age, I called Carly first, but there was no answer. I then called Matthew, and he did pick up. He couldn't believe the news, as it was five days short of being six months since this whole tribulation stated. Matthew was beyond ecstatic and so pleased to hear the news. As I was talking to Matt, Carly called me back on the other line. I told Matt to call in to his work and start packing, as I was going to get both Carly and him on a flight today. I got his passport information and told him I would call back with the details; then we said goodbye.

Next I called Carly back. When I told her the news we'd had been waiting for forever, she went into overjoy times ten too! It had been such a long journey with so many upsets, and it was unbelievable that we had reached this next step, the ultimate goal! I told her to make the arrangements with her work and that I was going to try to get them here as soon as possible.

With that being said, she was going to get all her things in order (if she could, as she was so completely overtaken with joy), and I would call back with all the flight info. That was the plan. We gained enough composure and said goodbye. I was so overcome with gladness and total gratitude; I was in awe of what God was doing, and I was overwhelmed. I prayed every time that I wasn't calling the next person on the list.

Next I called Chuck's sister's house, where Chuck's mom lives. I didn't reach anyone, but I left a message. Ger's place is like the central hub, so I knew that this long-awaited good news would be communicated and quickly shared.

Next on the list, I called my work. They had been so good to all of us from the very beginning. It was so early in Winnipeg that when I called my work, my boss was not in yet, but I did reach his voicemail. All I know is that I relayed the news on his message system and ran out of recording time. When D—— C—— (my boss) called back, he said my message was the best message he'd ever heard. I sounded so happy and excited that he called my coworkers into his office to listen to it, and they played it over several times. D—— C—— said that he kept my message on his phone for some time and would listen to it on occasion.

I looked at the time. It was now after 7:00 a.m. I wanted to call my sister, but it would be just after 5:00 a.m. in Alberta. Instead, I looked for flights and decided to book flights for Carly and Matthew before calling her. I called Chuck in between all the calls I was making, just to check on how he was doing. He relayed that the surgery prep had begun, which sparked some fuel in me to get over to the Heart Institute as quickly as I could.

I booked the flights that would get Carly and Matthew to Ottawa around 5:00 p.m. I called them with their flight info, and they shared with me that they both were almost ready to go. They asked me whether they would get to see Chuck before he went into the OR, but I disappointingly had to tell them no.

I couldn't wait any longer. I called my sister to tell her Chuck was going for his heart transplant. I woke her up, but she was so glad I had called her and thankful that the time had come. She told me to keep in touch and update her throughout the day, and I said

I would. I called and messaged a few good friends, and with that I was ready to go see Chuck.

I was so relieved when I reached Chuck's room and found he was still there. The morning had flown by with all the calls and booking the flights. I couldn't believe what time it was. The surgery prep had definitely started, and there was a lot happening in Chuck's room. They had already placed some extra lines in Chuck's body and shaved his chest once again. Although we were beyond pleased, joyful, thankful, eager, and relieved, we also knew that what lay ahead of Chuck was massive. The one thought that kept going through my head was that at one point in the surgery, Chuck would be lying on the OR table with no heart in his body. I couldn't grasp the concept; I didn't know how it would all come together. But one thing I did know was that I knew the One who did know how it would all come together, and I trusted whom He had chosen, especially the surgeon that God had put in our path. That's why I desired and needed to write a book about this time of the miraculous in our lives—because God spared us and saved us so many times. I want people to know that they, too, have access to the miraculous. I know He will do it for you and that God does help anyone who believes. Without God, our journey would have been a short, sad story.

Chuck and I were undeniably happy the time for the transplant had come, but without a doubt, anxiety was in the mix. This was a big one. Chuck had been through several open-heart surgeries on his valve before—four of them, to be exact. Is it any wonder that his heart couldn't handle the fifth? I kept on asking Chuck how he was doing. I told him Carly and Matthew would be here after the surgery was over. I shared with him all the well-wishes people had passed on and how happy they were for us. I kissed Chuck many times and told him how much I loved him and said I would be right here waiting for him.

It was just a couple of minutes after 11:00 a.m. when Chuck's surgeon, Dr. G—— L——, came in again to see him and meet me. He was there for only a few minutes. He asked whether we had any questions, which I did. I asked whether the heart was here, to which he answered no. They expected the heart to arrive around 6:00 p.m. He continued to say that they needed Chuck in the OR as soon as possible to have him ready for when the heart did arrive. With that, he shook Chuck's hand and mine and said to Chuck he would see him in the OR shortly. Dr. G—— L—— then left the room.

This surgeon/patient etiquette was different from any other surgery. In the past, Chuck's surgeons would come in a few days prior to the surgery to explain and discuss the surgery with us and sometimes even draw a picture to illustrate what was being done for a better understanding. Chuck had only met Dr. G—— L—— earlier that morning, when he had come in to tell Chuck they had a heart for him. Chuck thought that maybe the reason for that was perhaps because doing otherwise would overload the patient with fear. To imagine and discuss the subject of one's heart being cut out of one's body would bring fear to the bravest heart. The thought of lying on a table without a heart until a new still heart was placed in the body and then shocked to start it beating might be too much information for anyone, and it would instill fear. Who knows, perhaps sharing all that information might put the patient in a very vulnerable, fragile state of mind. In sharing all the details, it might affect the well-being of one's mind to courageously face the surgery with a positive mindset. Maybe in this case not knowing was best.

Chuck's nurse finished up doing everything she needed to do. She handed me a bag to gather up all of Chuck's belongings after Chuck left for the OR. After the surgery, Chuck would go back into the basement, where he had been placed when we first arrived in Ottawa. Chuck's nurse said she would give us a few minutes alone.

It seemed to me that Chuck and I had been in this position of saying goodbye before an enormous surgery a few too many times. I vividly remember each time; Chuck would have his surgery cap on, I would be sitting as close to Chuck as possible, holding his hands while saying all the things that were important at the time, and more importantly, praying to God to get Chuck and his surgeons through the operation. That "before time" together seemed to never be long enough. Somewhere deep inside me, I would wonder, *Will I see you again?* I was good at burying that thought, and I never spoke it. I can't even imagine what Chuck's deepest thoughts were, and we never spoke about them either. We chose to speak life.

This time was a little different, though. Chuck wasn't going into the waiting bay for the OR; he was going to the OR straight from his room. I heard the ward doors open and could see that Chuck's surgical team had come for Chuck. This was it; the time had come. With that, there was another big kiss and a "forever hug." I stepped back as they put the rails up on Chuck's bedside and unlocked the bed wheels. One more kiss and Chuck started to get wheeled away. I waited to see Chuck leave through the ward doors.

With Chuck and his bed gone, the room seemed empty. I looked around and saw the wheelchair, the stationary bike, and some of Chuck's personal belongings. With a deep breath and sigh, I started filling the bag with Chuck's things. I knew it was going to be a long day, but little did I know how very long it would be.

I made my way downstairs to the ICU in the basement. I knew the nurse at the desk, and I told her I had some of Chuck's belongings, as I understood Chuck would be coming here after the surgery. There wasn't a room ready for Chuck yet, as every room was occupied. For the time being, she offered to take Chuck's belongings and put them behind the desk until a room could be made ready for him. With that, I passed her the bag and thanked her. I left the ICU and walked up to the main lobby. I stood there for a moment and let my thoughts and emotions settle. I let God's words wash over me as I meditated on them, letting them renew my mind and absorb into my heart. I truly believed God had this, and He did indeed.

It was close to 1:00 p.m., and I needed to keep myself busy. I decided to go back and clean and tidy the apartment, as I had left in such a hurry to make sure I would see Chuck before he went into the OR. Carly had called me from the Winnipeg Airport to let me know that their plane was on time. I was so glad that they were coming and we could wait all together as Chuck went through his surgery.

I made my way back to the Heart Institute after I finished cleaning and tidying the apartment. Being in the same building as Chuck gave me some comfort; I don't know why, but it just did. When I arrived at the Heart Institute, I went up to the front desk to see whether they could give me an update on Chuck. All the receptionist said was that Chuck's surgery was in progress. She asked me to wait in the lobby, as a nurse would come up to meet and speak with me about the process for our family after the Heart Institute closed for the night. The remark about the hospital being closed surprised me. I guess it really shouldn't have; I should have realized how long the surgery would be.

CHAPTER 32

The Small Room

It wasn't long before the nurse was up in the lobby. She introduced herself and told me to follow her, which I did. She led me into the big family room, which housed a small family room within. She opened the door and said we would be able to privately use the room at any time through Chuck's surgery. She handed me the key, and I thanked her. She herself would be staying at the hospital for the duration of Chuck's surgery and would come by several times during the evening to give us updates. With that, she told me she would see me later, as she was going to drop by with some fresh clean pillows and blankets.

I sat down and stayed in the room for a while, feeling a bit overwhelmed. The room had two lamps, a small vinyl couch, and two vinyl recliners. The recliners were not the most comfortable, but I trusted they had been wiped clean; I'm sure that is the purpose of the vinyl, which is a good thing. There was a knock on the door; it was the nurse with the fresh pillows and blankets. I readily received them and thanked her, thinking to myself that the night ahead would be a long one.

It was nearing 5:30 p.m. when my phone rang. It was Carly calling to say that they had landed. We met at the apartment; it was so great to see them again. Life is always better when we have the ones we love close to us, in both the good times and, even more so, in the bad. They dropped off their bags, and then we headed directly back to the Heart Institute. Unrealistically, I was thinking, *What if Chuck's surgery is finished and we aren't there?* I guess I was wishfully thinking that would be reality, but it wasn't. The moment we were stuck in felt as if it were light years away from that wish.

When we got to the Heart Institute, I showed Carly and Matthew the small room we'd be staying in after the hospital closed. I looked at the time and saw it was now near 7:00 p.m. It had been almost six hours since I had my first update from the contact nurse, so I decided to make my first call to her to see whether she had any news. She answered her phone and said she would be up in a few minutes to speak with us. She came up to the room immediately. I introduced Carly and Matthew to her, and she introduced herself to them. She said the surgery was coming along, but Dr. G——L—— had noted that the enormous amounts of scar tissue from all the previous heart surgeries plus the most recent one were making accessibility to Chuck's heart a difficult task. She also mentioned that the heart for Chuck had arrived about a half hour ago. I asked her what information she could share with us regarding the heart; the only thing she could was where it had come from, which was Toronto.

At one time, the Heart Institute did share the name of donor with the receiving family, if the donating family agreed. But due to the sensitivity of the circumstance and upsetting situations that arose, the policy changed, and that information is no longer shared. At present you are allowed to write a letter to the donor's family and send the letter to the Heart Institute; in this case, the Ottawa Heart Institute would forward it to the donor's family.

The nurse told us we would have ample time to go get a bite to eat, but we would have to be back before 9:00 p.m. as that was when the hospital was locked for the night. So we decided to go for a walk, grab a bite, and be back for 9:00 p.m. The walk cleared the air, refreshed our minds, and passed some time. We arrived back at the Heart Institute just before 9:00 p.m. The hospital was dark and very quiet, and there was absolutely no one around. We went into the family room area, sat down, and watched the TV and flipped through magazines. I was wondering where the update nurse was, it was so late. The heart had arrived at the supper hour, and Chuck had gone in to the OR at 11:00 a.m. All these things were playing on my mind, and it seemed it was taking so long. I kept on having this vision in my head of Chuck lying on the table, chest cut and pried wide open, with no heart in his chest. I did my best to wipe away that thought every time it entered my head, and I wished I would have never thought of it, but let's be real—it was the truth. The only way I was able to settle myself was through prayer. My praying was pretty much constant at this time. I turned my entire focus to God: my mind, my heart, and my soul. Instantly peace and calm washed over me, and I continued to believe in victory for Chuck.

Time was passing very slowly. I guess it was about 11:00 p.m. when we decided to go into the smaller family room to see whether we could catch a bit of sleep. I think we had all dozed off and around 12:30 a.m. when there was a soft knock at the door. It was the update nurse. This moment was dreamlike, so surreal. She entered the room with her stainless-steel silver slate and told us that things were going much slower than Dr. G—— L—— had hoped. I had to ask her whether Chuck's new heart was in. She answered that they were in the process of doing that right now and that it was a tough challenge because of all Chuck's scar tissue from previous surgeries. She added she had no idea how much longer the surgery would be. With that, she asked us whether there was anything else we needed, which there wasn't. Carly, Matthew, and I all felt the same way—unsecure, not knowing where this would land. So, what did we do? We got up from the couch and chairs and got down on our knees. We all took turns praying out loud together, agreeing that Chuck's heart would be placed in his chest and would start so Chuck could live and function without any life support. We believed that God heard our prayers that were based on His promises, and that He could and would do this. We prayed hard and cried. There was no doubt about it; we were anxious and deeply concerned for Chuck. The delivery of the nurses' update was one of apprehensiveness; she definitely did not offer any victory promises.

But beneath all this heaviness—these past six months of upheaval of our formerly normal lives—even in this moment right here, right now, somehow there was still a small crack of light getting in. The light of God's Word and His promises was bringing hope and living truth into our spirits and hearts, which kept us believing in the impossible. We would have been dead people walking without God in all of this, but somehow we were able to push through, keep going, and even smile and laugh at times. The "somehow and some way" was God. For us, we couldn't have done it any other way.

After the update, none of us could fall back asleep, so there we sat, downcast in the softly lit family room. To comfort and strengthen us, we played some of our favorite worship songs on the iPad and listened intently to the words. As we listened, we were reminded and knew that God was in our midst, making a way. God was also there with Chuck and Chuck's surgeon and surgery team. We believed in the miracle taking place and God's promises being kept. We believed that the same power that raised Jesus from the grave lived in Chuck, and that it would be done for him. We listened to Jeremy Camp's song "Same Power" over and over again, and we believed the words.

Then there suddenly came a knock at the door. The time was just after 3:30a.m., and it was the nurse. She came into the room with her stainless-steel silver slate and said, "The surgery is over." Of course, we were all waiting to hear the words that would next come from her mouth. Then came those words I'll never forget. "Chuck's new heart is in, and his new heart is beating! His new heart has been beating for a half hour, all by itself and all on its own!"

It's difficult to explain how we felt—the feelings and emotions of Chuck's victory, our victory as a family. It was a moment that had us celebrating, jumping, hugging, and raising our hands and thanking God. Tears of joy and gratitude were streaming down our faces. Holy is the Lord and His miracle that was revealed before our eyes. Hallelujah to the King of Kings and the Lord of Lords. It was a moment that I'll never forget. As I write about it, I'm brought right back to that time as if I am there. The miraculous is etched in my mind forever, and I'm sure the miracle will go with me into eternity. This miracle will be the first I thank God for when I meet Him one day. The Holy Spirit saw us through all the way; there's no doubt about it. It was the one of the holiest moments in my life. It was a manifestation of everything we had hoped, prayed, and believed for. Our lives are dedicated to Him forever.

The nurse just stood and watched us celebrate this good, good, *good* news. As I hugged her, she told me how very happy she was for me and our family. She told us that we would probably be able to see Chuck in an hour or so. With that, she again expressed her happiness for us and left the room. I can't even explain our joy. There was no going back to sleep for us; how could there have been? We had made it through the tunnel, we had reached the gold bar that sat at the very top of the layered stack of "this first." All those to-do items had been ticked off the list one by one by Chuck's sheer determination and his faith. Chuck believed that God and he could get through all this one minute, one hour, and one day at a time, and here we were celebrating continued life for Chuck and, for us, life with Chuck.

Two specific incidents come back to me as I write about this victory moment. Way back at the very beginning, and in the middle and even near the end, it seemed as though we would never reach this day. My first memory about the possible length of the journey was from back in February. I remember Dr. S—— explaining that Chuck's path was going to be like traveling across Canada. He said for us to imagine Chuck was now on the east coast and had to make it all the way to the west coast before he would even be considered for a transplant. Dr. S—— wasn't trying to diminish our hope; he was only trying to communicate the time frame of the journey, should Chuck be able to make it that far. Dr. S—— added that Chuck had mountains to climb and that there were no guarantees. I think Dr. S—— gave a timeline of two years. We heard everything Dr.

S—— said, but to the knowledge and wisdom of all the doctors and specialists we added our belief and knowledge and wisdom of God. We believed that with God included in our circumstance during every minute of every day, we would make it to the finish line. And, to God be the glory, here we were.

The second incident happened in the elevator at the residency. As I was leaving the building to see Chuck, I met a woman in the elevator, and we started chatting. She asked me what I was here for. So I told her about Chuck needing a heart transplant. Then I asked her why she was here. Her answer was the same; her son was also waiting for a heart. Even though I really didn't want to know, I wanted to know, so I asked how long she and her son had been here in Ottawa. She answered me with "Do you really want to know.?" I nodded, and she told me they had been here for two long years! I remember hearing those words and my heart sinking deep within my chest. With a little more dialogue, she shared that her son was not placed in the same category as Chuck. Luckily her son was able to be out and about with a portable LVAD, which made a huge difference to priority. I was so relieved to hear about the difference between Chuck's and her son's situations, as Chuck would never have been able to survive waiting for two years. Also, I wasn't in a situation in which I could have stayed away from work and home for that amount of time.

But here we were; all that waiting and wondering was behind us. Chuck had made his journey across Canada, so we thought, and that's what we were celebrating at this time. It seemed as though we were waiting forever for the nurse to come back and tell us we could go see Chuck. But then came the knock at the door. It was her. The time had come. The best way I can describe the walk to see Chuck is to say it was like walking on clouds and air. I felt as if I were floating. Just thinking Chuck was out of the OR and back in a room was surreal and spine-tingling to me. We reached the ward, walked through the doors and down the short hall, and there we were, standing in Chuck's room.

CHAPTER 33

The Miracle Is Real

The post surgery nurse welcomed us in. I remember seeing Chuck from the doorway as I stood there gazing at him. The light in the room was soft and glowing, as if it radiated peace and calm. I felt an enormous amount of overwhelming gratitude, especially now that we had reached this part of the journey. I walked to the bed and took a look at Chuck. I was so surprised, pleased, and contented with the look on Chuck's face. Chuck's eyes were still closed, but his skin was pink, and for the first time there was peace and comfort on his face. I had seen Chuck after many surgeries, and he always looked distressed and in pain, as if he had been on a battlefield and had gone through torture and agony. But not this time; this time his look and aura were different; they reflected ease and well-being.

I asked the nurse when they would start waking Chuck up. To my surprise, she said they had already begun backing off the sedation. I was taken aback by his awakening taking place so soon after surgery, but I was so excited and happy. Slowly, Chuck began to stir. The nurse wiped away the surgical gel from Chuck's eyes, and slowly they began to open and close. Every time Chuck opened his eyes, they stayed open a little longer, and he soon was beginning to look around the room. I began by saying hello and telling him that the transplant surgery was over and that he had made it and we were all here, right beside him. Both Carly and Matthew were telling Chuck how well he had done and how strong he was and how happy we were. We told Chuck how good God had been to us, and Chuck raised his hand, acknowledging God as an act of worship and giving thanks to his Divine Physician. Chuck, to this day, five years later, declares that while he still lay on the table in the OR, the minute his new heart started, he raised his hand in honor and supreme gratefulness to God. That could be why Dr. G—— L——, the transplant surgeon, called Chuck "the real deal." I will explain more about this a little further along in the story.

We asked the nurse whether we could play some music from the iPad, and she said that would be an awesome thing to do for Chuck. So we played Chuck's favorite worship song, "How Great Is Our God," by Chris Tomlin. When Chuck heard the music and that song, he immediately raised his arm in the air again. Our eyes filled with tears, and Chuck's eyes were staying open. He focused on us, and he smiled. Remembering this moment stamps and seals everything for me as to why we believe what we believe. There is a song I love called "Better is One Day," and the lyrics of one line reside within every part of my being. It says, "Better is one day in your courts, better is one day in your house than a thousand elsewhere." That's how I feel every day.

The nurse looking after Chuck was exceedingly attentive to him. She told me she had read through Chuck's huge binder of his medical records, and she asked whether one of us would be writing a book. She said that if we would, she'd be the first to buy a signed copy. In all her years of experience and working at the Heart Institute, she had taken care of many people who had undergone heart transplants. But never had she seen, known, or heard of another patient like Chuck—with so many complications, problems, and issues—who survived. She said she was as amazed by Chuck as everyone else.

Chuck kept opening and closing his eyes; he needed to rest. And with us there, him sleeping was very unlikely. We felt that the best thing to do would be for us to leave so Chuck could rest. Also, the three of us were tired. Even though we were feeling good, healthy, and energized from seeing Chuck after his transplant surgery, we needed to get some sleep too. With that, we said our goodbyes and gave kisses and hugs. Chuck responded well and gave affection back. As we were leaving, the nurse told us that tomorrow, later in the morning, Chuck would be taking off his respirator and would be breathing on his own.

Walking back to the residency, we felt as if we were walking on air. We kept on reflecting on Chuck raising his hand and how peaceful, rested, and happy he looked. We decided that we needed to make a video update and share it on Facebook. As much as I have written in this book, I don't know if I've really communicated just how vast or how full-sized of a miracle it is that Chuck has his life today. I can't tell you enough that the only way Chuck is here and made it through all the trials, tribulations, and complications is because of the Divine Physician and Healer, Jesus Christ. Our short Facebook video had over five thousand views in a couple days. Our family and friends, coworkers, acquaintances, and unknown followers that we had picked up along our journey were so overwhelmed and overcome with joy for Chuck and us. Everyone thought we had reached the light at the end of the tunnel, as did we.

Morning came fast. Our sleep was short, but we felt rested and were anxious to get back and see Chuck. We got ready and headed back to the Heart Institute. We walked down the hall into the ward, past the front desk, and entered the room. Chuck was awake, with no respirator, and greeted us with a big smile and a hello. Chuck was what he himself termed as "unleashed," and really that was what he was, and exactly how he felt! I can't even imagine how freeing it felt for him to have most of his tubes removed: tubes from his stomach, neck tubes, respirator tubes, and all the other tubes except for his chest tubes, which were draining the fluid from his chest and his intravenous site. Chuck looked clean, refreshed, soft and new lying under his white blankets. He looked renewed and restored. He could talk once again. It was like a flood of victory washing over all of us in Chuck's room. This atmosphere was filled with the presence of the Almighty. Every miracle was real and clearly visible to our eyes and minds. I'm sure it was this way so that we could see and share what God had done in our time of crisis. There was no denying we came through unscathed and not even smelling like smoke.

If you're wondering, "What does she mean by 'not even smelling like smoke'?" let me explain. The book of Daniel, chapter 3, tells a story of three Hebrew teenagers: Shadrach, Meshach, and Abednego. These three teenagers were thrown into a fiery furnace by Nebuchadnezzar, king of Babylon, when they refused to bow down to a nine-foot pure gold statue of the king's image. They knew that bowing down to the king's statue would defile the Almighty God. These heroic teenagers had a choice to make. To not bow down to Nebuchadnezzar was to defy and defile the king, but to bow down to him would be to defy and defile the Almighty God. It's a choice we will all visit at some point in our lives. These three Hebrew teenagers chose to remain standing in a crowd of three hundred thousand who bowed down to the golden statue at the sound of a trumpet. Their refusal infuriated the king. The three were arrested by the king's officials and thrown into a furnace that was made seven times hotter than normal. Then Nebuchadnezzar, looking through the furnace window, then saw four figures walking unharmed in the flames. The fourth being looked like the Son of God. Confused by what he was seeing, he said to his officials, "Were not three men thrown into the furnace?" The officials answered, "Yes."

Seeing this, Nebuchadnezzar brought the youths out and saw that the three Hebrew teenagers had no signs of being in the furnace. Their clothing was not scorched, their hair was not singed, and they did not even smell like smoke. The only thing that had burned in the fire were the cords that had bound them. Nebuchadnezzar then realized that the fourth figure was not *like* the Son of God; the fourth figure *was* the Son of God. The king was astonished and realized that all of this was due to the delivering power of God. Nebuchadnezzar became a believer again and promoted Shadrach, Meshach, and Abednego, and no one was allowed to speak against the one and true God that Shadrach, Meshach, and Abednego worshipped.

This lesson from the past is an inspiring example and has something we can take away. Even when the penalty was death, the three teenagers stood for what they believed, and God delivered them. The lesson for today is that we must determine in advance how we will respond to our trials.

In our journey, I decided for myself, Chuck for himself, and our kids for themselves that no matter what the report from medical powers that be or what we saw in front of our eyes, we would believe in the never-ending, never-stopping, ever-reaching power of God. In every room Chuck was in, I always pinned up my beautiful portrait of Jesus Christ given to me by my treasured lifelong friend Cindy. I always focused on that portrait when it seemed there was no way. The picture was a visual reminder that there was a way in Him. Jesus Christ is the way, the truth, and the life. That's how I felt in taking that stand in contrary times. I know we were brought through all this unharmed, with everything seeming to fall into place. Many times, we had to take that stand and make it known who was directing our steps.

Shortly after that moment, and being wholly present in the revealing confirmation of the miracle in the Chuck's room, Chuck's head transplant surgeon and assisting surgeon came into the room. Dr. G—— L—— looked energized and was excited to see Chuck. He shook Chuck's hand and asked him how he was doing. Then Dr. G—— L—— said, "Mr. Haarsma, I thought I had seen miracles in my profession, but you, sir, you are the real deal." Dr. G—— L—— then stepped back, and the second doctor shook Chuck's hand and said, "Mr. Haarsma, God must have great plans for you. I hope you continue doing well."

I commented, "Yes, I understand Chuck was over the line one time."

He looked at me and answered, "Oh, Chuck was over the line

more than one time. Chuck was over the line several times. That's why I believe God definitely has saved Chuck's life for a purpose."

With that, Chuck's surgeon said that he would check on Chuck tomorrow, and both doctors left the room. Carly, Matthew, and I couldn't thank them enough for what they had done for Chuck and us. I knew deep in the deepest part of my heart that all the surgeons who operated on Chuck had been chosen and handpicked by God.

To be honest, I was taken aback by both doctors' comments, especially those of the second doctor. He was only speaking from his time with Chuck in the transplant surgery, not even knowing of every previous miracle poured down and washed over Chuck back home in Winnipeg. I knew of the miracles, but hearing these words from Chuck's two transplant doctors sent chills down my spine and revealed even more the miraculous in our lives. Especially when the very brilliant and gifted saw the miracle did I know it was indeed just that—a true holy miracle. I knew that Chuck and our family had been spared from Chuck's death and that Chuck's life had been saved by the world's Saviour, Jesus Christ.

As the day went on, things just kept moving forward. Chuck's chest tubes came out, and Chuck was fully "unleashed." Next up was what Chuck had waited and longed for since day one, from the very beginning of all of this, and that was an independent walk. It was time to walk with absolutely no "short ropes" of any kind: no tubes, no lines, and no machines—just a walker for support. To experience and see Chuck's very first walk with his new heart was surreal, and the vision is etched in my mind forever. Chuck in our eyes and the eyes of those surrounding him and those back home, including medical staff, friends, family, and anyone else who knew him, Chuck was a real-life superhero. Chuck was in high spirits and enormously relieved to be able to walk again all on his own. Chuck had told me that one of the hardest parts about being so sick and being bedridden for such a long time was not being able to walk. Both Chuck and I now have even more compassion, kindness, respect, and consideration for people of all ages who are in wheelchairs. I can't even imagine how it is for parents of children who need wheelchairs. The first two words that come to mind are "devastating" and "heartbreaking."

When Chuck would see people walking in the hallways of the hospital, no matter how slowly they moved, he really envied their ability to get up and go. He longed so much to be able to do the same, and here he was. No longer did he have to wish or hope to walk. Chuck was up and walking. Chuck's second time up, he left the walker behind and managed to walk on his own, and he walked strong and fast. At one point it seemed he was almost running. As Chuck walked through the ward, I noticed the other patients (the ones who were conscious) watching him. I'm sure they had that same feeling that Chuck had of hoping and wanting to be able to walk again one day. There were some in their beds that waved or gave Chuck a thumbs-up. I think Chuck inspired them, as he did so many along the way. In fact, back home in Winnipeg, the doctors and nurses would share Chuck's story and determination with other patients to encourage them and give them hope. They shared that victory could be theirs if they didn't give up. One thing that is for sure is that Chuck never gave up—never.

Carly and Matthew would be leaving tomorrow for home, so between Chuck's rest times, we had great visits. Our family basked and lingered in the atmosphere of the miracle. Before we knew it, the day had come to an end. Early the next morning, Carly and Matthew left. Chuck and I were sad to see them leave, but we thought we would be home in a week, so that made their leaving a bit easier.

CHAPTER 34

This Really Can't Be

Chuck's voice was returning to normal, but when he talked there was a squeak; it sounded like a faint whistle. I didn't want to say anything, but there was no denying it was there. I didn't mention it to Chuck or his nurse, as I was hoping it would disappear on its own. I was thinking that maybe a vocal cord had got scratched or somehow damaged from being intubated this time. But as time went on, the squeak got worse.

On top of that, there was *C. diff* going around the ward, and Chuck unluckily got infected. He was quarantined for five days, which meant the obvious—no walks. The fact that Chuck couldn't walk and work to gain his strength back was weighing heavily on my mind. Then, on top of the *C. diff*, it seemed that there was seepage from Chuck's incision on his chest. The wound looked very painful and very red around some of the stitches. I knew we would not be leaving for home in a week. But much larger than that was the fact Chuck was still going through so much suffering and anguish. I don't even know how Chuck mentally handled trouble after trouble, never mind all the pain in his body. But then again, I do. Chuck's faith got him through. There's no doubt about it, and I'm so grateful for Chuck's strong will, sheer determination, stubbornness, power, and strength. Those characteristics served him well when he needed them most. But there is no denying that all these new health issues were pushing our spirits down. I thought to myself, "This really can't be. How can this be?" But it was, and we would have to deal with it. I know I had the easier position, as I wasn't the one going through the physical pain and suffering, but this made my spirit crash somewhat. My heart was breaking for Chuck, and I was longing for home immensely. It seemed to me that the prospect of going home was getting further away with each passing day.

All these issues that arose after Chuck's transplant surgery were frustrating and hugely disappointing. I was concerned for Chuck's mental well-being. Actually, when I asked Chuck how he was doing with all these things, his answer was calming for me. He usually answered with something like "Just a little hurdle." To hear Chuck meet his challenges so courageously built me up and gave me strength to carry on and confront all these difficulties, which is ironic, as you would think Chuck would need more encouraging than I would.

As a couple days passed, there was no doubt about it; Chuck's whistle when he spoke had grown louder, and his chest incision was unquestionably infected. Dr. G—— L—— had been coming in to check on Chuck and he popped by early in the afternoon of Thursday, June 6. Dr. G—— L—— took a look at Chuck's chest, listened to Chuck talk, and heard the whistle every time Chuck spoke. Dr. G—— L—— looked at Chuck and me and said, "There's no way we can get around this. We have to go back in and see what's happening under there. Instantly the room started spinning, my body got warm, and I felt as if I were going throw up. Chuck asked some questions as to whether or not there was any other way to deal with these two problems, but the devastating answer was no. Dr. G—— L—— said the OR would be booked for the next morning, and the surgery would take place then. This news was an enormous blow to both Chuck and me, but we knew there was no other way. We couldn't chance an infection running through Chuck's entire body again, so together we prayed and agreed this would all work out. I can only imagine, though I really can't imagine, how Chuck felt about his chest being cracked open another time. We talked about it only once and then didn't discuss it further, because talking about it wasn't going to change anything; it would only build up our anxiety. Instead we prayed; that was and still is the answer to everything. Trust me; it works. It truly activates power that cannot be accessed any other way.

The day was definitely a somber one. I think we both wanted it to pass so that what needed to be done would be done and over with. But then again, Chuck having to undergo another surgery was a lot to take in. The only way we moved forward was by believing we were covered and protected by the wing of God.

Morning came, and I made sure that I was there to bid Chuck farewell before he left for the OR one more time. I wasn't fearful that Chuck wouldn't make it through the surgery, though I was worried and deeply concerned about his pain and suffering. Think about it for a second; the discomfort we feel from a tiny sliver, a piece of glass, or an oven burn on our skin—these small wounds are bothersome and cause pain. I can't even imagine the pain Chuck was experiencing, as his body as it looked like a war zone, cut, bruised, marked, and scarred. There were wounds everywhere on Chuck's body: the back of his head, his back, his feet, his butt, his neck, his arms, his abdomen, and, of course his chest. My heart was broken again, but I had to lift my head and realize this wasn't finished yet. I couldn't believe it, but there was no choice; we would have to keep going through until it we were done.

I told Chuck I would be waiting for him when he was finished in the OR. We kissed and said our goodbyes. Chuck's nurse actually said that it would be quite a long time until Chuck would be back from the OR; her best guess was that he would return around 5:30 p.m. So, with that info, I asked her about any malls she would recommend for me to go walk around. She did suggest one quite far away, and the bus ride would take me down a beautiful street of flowerful outdoor cafés and past the Parliament building. I took her suggestion, left the ICU, and made my way to the bus stop. I really didn't want to go, as my heart was definitely not in it, but I needed something to pass the time. The bus came, and away I went, with only one thing on my mind, and that was Chuck.

The bus ride took my mind off things somewhat. I watched people getting on and off the bus. There was at least a few miles of outdoor cafés with the most beautiful flowers in baskets, hanging baskets, and pots, big and small; it was beautiful. The bus ride was worth it just to see all the flowers and ride past the Parliament building, which I had never seen before. The building was architecturally magnificent.

I reached the mall, and it was nice, clean, and airy, but I really didn't feel like being there, and I sure didn't feel like shopping. I quickly walked around, the entire time thinking that I really should be at the hospital or at least closer to Chuck. *What if Chuck needs me?* With that thought, I grabbed a bite to eat at the food court. I watched people around me, wondering to myself what was happening in their lives, taking into consideration my own circumstance. No one knew my husband had just survived a heart transplant and now was back in surgery because of complications. As I looked at all these people, I realized I had no idea what challenges they may be facing or what they may be going through or had gone through. That's why kindness is so important, because we really have no clue what others have going on in their lives or what they have been through in the past.

It was time for me to go; I really needed to get back to the hospital. I made sure to sit where I would see the opposite side of the flower-lined streets. It wasn't too long before I was back where I needed to be. I made my way back to Chuck's room but was disappointed to find that it was still empty. Chuck's nurse said Chuck's surgery was over and he'd be coming back to his room shortly. I sat down in my chair and waited once again.

CHAPTER 35

Grim

I could hear the ward doors open and the wheels of a bed rolling in the hall. Yes, it was Chuck. The transporters wheeled Chuck in the room, plugged in the machines, and did what they had to, to set Chuck up. When they were finished, I walked over to the bed to take at look at Chuck. I was so taken aback by the expression on Chuck's face. It was one of excruciating pain, and it looked as if he was wincing in his sleep. It made me wonder whether somehow Chuck had felt the surgery. I instantly felt sick to my stomach, sat down, took a deep breath, and tried to settled myself down. Right then Chuck's surgeon came into room. I'm certain that Dr. G——L—— noticed the sick look on my face.

Dr. G—— L—— started by saying that Chuck was definitely a fighter and that he recognized how much Chuck had gone through in the past six months. He continued, saying that, regrettably, when they went in, they found that Chuck's sternum had become severely infected. The only way that they could stop the infection was to shave down Chuck's sternum. As he spoke those words, I could feel the pain in my own chest, and my eyes welled with tears. Dr. G—— L—— then further explained about the whistle that was noticeable when Chuck talked. He'd found that Chuck's lung must have accidently and unnoticeably been punctured during the heart transplant. Dr. G—— L—— walked over to Chuck's bed and then gently opened Chuck's gown, which was on backward, with the opening to the front. I thank God that Chuck remained sleeping. I took one look at Chuck's chest and thought I was going to hit the floor. I had to sit down again. To this very day four years later, even as I write this, I vividly can see Chuck's chest, and it makes me cringe and grab my own chest. The pain on Chuck's face is etched in my mind forever.

Dr. G—— L—— said that this was going to delay us going back home for some time, maybe up to two to three weeks, as he would have to oversee how Chuck's sternum would heal. At this point three weeks seemed like eternity to me; that in itself was a massive downer. But then came the real blow, when he said that in the worst-case scenario it could be two to three months, should Chuck's sternum not heal. At that point plastic surgery would be the only option; they would need to build Chuck's chest up with prosthetic pectoral muscles and a prosthetic breastbone. My heart dropped to the floor even thinking of Chuck having to go for yet another surgery, and I definitely couldn't fathom staying in Ottawa for another two to three months. I just couldn't. The thought of both of those possibilities made me sick.

The days passed by, and Chuck was alert and, as always, brave and courageous, and he never complained. But I could see that all these extra complications were piling up on his state of mind. Chuck's chest was extremely painful, and he was bandaged with dressings to the max, starting from the middle of his neck right down to his belly button; this was to prevent any germs or bacteria from getting into his incision. The good news was that Chuck was back up to walking, so there was some progress being made amid all this regression.

It was early afternoon when I heard the phone buzz at the ICU nurse's station. Not long after that, the charge nurse came in and gave me the message that some people from Winnipeg were upstairs in the lobby, hoping to see me. I was totally shocked and surprised; I couldn't even guess who it might be. Both Chuck and I were anxious to find out who it was. With that, I made my way to the lobby. I turned the corner to see a couple that we'd once had a close relationship with from a church we had been members at. I was completely surprised and so happy to see someone I knew. I felt so grateful that they had come to visit with me and check on Chuck while they were here in Ottawa. I had to call Chuck to tell him who it was, and he was so surprised, as was I. They bought me a coffee, but more than that, they brought me comfort and hope. Our time together passed quickly. We said our goodbyes and said we would see each other back in Winnipeg.

I was feeling very anxious regarding what Dr. G—— L—— had said about possibly being in Ottawa for another two to three months. I was beyond antsy, restless and fretful about staying any longer than another two or three weeks. I guess the word traveled around the ward, so the Ottawa social worker and psychologist came to visit me. She suggested that maybe I could go home for a week and then come back. As much as it sounded like a good idea, it wasn't feasible, as I could not and would never leave Chuck here by himself. I told her that I would keep the idea in my back pocket, well knowing I would never use it. The good news was that Chuck was getting moved from the ICU to a room n the regular cardiac ward, as he no longer needed intensive care. To us that was a huge step in a positive direction. Again I moved some of our personal things; most importantly I took down the picture of Jesus Christ from the cork bulletin board. I absolutely needed to physically see that picture. More than ever, I needed to focus and dig deep into the promises of the One who could make the impossible possible.

Moving upstairs to the cardiac ward was part of the process of getting out of the hospital, but it was different from the care Chuck had been getting for the past six months. Some days it seemed the only time we'd see a nurse was when it was time for medication. Time passed, and we hadn't seen Dr. G—— L—— for days. Sometimes I would think, Has he forgotten about us? I looked at Chuck's chest when the nurse would change the dressing. His incision was not as red as it had been before, but there was one area where I could see his skin was not healing together; there actually was a half-inch hole. The nurse didn't like what she saw, so she requested that Dr. G——L—— come and take a look. In the back of my mind, I was not getting a good feeling about how Chuck was healing. The thought flickering in and out of my mind was that we were moving toward having to stay the two to three months longer.

A few times, I mentioned to Chuck that if he landed up staying longer, I would need to go home for a week. By the look on his face, I could tell he knew I was serious. I knew Chuck wanted to get home as badly as I did. So we both agreed and fervently prayed with each other that soon we would be going home together.

Dr. G—— L—— came in to see Chuck the day following the nurse's request. Dr. G—— L—— looked at Chuck's chest, slightly shook his head and pressed on Chuck's chest, and through the hole spurted fluid. It was absolutely dreadful, and the amount of fluid was alarming.

Dr. G—— L—— looked at me and said, "I'm sorry; you won't be going home. I can't send Chuck home like this. I'm going to put you on some different antibiotics, and I'll check you next week." I can't explain my emotions and feelings that welled up in me; I thought I was going to explode—not with anger but with huge disappointment. The situation made me want to scream, get up, and run.

Neither Chuck nor I asked any questions; there was nothing to say. But the situation was what it was, and we had to accept it. But beneath and inside, I was having a hard time doing so. We thanked Dr. G—— L—— for coming by and watched him leave Chuck's room. To me, hearing Dr. G—— L—— say we would be here at least another week was like hearing a judge give us a sentence of life imprisonment. I realize how overstated that sounds, but that's how it felt for me. Chuck turned to me and said something like, "So that's sure not what you wanted to hear." He might have even said, "So when are you leaving?" Even though I wanted to leave physically, my heart wouldn't let me go. What if Chuck passed away when I went home? I couldn't handle it, and I would never forgive myself. Deep within, I knew that the minute I reached home, I would turn around and come right back here to Ottawa. For now, I needed to stay put and manage my disappointment the best way I could.

The next few days were quiet and very routine. Chuck and I did his daily walks, completed word searches and crosswords from time to time, and occupied ourselves in various ways. A friend of mine from back in our teenage years who now lived in Ottawa had reached out to us when she learned we were here. She texted me asking whether it would be okay for her and her husband to drop by the Heart Institute and come see me. Sometimes you receive a gift, a call, a word, a smile, a surprise visit, a card—just something that comes at the right time. Well, this text was exactly that. Her reaching out was uplifting and added normalcy into my life. I hadn't seen her for years, so to meet up with her was a welcome distraction from everything going on around me. I texted back saying I'd love to see her. So we made a date, and she inquired what Chuck and I liked in the way of Chinese food, which is anything except squid, or calamari. I was excited and so looking forward to seeing her and meeting her husband. Chuck wasn't sure whether he'd be up to going down to meet them, but he'd cross that bridge when they got here.

Having something to look forward to made a huge difference on my outlook; this day didn't feel like drudgery. I was energized, and it took my mind off the complications that were delaying us from going home. Don't get me wrong; Chuck and I were still having laughs, and we were good at killing time together. It just had been a very long journey. Thinking we were going home a week after the transplant surgery to now talking about possibly staying two to three months longer was discouraging and dampening, and it lowered my spirits. But I had been praying, as had Chuck, for God to pull me up from this disappointment, and I'm sure that this friend visit was an answer to that prayer.

I remember that when my friend texted me that she had arrived, I was instantly happy and motivated. I asked Chuck whether he was gong to come down. Totally unexpectedly, Chuck said he was coming down with me to see them. I was elated, and this seemed somewhat normal. I joked that this was our first double date with Chuck's new heart, and Chuck agreed it was. My friend didn't think Chuck was coming down, so we decided to run with that and thought we'd let Chuck's appearance be a surprise. Chuck looked pretty good for someone who had been through all he had; in fact, Chuck's hospital bedhead was stylish and looked awesome.

We were ready to go. We made our way to the elevator and went down to the main floor. My idea for the big surprise was that I would go alone into the lobby first, and then Chuck would round the corner a few seconds later. So I made my way around the corner, and we spotted each other. I can still see the expression and smile on her face. But when Chuck rounded the corner, her excitement went to an entirely different level. The expression on her face was one of disbelief and complete shock. She started trembling, and tears filled her eyes. She really couldn't believe what she was witnessing as Chuck was walking toward her. She stood up and held her face in her hands and cried. She wiped the tears off her cheeks as she introduced us to her husband, and we hugged our way through our reunion. During our entire visit, she kept repeating how she couldn't believe her eyes. Seeing Chuck up was like seeing a dead man walking. Every time I saw Chuck up and moving around, I myself was overwhelmed with gratitude; I can't imagine what it was like for others. Catching up on each other's lives, the delicious Chinese food, meeting her husband, and reminiscing about good times gone by—it was all fun. But the best thing was the in-person contact with someone we knew; it was like fresh water pouring into a dry well. Their visit was so elevating. It was like a shot in the arm. I will never forget it; the memory will dwell in my mind and in the depths of my heart forever.

CHAPTER 36

Going Home

Chuck and I talked about our friends' visit for days; it was such a highlight. We continued to do Chuck's walks and ventured to the cafeteria and TV room a few times to get a change of scenery. There was no way for Chuck or me to tell whether Chuck's sternum infection was healing; even Chuck's nurses didn't comment on the status of his chest when they changed his dressing. All I knew was that I was counting down the days, hours, and minutes until Dr. G—— L—— would come back, assess Chuck, and hopefully let us go home. That day couldn't come fast enough, but it finally did arrive.

Chuck and I were in his room, and I could hear two sets of footsteps coming from down the hall. They stopped just outside the door, and then came the moment we'd been waiting for; Dr. G—— L—— entered Chuck's room with the nurse to assess his chest. Once again my heart rapidly moved up from my chest into my throat. Dr. G—— L—— was energetic as always, with no time to waste. He asked Chuck how he was feeling and then proceeded to remove Chuck's dressing. He looked at Chuck's chest, and what probably was seconds seemed like forever before he spoke.

"Well," he said as he pushed down on Chuck's chest, "How does that feel for you, Chuck?"

Chuck replied, "Sensitive."

Dr. G—— L—— said there hadn't been as much progress as he had been hoping for, as he stood silent, thinking with his hand on his chin.

He then spoke. "I know how badly you want to go home. I see some healing, but not as much as I would have anticipated. I want you to know that if I send you home, there's a good chance you may have to come back for prosthetic surgery. Are you still wanting to go home knowing there is a possibility you could be right back here within two to three weeks?"

Dr. G—— L—— was talking to both of us, but more so to Chuck. I spoke out of turn and immediately answered with a yes.

Dr. G—— L—— looked at Chuck and said, "You, Mr. Haarsma?"

Chuck answered, "Yes, I would like to go home."

There was a long, drawn-out pause, and I was thinking, *We're staying.*

Then Dr. G—— L—— suddenly said, "Well, I guess you can start packing your bags. I'm going to send you home, back to St. Boniface Hospital, and hopefully things will keep going forward. As much as it's been a pleasure to have you as a patient—you well tested my skills and made the miracle real—the time has come to say goodbye." Dr. G—— L—— shook Chuck's hand and then shook mine. He then turned to the nurse and told her she could start arranging for Chuck's discharge, which would happen in the next couple of days.

I couldn't believe what I was hearing. I was over the top and bursting inside with so many emotions. The overall emotion encircling everything was one of immense gratitude. I was so overjoyed that this moment had come.

After Dr. G—— L—— and the nurse left Chuck's room, I jumped up and did my happy dance, we were going home! I called Carly and Matthew, and I called Chuck's mom. I texted my sister, Chuck's sisters, and our friends. If I'd had the opportunity, I would have shouted from the hospital rooftop and let the world know Chuck and I were going home. I was ecstatic.

In the next couple of days, the arrangements were made for Chuck to leave on Thursday, June 23. Somehow Chuck had convinced me to fly back home in the four-seater plane with him, as there was room for me now since there were no medical people required other than a paramedic. In the evening, I went back to the residency, and while packing my things I started thinking about it a bit more.

The truth is that there was absolutely no way I could fly in that plane because of an experience I had back in high school. From the moment I went up in that small aircraft, I wanted to come down and my joy flight to be done. The bad thing that has made me fearful to this day was when my schoolmate tried to land the plane. He couldn't land the plane the first time because of a strong tailwind, so we'd had to pull back up at the last moment. With the plane teetering from side to side, the thin walls shaking, I promised myself that if I should touch the ground again, I would never get into a small plane again. Obviously we landed safely, as I'm here today. But even at such time as this, in the midst of all our joy, I was keeping that promise to myself. I would make arrangements to go home on a commercial flight. I called Chuck and broke the news to him.

Actually, Chuck wasn't too surprised and understood my change of mind. So I ran with that and booked the earliest flight and called in for a taxi pickup. As I looked around the residency suite, I had no remorse about leaving; it had never felt like home or become a personal sanctuary; it was just was a place to lay my head. I packed everything except the things I needed for the morning. This was it; I was going home. I was going home to my kids, my house, and my life; and best of all, I was going home with my husband, Chuck.

Chuck and I had a short conversation, as it was very late, close to midnight. The plan was that he'd be leaving sometime the following morning. We said our good nights, and I promised I'd call when I got to the Ottawa airport.

Morning came fast. I called Chuck, but he didn't have a time yet when the paramedics from the air ambulance would be picking him up, all he knew was that it would be sometime in the morning. That sounded good to me; I'd call again to check in when I arrived in Toronto.

It seemed like it was within minutes that I was in Toronto to catch my connecting flight to Winnipeg. As soon as I could, I called Chuck to see whether he was on his way home too. I was surprised when he answered the phone, as I thought he'd possibly be in transit, making his way to the airport

I honestly couldn't believe what Chuck was telling me. Chuck had a lump under his skin in his groin area. A doctor Chuck had never seen before had dropped by to give him one last exam before bidding Chuck goodbye. Chuck told the doctor about the pocket, and when the doctor pressed on it, it burst, spraying fluid all over Chuck's clothes and the doctor's clothes and his shoes. Because that happened, they said that Chuck should not go home! The ambulance and paramedics had just arrived for Chuck's transport to the airport. Chuck said that he had already been discharged and told the doctor and nurse just to bandage him up, as no matter what, he was leaving to go home to Winnipeg. I thank God Chuck was aggressive about it and they allowed him to continue to come home. I honestly can't say whether I would have continued to come home or headed back to Ottawa. All I know is that I was relieved I didn't have to make that decision; we were both still going home. Chuck was on his way, and I was on mine. This day was unforgettable; it was my jackpot, my winning lottery ticket. I'm sure Chuck felt he had just escaped a narrow getaway, and in fact he had indeed, and at this time, that was all that mattered.

CHAPTER 37

The End before the End

Nothing came easy in this journey, not one thing; but suddenly, good things and good outcomes always came.

I arrived in Winnipeg and felt like kissing the ground once I stepped off the plane. I was home! I really can't remember how I got home from the airport. But I do know that when I put my key in our front door and opened the door, the known comforts of home flooded all around me. Actually, the truth is I fell to my knees and cried in gratitude. I was home, and soon after me, Chuck would be home in Winnipeg too, or so I thought. There were heaps of mail on my dining room table, and all my plants were good except one that in no time made a comeback. The house was clean, and the grass, let's say, left something to be desired; but who cared, we'd fix it. All that mattered was that I was home.

Chuck's journey home in the small medical plane would be better described as an adventure or an undertaking. I absolutely knew I had made the right decision flying home in a big jet airliner, as it was extremely windy on our travel day.

Once I dropped off my bags, I wanted to make it back to St. Boniface Hospital to be waiting there when Chuck arrived. I did exactly that and made my way to the hospital. I guess it was near 5:00 or 5:30 p.m. when my phone finally rang, and it was Chuck.

I asked him, "Where are you?"

I was totally speechless when Chuck answered, "Thunder Bay."

I was totally blown away at Chuck's response. Chuck explained that because of the winds, they'd had to stop to fuel up the prop plane. Chuck was, in fact, walking around on tarmac in Thunder Bay as the pilot fuelled up the prop plane at the self-serve pump! It was a blessing that I wasn't on that plane. There's no doubt in my mind I would have gotten off in Thunder Bay, rented a car, and driven the rest of the way to Winnipeg.

Chuck finally arrived at St. Boniface around 8:30 p.m. He now was home too. We celebrated that we were both in our hometown! Chuck was getting closer to coming to his own home and his own bed. Unfortunately, there were unexpected hurdles that we would need to get over. Honestly, I thought we had reached the end of all this and were done, but the journey was not over yet. The things to come were some of the hardest. I needed God more than ever—so much more than words can say, and so much more then ever before. I believe the massiveness of this fight was to prove and confirm our Living God's miraculous power to me, us, our family, our friends, our fellow believers, and all those around us. There's no other explanation. There isn't a secular explanation that makes sense. At times even all the medical people were speechless at Chuck's journey and the never-ending stream of miracles. Little did I know I would now have to dig further into the God's Word for direction. What I needed most were strength, energy, and wisdom of the kind that only God could give. I needed God more now than anything. I needed Him more than I had they day before more than words can say.

In a few days, Chuck was moved up into a regular cardiac ward. We both thought that was a step in the right direction. We thought for sure he was closer to getting his foot out the door. Well, to our huge disappointment, it was just the opposite. What began was an onslaught of nightmares, to say the least. When I tried to speak up about the things going on that were just plain wrong, no one would listen to me. Chuck was not in a frame of mind in which he could speak for himself, as a sea of drugs started to be administered to him. The drugs were wreaking havoc on him; they were pretty much making him frenzied and unruly. The nursing staff were overloaded with their patients; all they really had time for was to deliver medications. No one had time to listen to me or my concerns as I realized what was going on with Chuck and the drugs. "Bad" doesn't even begin to describe what was taking place. The nurses were constantly on the run and had way too many fires to put out. Even when they said they'd be right back to discuss issues further, they never returned; they were just too busy.

It was enormously difficult for me to accept what was going on with Chuck. I mean, think about it; his journey had been a struggle with several near-death experiences, and now this? The situation escalated to the point where Chuck, in his drugged mental state, was back to needing a Constant Care health-care worker assigned to him 24-7. At this point Chuck couldn't even have a roommate because of the intense situation. I've chosen not to go into detail because what we were dealing with was so heart-wrenching and personal. I knew in my heart of hearts that there had to be a change, as Chuck had been through an absolute nightmare, and this was not how his story was going to end.

Things were going from bad to worse. Chuck's sister Janice and I were sitting with Chuck when the nurse came in to tell me that one of the doctors from Chuck's team wanted to meet with me. I thought it was odd that he just didn't come up to Chuck's room, and I was wondering what it could be all about. I asked Janice to come with me so there would be two sets of ears to hear what would be said. So we left Chuck with the Constant Care person, and to the meeting we went. What I was about to hear were the most unexpected words I could ever have imagined.

The nurse guided us to the room, which was on the same floor but in a different ward. The ward was called the Acute Critical Care Unit (ACCU). When we walked into the room, there were two doctors—one I knew and one I had never seen before. Dr.

C—— (the one I knew) welcomed us in and gestured to us where to sit down. To be candid, Dr. C—— and I never connected. I felt that he would let me talk but never listened to me; I was an interruption to him. To say the least, I was quite taken aback that it was he who wanted to meet with me. Right from the get-go, I was leery of where this meeting might go.

Dr. C—— started by reviewing Chuck's current condition, which we all recognized was declining in all aspects. I was sitting at the edge of my seat, waiting to hear what Dr. C——'s game plan was to help Chuck out of this dark state he was in. But what came out of his mouth was outrageous and shocking to both Janice and me.

Dr. C—— said there was really no medical reason for Chuck's behaviour. Then he went on to say that the amount of trauma and the ICU delirium (which I never once believed or accepted) that Chuck went through could cause permanent damage to his state of well-being. I could feel myself getting fired up inside, because as I knew now and back then, when Chuck was in the ICCS, all of Chuck's delirium was drug-induced. Dr. C—— continued on by comparing Chuck's state to a ship on the sea that makes it through many wicked storms but, at the end of it all, sadly never reaches the port.

I had to ask Dr. C—— what, exactly, he was saying.

He then said to me, "Chuck may not make it home; this could be the end."

With what I heard, I felt that I was catapulted into the twilight zone. I'm not trying to be funny; that is exactly how I felt. My head was whirling. The funny thing about it was that Dr. C—— didn't stick around whatsoever, not even for five minutes. I looked at Janice, who was feeling just as confused as I. Janice's eyes were filled with tears as she said, "I can't believe this."

I really didn't know what to do. After all we had been through as a family, how was I going to tell Carly and Matthew this news? I needed to tell someone of this change in Chuck's medical assessment, of this 180-degree change of direction. I was floored and flabbergasted. I called "my sister Barb." I really can't even remember what I said to her in my state of shock. But I do remember that both Janice's and my eyes were full of tears, as we were both so traumatized and upset about what we had just heard. I honestly couldn't accept it. There was no way I could or would accept this bad news. The question now was, What was I going to do about it?

I was going to do what I always did. I prayed. It had worked every other time, and somehow the God of miracles just kept His goodness and faithfulness flowing over us. I was not about to change the process now. Almost immediately, fiery courage rose in me, bold and strong. It was actually bursting inside of me. But let me be clear; it definitely wasn't of my own strength or confidence. If I had relied only on myself, I would have curled up into the fetal position and fallen apart.

I was trusting on God to answer my prayer with an idea or word on how to move forward from here and give me the stamina not to give up. As quickly as I had prayed, the answer came to me. I was going to request a meeting with Chuck's team and tell them to take him off a certain antirejection drug (acyclovir) and all the opiates, narcotics, painkillers—any possible mind-altering drugs—and I would sign the papers and would be 100 percent responsible and accountable for the outcome. There was nothing else I could do. God gave me the wisdom to realize that this was the biggest fight of my life for Chuck's life. He graciously gave me the energy to take on the challenge and keep on going.

CHAPTER 38

The Home Stretch

In all of this mayhem, things were escalating with Chuck. I was able to take Chuck home a few times on day passes. These experiences were great challenges and included a few alarming incidents. I began to notice that just prior to leaving on a day pass, there was one particular drug that was administered to him. Within forty-five minutes, Chuck was flying high, and believe me when I say it wasn't a good or very manageable situation. All of these incidents taking place (which I've chosen not to go into detail about) were so far from Chuck's real personality and behaviour. I knew it was the drugs, but absolutely no one was listening to me. Actually, that's not true; some of the doctors were listening. But every Monday, when the managing doctor overseeing Chuck changed (which occurred weekly), the cocktail of drugs would change, causing chaos and turmoil. Chuck himself knew that this was not him.

As the battle was fiercely intensifying, I couldn't keep quiet about what was going on; it wasn't fair to Chuck or us. We were on the home stretch, and I knew we were supposed to reach the finish line. Finally, the pharmacist agreed to call in the head pharmacist to come and see Chuck. When he walked in the room, he was very tall in stature, and to be honest, he looked as if he had been on an all-night bender. He was a man of very few words and had a great head of unruly gray hair. I'm sure he was seventy years or older. He asked me some questions; I think it was a total of two. Before I knew it, he said to the other pharmacist and nurse, "Yeah, take him off ..." and he named a drug and then left the room. When I heard him say those words, I was so relieved. But it didn't deliver the results that I thought and hoped it would. In fact, disappointingly, it didn't change a thing.

To my surprise and huge disappointment, Chuck was moved into the ACCU, where the ratio of care of nurses to patients was lesser, but the reality was that Chuck was going backward. I still refused to accept and believe that what Dr. C—— had said was either real or true.

I was disillusioned, exhausted, and just plain overloaded with all the setbacks and difficulties. As Chuck was feeling so unwell and out of sorts, it was my desire never to leave him alone without a family member present with him. The Constant Care workers knew he was a heavy care patient, and when I think about it, Chuck was now having only male Constant Care workers. I guess that was in case things became boisterous. Chuck never liked Constant Care at the best of times, and now at the height of this condition of psychedelic confusion, Chuck was now in a state of paranoia and didn't trust anyone or want anyone near him. To add to the pandemonium, Chuck was starting to refuse his drugs, as he was feeling so mentally and physically departed. The problem with that was that Chuck required, as he will for the rest of his life, antirejection drugs so his body wouldn't reject his new heart. But the fact of the matter was that they would have to agree and change from the one drug that was making him so sick back to the other that had worked well for him. Despite the doctors' differences of opinions, drive, competition, and ambition for success and triumph, they needed to come together and do what was best for Chuck. Through prayer I had the revelation that the power struggle was real, and I knew that was what I would have to press against and combat.

It was getting very late, and I was so very tired, as my hours at the hospital were increasing every day. Chuck's sisters had been supportive and good to us and always offered to come and stay with Chuck if I or Carly and Matthew couldn't be there. This night I needed to call on a sister, as I needed to step away, get some rest, and clear my mind and tend to my soul. I called my sister-in-law Ger to see whether she could come and stay the night. Ger, who is always so very loving and giving, didn't even ask a question; she just answered with a yes. Her yes was like medicine to my soul and entire being. Chuck was comforted that she would be with him, as was I. It didn't take her long to get to the hospital. Ger hugged me and immediately zoned into Chuck. I gave her an update on where things were with Chuck not wanting the drugs and really wanting no one near him. After that, I said goodbye to Chuck and Ger and I left to get some very much needed rest.

Before I knew it, I was back at the hospital, but still the break was so greatly appreciated. Ger said Chuck didn't have a very good night and didn't get any sleep. I'm sure that was another contributing factor in his agitation and restlessness. Chuck absolutely hated the hospital nights and barely slept through any of them; he only caught some very short catnaps through the days.

It was early afternoon when Chuck's nurse (a male, which I'm sure was intentional) came into Chuck's room with a stretcher and told me he was taking Chuck for an MRI. I noticed he popped two syringes into his top pocket. I asked him what they were. His reply was Haldol, in case Chuck needed to be relaxed. I guess you could say I went on high alert, as I knew that it was an antipsychotic medication used for sedation. I couldn't understand why these people weren't understanding that these kinds of drugs had completely the opposite effect on Chuck, as most everyone had experienced the frightening, intimidating outcome. I told him I thought it would be best not to administer them to Chuck, and he did say he hoped he wouldn't have to.

Chuck was on the stretcher, and we were off. I had a hard time keeping up with the nurse; he was flying through the hallways and tunnel to get to the MRI screening, which was in a different building. When we reached the building, Chuck was basically whisked away, and I needed to find a washroom. To my dismay, and to add even more frustration to what I was already feeling, my phone, which was in my back pocket, fell into the toilet bowl. I grabbed it out very quickly, but it was done, dead, not working. Maybe it was a good thing to shut myself off for a while. I let both Carly and Matthew know what happened and told them they could notify the family as to why I would be unavailable. There's no doubt I was upset, but there was nothing I could do about it right at this time.

It didn't take long for the MRI to be done, and the good news was that Chuck's nurse did not have to administer the Haldol to Chuck. With my phone now being dead, I now had more uninterrupted time to think. The outcome was that I came to the decision that I was going to request a meeting with all of Chuck's doctors. I would insist Chuck be taken off acyclovir. Through consistent, hard, pressing prayer, my deepest innermost voice was telling me that would be the only way Chuck would come out of this black hole. We made our way back to the ACCU. I notified the charge nurse of my request as soon as we got back into the ward. The nurse came back to me later in the day and said I was to be at the hospital for 8:00 a.m. rounds. It was time for me to prepare and do my homework.

CHAPTER 39

Breakthrough

The day had finally come for me to make my case that Chuck's care had to change—specifically his medications. From the very beginning, I had studied and researched every drug Chuck was on. This helped me understand why some drugs were necessary. But more importantly, it educated me on the drugs that were wreaking havoc, causing the madness and having major ill effects on Chuck. Before I left for the hospital, I reviewed a few of them. I was ready, my spirit was strong, and I felt confident.

Chuck's sister Janice offered to meet me at the hospital at 8:00 a.m. I appreciated her support and took her up on it. I thought it was good to have two sets of ears to hear what would be said. I got to the hospital around 7:45 a.m., and Janice was already there. Chuck was so sick. He was frail and white, and his skin was clammy; he wasn't well at all. Chuck was suffering terribly, to say the least.

I saw the doctors starting to gather around nurse's station, it seemed to me there were more of them than the usual number. To remain calm, I said a silent prayer. During this entire journey prayer was always the way I prepared to fight my battles. I was calm, and even though I was up against a team, I was partnered up with the Waymaker, Christ Jesus. He would make a way and turn this page so our story could keep going. With Jesus, we could claim victory, giving all praise and glory to Him, the King. Like no other, Jesus is the True Victor. His name is all powerful and can do the miraculous, the unimageable. He never let me down, and I stood on my belief and trusted in Him as my firm foundation.

Before I knew it, the doctors were standing outside Chuck's room, going over his chart. My heart quickened as Dr. C——— opened the door and the eight, or maybe ten, of them entered the room. This was it; the time of opportunity had come for me to try to make things better. I stood up and said good morning. I felt calm but was very passionate in what I was about to say. I basically acknowledged each doctor and each specialization in the room. I started by recognizing their dedication and verbalized how they must have studied and committed their lives in vigilantly working to become who they were. I expressed my gratitude as I thanked all of them for everything they did for Chuck. We realized that without them, we wouldn't be here today.

As I knew their time was short, I turned the focus to Chuck. I told them to look at Chuck. His skin was clammy looking, transparent, and beyond pale. He was thin and not looking well at all. Truthfully speaking, he looked as though he was one step away from no return. I continued by saying that since we had come home from Ottawa, things had become chaotic and unmanageable. Chuck had gone from someone who beat all odds to someone who might "not make it to the port," to quote Dr. C———.

I continued in saying that Chuck had survived so many risky procedures and surgeries performed by many doctors, and that the word "miracle" had been used to describe the success of some of the procedures. But now we had come to this. I told them that I couldn't and wouldn't accept that Chuck was suffering from ICU delirium. I said that in my opinion what we were seeing in Chuck was all drug-induced behaviour, and this could no longer go on. I explained that I knew they all wanted the best for Chuck. But as Chuck's wife, and as a witness to everything happening to him, I was insisting that he be taken off acyclovir and put back on the other antirejection drug that had worked well for him. To add to that, I also wanted Chuck taken off all other drugs that were classified as narcotics. I added I was comfortable signing the papers and would take full responsibility of the outcome. But this needed to happen immediately, before Chuck's next dose of his antirejection drugs that he was now beginning to refuse because they made him so sick.

To my surprise, and from straight out of left field, Dr. C——spoke out. He said I wouldn't have to sign any papers and that he himself would stop the antirejection drug that I was insisting was making Chuck so sick and would start Chuck on the original antirejection drug that he had been on at the beginning. Dr. C—— also said that all opioid and antipsychotic drugs would be stopped. This would be tried to the end of the week, and we would see what the results would be. I was flabbergasted and shocked that Dr. C—— agreed to move forward with what I had said. Maybe he had no choice, but he didn't fight, rebut, or challenge me at all. I was so relieved; the load had been lifted from me. I felt as though I could fly and as if the heavy weight that I had been under and carrying around had been removed. I knew God had sustained me once again. He had given me the words, the courage, and the confidence to challenge this last diagnosis, which I knew was completely wrong, *only* through His wisdom. God was making a way where there was no way. He was paving the path; I now see it as our family's parting of the Red Sea.

The meeting was over, and the doctors left the room. Janice, Chuck, and I were satisfied, and poor Chuck just nodded his head, as he was feeling so ill. I was greatly comforted and beyond pleased that finally a change was taking place and we were moving forward. We anticipated that Chuck would be feeling a whole lot better in the next few days. I really felt that soon we'd be on the way home. The best part was that I believed we'd be going home together.

CHAPTER 40

A Long Haul

A couple days passed of Chuck being on the new antirejection drugs and absolutely no narcotics of any kind, and he was doing so much better, exactly as I had thought he would. He was moved back to the regular cardiac ward and placed in a very small room with another patient. Chuck was still hooked up to an IV 24-7, so moving around was like an obstacle course for anyone in the room, never mind trying to maneuver with an IV pole. One night when Chuck had to get up and use the washroom, he got tangled up in the small space and fell hard, which caused a call to me around 2:30 a.m. The nurse on the other end sounded frantic and very frustrated. She said Chuck was extremely upset. She wanted to send him for a CT scan immediately, and to put it bluntly, Chuck wasn't having any part of it. The nurse told me that someone from the family had better get to the hospital immediately or she would have to sedate Chuck and put him back on a ventilator.

As you can guess, this did not sit well with me. There was absolutely no way we were going back to that. I knew that if Chuck was put back on a ventilator, he'd never be able to wean himself off it. I genuinely couldn't go back to the hospital, as I was so spent. I got out of bed and went to wake up Matthew to see whether he'd go. Matthew came to my rescue and went to see what was going

259

on with Chuck. When Matthew arrived at the hospital, Chuck was so relieved and grateful to see him. I think Chuck was done with his hospital stay; he desperately needed to get out and come back into his home. Matthew stayed the rest of the night and into the morning, until either Janice or Kristen arrived at the hospital. I went to the hospital a little later, and to say the least, the entire day was intensely restless for Chuck. Janice, Kristen, and I had a day of strong negotiating, and at times, Janice actually had to stand in front of the door to keep Chuck in his room. It was another one of those days one never forgets but wishes one could.

Chuck so badly wanted out, and the jostling was, to say the least, exhausting. So, taking matters into my own hands, I thought maybe it was time to take Chuck out on a day pass. My reasoning for this was that if they would allow Chuck out on a day pass, there didn't seem to be much point in debating all day with Chuck about why he couldn't go out. Moving forward with my bright idea, I told Chuck I was leaving the room to go inquire whether he could go out for the rest of the day. I thought maybe a drive and a change of scenery would give him a sense of freedom and some power over his own life.

I went and inquired at the nurse's station about taking Chuck out, and after some discussion, they said yes. I didn't know whether I was doing the right thing, but I figured that getting out for a bit could only make the situation better. Quite frankly, I think we all needed out. The struggle to keep Chuck in the room was real and daunting and extremely exhausting. I made my way back to Chuck's room and shared the good news (so I thought) that we were going out.

Chuck seemed happy and was game for the idea. We gathered a few of his belongings and we were ready to head out. Surprisingly, when we were wheeling Chuck out of the hospital, which is normal hospital protocol, Chuck seemed to have a change of mind. As we reached outside and Chuck got up to walk, he decided he wasn't going anywhere. He wasn't going home, but neither was he going back into the hospital. Chuck grabbed the wheelchair ramp rails and wasn't letting go anytime soon. Janice, Kristen, and I tried talking to Chuck, but his mind was set to stay exactly where he was on the wheelchair ramp. I thank God that my son-in-law Chris showed up from out of nowhere. As Chris got closer to us, he could see that there was a debate of sorts taking place.

Chris nonchalantly asked Chuck what was going on. Chuck didn't have a concrete answer, but he also refused to either go to Chris's truck or for Chris to take him back to his room in the hospital. When Chris asked Chuck what he wanted to do, Chuck answered with "Wait."

We asked what seemed to be a million times, "Wait for what?" But there was no answer to this. This went on for a couple hours, with many bypassing spectators. Then along came a man; actually, I would better describe him as an angel. He came up and asked us what we were trying to do.

"Trying to get Chuck back into the building," I said.

He calmly said, "Why don't you sit him down and wheel him in backward."

So, with a bit of jostling, Chuck was in the wheelchair immediately; and with lightning speed, we pulled him back into the hospital and up onto his ward. This day was undeniably one of the most gruelling ones after Chuck's heart transplant; it had been a long haul, and it felt as though we had hit rock bottom. In my mind, the only way up and forward from here was to get Chuck out of the hospital and back home.

The day was long and arduous, and I was looking forward to its end. As the evening went on, Chuck fortunately settled in. Only when I was sure Chuck was peaceful and calm did we say our good nights and goodbyes. All along my drive home, I prayed and wished for a better tomorrow. I pulled up in the driveway, went into the house and up the stairs, and fell into bed. I was out like a light.

CHAPTER 41

Victory Day

O Lord my God, you have performed many miracles for us.
Your plans for us are too numerous to list.
You have no equal.
If I tried to recite all your wonderful deeds,
I would never come to the end of them.
—Psalm 40:5 NLT

When I awoke, I was greatly relieved that I hadn't received a phone call during the night. This meant that things must have been peaceful, with no calamity or situations. One thing that became a life-changing revelation over and over again was how our everyday normal is such an overflowing blessing. I think I can safely say that most of us, at some time in our lives, forget and take for granted how our everyday normal is an abundant godsend. Then something happens or we hear of a tragedy that makes us remember and refocus our lens on how fortunate we are and how really good we have it. The goodness in our lives appears more tangible as we recognize how much we have been blessed. I think gratefulness is so important and vital to our mental and emotional health, which is directly linked to our physical health. Our well-being is absolutely connected to our thoughts and perspectives.

As I drove to the hospital, I wondered what would be on the slate for today. When I reached the hospital, Chuck seemed to be well rested and in a great frame of mind. It was already the end of July; we had been home from Ottawa for almost one month—since June 28, to be exact.

This definitely wasn't the way the post surgery was to go. We were told we'd be home ten days after the transplant, and we'd hoped that would be the case. Although it would have been very easy to slip into self-pity and walk around asking, "Why us God, why?" we instead chose to continue and believe that with every day we were one day closer to Chuck's homecoming. Chuck's homecoming was coming; we believed it, and more importantly, we spoke it. Little did I know it was closer than I knew.

It seemed exceptionally busy in the ward this morning. Chuck's nurse came into the room to notify us that the occupational nurse was coming up to see Chuck. It was not long before she arrived, and when she did, she greeted us and said she had some questions for Chuck. As I mentioned, it was noisy, busy, and distracting in the ward. Plus, Chuck's roommate had a lot going on, so there was a continuous flow of people coming into and going out of the small room. The occupational nurse started her questionnaire, and I couldn't concentrate on what she was saying because of all the distractions around us. I could see Chuck was having a hard time focusing, so I asked the nurse whether it would be possible to find Chuck a quieter location. She said she was comfortable with finishing in the room. I mentioned that there were so many interruptions taking place that it was unfair to Chuck. The questionnaire was a mental assessment, and this was not a room where anyone could think and concentrate clearly. Regardless of what I said, she finished the questionnaire in the room, which made me very anxious about what the outcome would be. She then gathered her things and thanked Chuck for his time. She said she'd be back after lunch for part two, during which she and Chuck would be going on a "field trip."

Lunchtime came and went, and the occupational nurse was back. She explained that she and Chuck would be going down to the main lobby area, where there was a cafeteria and a Shoppers Drug Mart. Chuck was about to do some daily living tasks and run some errands. Deep within my soul, I felt rumblings that maybe something good was going to happen with all of this. So off Chuck went, and they were gone for about a half hour. When they returned, she said she'd be writing her report and she wasn't sure she'd see Chuck again. Then she shook his hand and wished Chuck the very best. I could feel hope rising within me. Her words were giving life to Chuck's and my bones! Was I really hearing what I thought I was hearing? When she left the room, I couldn't help but say, "Chuck, I think you might be coming home soon!"

Not surprisingly, Chuck's reply was "I can only hope."

With the occupational nurse's remarks, our souls were stirring. She made it sound as if the possibility of Chuck's homecoming could be right around the corner. With this tiniest glimpse of hope, we had a hard time staying in Chuck's small room. We were on about our third or fourth walk in the ward that afternoon when we decided to sit in the two chairs at the end of the hall. As we were sitting chatting, we spotted Dr. Z—— walking her usual hundred-mile-an-hour sprint. She spotted us and said, "Well, that's exactly who I'm looking for." Our expectation multiplied a hundredfold.

Chuck answered with, "Oh yeah, why's that?"

"Well, Mr. Haarsma, you can start getting ready to go home." Dr. Z—— replied.

Ecstasy, excitement, euphoria, shock, and disbelief are only some of the emotions we were both feeling. But more than all the other emotions, gratefulness, thankfulness, and appreciation were spilling over to what our ears were taking in. Since January 6, 2016, this was the day we had hoped, prayed, dreamed, and longed for, and it was here! It was the kind of moment in which you hope that no one comes along, pinches you, and wakes you up. This moment in time felt like a dream. January 6 to July 28, 2016, had been a very long haul. It had been a time of continuous trials covered by faith, prayer, and hope through countless surgeries, procedures, close calls, and code blues. But because of God's supernatural power, protection, and grace, along with all the excellent, incredible, extraordinary, and above-and-beyond doctors, nurses, specialists, health-care aides, cleaning staff, fellow patients, and families, we were hearing these words this day.

Dr. Z—— went through some details with us. It wasn't as easy as skipping down the hall and packing Chuck's bag. We would be going home with a bag full of dressings, prescriptions, and a two-month daily IV program. But nonetheless, Chuck was coming home. As soon as I could, I called Carly and Matthew, who were beyond exultant and surprised. It was truly hard to believe that the day had come which in so many ways had felt as if it never would.

Philippians 4:4 (NIV) reads, "Rejoice in the Lord always, I will say it again: Rejoice!" This verse says to rejoice in God Himself, to rejoice in the Lord and His character, His compassionate grace, and His justice and mercy. It's not a call to rejoice in our circumstances; it's a call to rejoice in Him who is with us in our circumstances. This is a very important distinction, as many of our circumstances are unwanted and truly terrible. None of us enjoy bad news or trials, but the one thing that can change our paths is knowing that God is our Good Shepherd who will lead us and see us through our times of trouble. God will give you peace and be with you in the middle of the circumstance. We need to center God and decenter ourselves in our circumstances. We often are a perspective shift away from changing our entire days and the ways in which we handle our trials. We can make everything easier on ourselves by trusting God. I will testify and bear witness to what I've written and what you've just read; that is solely the primary reason for this book.

Five years ago, when the miracle became real, I was so amazed and astonished, and we continue to live in awe and wonder every day. After receiving all the miracles and living under the wing of God, I made a vow and a promise to God that I would tell the world of what He had done for me, for Chuck, and for Carly and Matthew. I now feel that I have accomplished what I set out to do. You may think of, have heard of, or know of unbelievers that have had heart transplants. I believe there are many, and I can assure you that they, too, are also very grateful to have received extended lifetimes. I also believe that many unbelievers, after having gone through life-changing hardships bigger than themselves, soon begin to awaken to the idea that there has to be a higher power that saw them through their trouble. But regardless of all that, with Chuck the odds were stacked against him in the beginning, in the middle, and right to the end.

At the very beginning, there was only one doctor who said he could and would do Chuck's surgery; the others declined, as they said Chuck would not survive. The surgery in January 2016 would be Chuck's fourth valve surgery because of a second infection of endocarditis. Chuck was in a weakened state and was critically ill because of the endocarditis. After the valve replacement surgery in January, Chuck's heart beat on its own for only half an hour before he went into cardiac arrest and frantically was put on ECMO. Chuck was in a coma and was to stay on ECMO only for the maximum seven days, in hopes that his heart would start to beat and pump. When that didn't happen, they decided to keep Chuck on ECMO for five more days, pushing the envelope. Disappointingly, Chuck's heart didn't start. Chuck was to be put on a portable on LVAD on the thirteenth day, but that couldn't happen because of his circumstances and his fragile state. Therefore Chuck was put on a CentriMag LVAD that was not portable. It looked a lot like an old VCR with ¾" hoses coming from it, which were crimson in color because Chuck's blood was flowing through them. This would keep him in an ICU for the rest of his life or until a possible transplant. He was kept in a coma for three weeks or more; once that time had passed, he was "prepared" for us to come and see him on the day the hospital staff believed would be his death. Chuck's hands and feet were discoloring, and all the signs that were before our eyes undeniably spoke death. But to everyone's disbelief, and with all honor to God's mighty power and miraculous hand, Chuck was kept alive, not by medicine or luck, but by God and only God.

In early March, Chuck's case for transplant was submitted to Ottawa. A meeting was called with us on the morning of Good Friday, March 25, 2016, which we took to mean good news, because it was Good Friday. But that day didn't mean good news for Jesus Christ, and it sure wasn't a day of good news for Chuck in 2004 or 2016. In 2004, Chuck ended up in the hospital on Good Friday and had his third heart valve replacement. His stay that time was forty-five days long, with many hurdles and roadblocks of its own. On March 25, 2016, we were told Chuck had been denied for a heart transplant because he was too sick and weak to survive the process. I'll never forget the look on Chuck's face and my kids' faces, and the feeling in my heart and ill feeling over my entire body. I remember one of the doctors gently saying that we might have to accept that fact and we would have to just make the best of the time Chuck had left. I'm sure most of the room saw the wince and grief on my face when I heard those words. The doctors beside me spoke a bit differently, saying that if Ottawa didn't accept him, they would try again in six weeks, maybe again with Ottawa, maybe with Edmonton.

Then another doctor spoke up, saying that there was a long to-do list of items to accomplish for Chuck even to be considered. Chuck would have to gain strength and learn to walk again, and he would need to be able to walk two laps around the unit. At that point, Chuck couldn't even stand, but with God he did. There were many firsts that were accomplished for Chuck to achieve most of the list items. For one, they stitched Chuck's tracheotomy hole up; they had never done that procedure before, but with God, they did. Chuck experienced two code blues, but with God, he survived. Chuck had many life-threatening procedures performed on him, such as a thoracic team from the Health Sciences Centre Winnipeg being called in to remove blood clots from his lungs; and with God, the procedure was successful and Chuck survived. Chuck had to be on dialysis, with just a small chance that his kidneys would come back; but with God, they did. Just the fact that Ottawa accepted Chuck the second time is a miracle. When we arrived in Ottawa, Chuck wasn't on the transplant list, and we were told they couldn't and wouldn't make any promises either. The Heart Institute ran every test that Winnipeg had done. I'm positive it was because of their disbelief of the positive results compared to six weeks prior. Then, on the fourth day, the doctor opened the door to Chuck's room and delivered the news that changed Chuck's destiny forever. With God, the impossible was made possible! Chuck's name was on the list—and at the very top of the list! He was number one in North America!

I could go on and on, but in my mind—and more importantly in my heart—I know God made it *all* possible. *He* did. He made everything fall into place just at the right time and in time. It all happened in His perfect timing. His hands picked every person, every place, and everything. Matthew 19:26 (NIV) resides deep within me. it reads "With man this is impossible, but **with God all things are possible.**"

I'm sure that after reading this book, you, too, must feel and know that the miracle is real. I realize how blessed I am, as I get to see and live the miracle every day. As I think back to this time in our lives, I realize that the presence of our Holy, Mighty, Loving, Miraculous God was never so present or real as it was back then. My guess is that the reason for our awareness was because we were desperately in need for a miracle almost every day. So we prayed throughout each day, expecting to receive what we were praying for. We never wandered away from God for a minute.

The One True God; His Son, Jesus; and the Helper Holy Spirit were all there, very present in our time of trouble. When I cried and prayed in solitude in the chapel, I knew that God was listening to my prayers and my pleas and that He heard the pain in my heart. As I prayed, the one thing that kept coming back to my mind was the year 2004. Back then, that forty-five-day journey of Chuck's heart valve replacement surgery seemed so big, so critical, and we almost lost Chuck. Never in a million years would I ever have thought I'd be back in the same small chapel, looking at the huge cross with Jesus on it above the altar. This crucifix is different from others, though; it's like no other I've ever seen. On this beautiful cross, Jesus's hands are not nailed to the cross; instead they are extended outward, inviting and welcoming anyone who prays to Him. It spoke to me in the way that symbolized that He embraces us and all of our needs and is there to hold us when we need Him the most. He's no longer nailed to the cross; He's alive and well and here to help us, hold us, and carry us through this life, especially in our times of trouble.

I want to share some scripture with you that spoke life and truth to me back then and still speaks life and truth to me now. I am hopeful it will lift you up and encourage you when you need it most. Scripture can see us through our darkest times if we study and believe it. But it's up to every one of us to seek the Lord and His greatness on his or her own. No one can do it for us; we have to seek Him to have our own relationship with Him. Every relationship with Him is unique; mine and yours are different. Every relationship is individual, but the promises and goodness of the Lord are for everyone. Here are a few.

> [3] Praise be to the God and Father of our Lord Jesus Christ, the Father of compassion and the God of all comfort, [4] who comforts us in all our troubles, so that we can comfort those in any trouble with the comfort we ourselves receive from God. (2 Corinthians 1:3–4 NIV)

> [19] Then they cried to the LORD in their trouble, and he saved them from their distress. [20] He sent out his word and healed them; he rescued them from the grave. (Psalm 107:19–20 ESV)

So do not fear, for I am with you; do not be dismayed, for I am your God. I will strengthen you and help you; I will uphold you with my righteous right hand (Isaiah 41:10 NIV)

Be strong and courageous. Do not be afraid or terrified because of them, for the LORD your God goes with you; he will never leave you nor forsake you. (Deuteronomy 31:6 NIVUK)

For I know the plans I have for you," declares the LORD, "plans to prosper you and not to harm you, plans to give you hope and a future. (Jeremiah 29:11 NIV)

I can't explain the almighty power of Jesus, but I know it is real because of what we experienced. We were able to proclaim victory. We will always proclaim God's victory while we are here on earth and eternally in heaven. Once again, Christ defeated the enemy. In those really tough moments, hours, days, weeks, and months, we came through all the valleys because of Him. Jesus Christ is everything that He claimed to be over two thousand years ago, as He is today. He was and is the anchor in the wind and waves. Jesus is eternal and alive. He is Healer, Restorer, Redeemer, Divine Physician, and Miracle Worker. He is the Shepherd welcoming the lost, the successful, the sick, the healthy, the rich, the poor, the confused, the intelligent, the addicted, and the overachieving. Whosoever—yes, whosoever—will seek Him, may be assured that He can make us whole again and that He promises to do so. His love is like no other; He is there when no one else is. Jesus empowers us with the Holy Spirit, also known as our helper. I myself could not go through life without Him. Even what I may face in my future does not scare me, because I know He will be there will see me through any challenge. His presence is my weapon, pushing away darkness and breaking every chain. No weapon formed against me shall prosper. As I near the end of this story, I can only encourage you to become a believer and a follower in Christ Jesus. I'd like to give you the opportunity to do so.

If you read this prayer and accept Jesus Christ in your heart, you will become born again.

Dear Lord,

I'm a sinner.
Please forgive me.
Come into my life and cleanse me from my sin and unbelief.
I believe in you and in salvation through the blood of Jesus.
I turn from sin and trust in Jesus alone as my Savior.
In Jesus's name I pray.

Amen.

Congratulations, welcome to the family of God. This will be a new beginning for you. Things won't change in your life overnight, but as you seek Him, you will renew your mind and heart to the perfect truth, and you will see gradual changes and experience gifts and blessings that will be new for you. You will be charged with a fire on the inside. You will have renewed energy from having new hope and strength. The light will become stronger, and fear will subside as you know you are walking through this life with your Heavenly Father. I hope you start this journey today. God bless you, and may His blessing be over you and your loved ones and generations to come.

CHAPTER 42

Home and Life Thereafter

To conclude, "that day" had come; Chuck was discharged, and we were on our way home. To me, walking out through those hospital doors with Chuck was superior to winning a lottery. I decided that we would made one pit stop at the hairdresser to get Chuck's hair cut. You have to remember that to my eyes, Chuck looked healthy and restored, as I had seen where Chuck had been. As I stated earlier, Chuck had pretty much been lying on death's doorstep for the entire seven months. Seeing Chuck walking out of the hospital with no tubes, no lines (other than his IV site for antibiotic treatment), no poles, no machines, and even no hospital pajamas, to me Chuck looked as if he was on top of the world. When we got to the hairdresser's, I could see that my dear friends at the shop were taken aback at Chuck's physical stature. Although they were very glad to see him, it was a bit of a shock, as Chuck had lost forty pounds, and I guess that to others who hadn't seen him for some time, he looked very drawn. As one of his good friends from the lake said, "Man, I was so happy to see you, but I have to tell you, when I saw you, I thought you looked so bad." It's true; Chuck probably looked very sickly to everyone, but not to me. To me, I had my baby back—the handsome guy I loved and had married.

We returned to life at home, but in the beginning it was very different from what we were use to. Chuck had a wound that needed dressing every several hours; he went for daily IV antibiotic treatment for six weeks; and his sleeping pattern—well, there wasn't any. Chuck had hated the nights in the hospital, and he never slept during the dark hours. He'd lie awake pretending to be asleep and would doze off only when it started getting light out. Now that he was home Chuck would frequently wake up during the night startled, thinking he still was in the hospital. Now Chuck has restful sleeps, which is good for both of us.

In June of 2021, we celebrated Chuck's five-year heart anniversary. I can't believe how time has passed. Since then, Chuck has retired from work and lives life to its fullest every day. Through his strong and unwavering sheer determination, plus a lot of hard work, Chuck is healthy. Chuck has strength back, as he chooses to live a healthy lifestyle every day. Every day as a couple, we are living a real miracle. Our daily life has pretty much returned to normal. Actually, life is better than our previous normal, because we look at life a bit differently now. Every moment matters; every normal day is special. As we've all heard or read on a card or plaque, "Every day is a gift." And it truly is. We can all think of friends, relatives, celebrities, and other people we know of who've passed away as a result of age, disease, or tragedy. Our hearts are heavy and sad we when learn of their passing. That's why it's so important to be present in every moment and to enjoy each day.

I don't know why, but I am naturally excited each morning and look forward to taking on each day. I often say to Chuck how excited I am. He'll ask me why, and my answer always is, "I don't know; I just am."

If you and I are still here, I'm sure we're here for a good reason and purpose. And for Chuck to survive the traumatic journey he went through, his reason and purpose must be on an entirely different level.

I hope our story encourages you to press on through life's hard times and challenges. I hope that you never have to go through a huge event, as we did. But should you find yourself in a hard spot, don't go it alone; go with God. No one loves you like He does. His ways are amazing, and He is faithful. Just remember: you don't have to be cleaned up and spotless; you come as you are, one step at a time. Don't wait for "the event" or heartbreak or loss. Living with God in your days, weeks, months, and years gives you your best life possible.

No matter what life brings you, never give up, and keep growing and using your faith. Remember: God will never leave you or forsake you. Now go enjoy your life, and remember that with God all things are possible!

God bless you and keep you.
May His grace, His favor, and His peace be upon you
for ALL the rest of your days.
With love,
Tannis

With God's power, life can exceed every earthly expectation.
Faith is believing in the impossible and knowing
it will come to pass as promised.

"A Special Thankyou"

We are forever grateful, thankful and give honor to Chuck's Organ Donor. His selfless decision to become an Organ Donor saved Chuck's life.

The End

Lightning Source UK Ltd.
Milton Keynes UK
UKHW012152130223
416920UK00002B/405